To Audrey

My forever inspiring
& thoughtful Torah
student.

Fondly -
Sally

The
Modern Men's
Torah
Commentary

Also by Rabbi Jeffrey K. Salkin from Jewish Lights

A Dream of Zion
American Jews Reflect on Why Israel Matters to Them

Righteous Gentiles in the Hebrew Bible
Ancient Role Models for Sacred Relationships

Being God's Partner
How to Find the Hidden Link between Spirituality and Your Work

Putting God on the Guest List, 3rd Ed.
How to Reclaim the Spiritual Meaning of
Your Child's Bar or Bat Mitzvah

For Kids—Putting God on Your Guest List, 2nd Ed.
How to Claim the Spiritual Meaning of Your Bar or Bat Mitzvah

The Bar/Bat Mitzvah Memory Book, 2nd Ed.
An Album for Treasuring the Spiritual Celebration

The
Modern Men's
Torah
Commentary

New Insights from Jewish Men
on the 54 Weekly Torah Portions

Edited by Rabbi Jeffrey K. Salkin

For People of All Faiths, All Backgrounds

JEWISH LIGHTS Publishing

Woodstock, Vermont

The Modern Men's Torah Commentary:
New Insights from Jewish Men on the 54 Weekly Torah Portions

2009 Hardcover, First Printing
© 2009 by Jeffrey K. Salkin

Library of Congress Cataloging-in-Publication Data
The modern men's Torah commentary : new insights from Jewish men on the 54 weekly Torah portions / edited by Jeffrey K. Salkin.
p. cm.
Includes bibliographical references and index.
ISBN-13: 978-1-58023-395-8 (hardcover)
ISBN-10: 1-58023-395-3 (hardcover)
1. Bible. O.T. Pentateuch—Commentaries. 2. Judaism—20th century. 3. Jewish way of life. I. Salkin, Jeffrey K., 1954–
BS1225.52.M63 2009
222'.1107081—dc22

2009007975

10   9   8   7   6   5   4   3   2   1

Manufactured in the United States of America
Jacket Design: Tim Holtz
Jacket Art: *Heritage III* by Shraga Weil, signed and numbered serigraph published by Safrai Gallery, 19 King David St., Jerusalem, Israel; www.safrai.com

For People of All Faiths, All Backgrounds
Published by Jewish Lights Publishing
A Division of LongHill Partners, Inc.
Sunset Farm Offices, Route 4, P.O. Box 237
Woodstock, VT 05091
Tel: (802) 457-4000   Fax: (802) 457-4004
www.jewishlights.com

To my sons, Samuel Asher Salkin
and Gabriel Adin Salkin

"Be strong and show yourself a man."
(1 Kings 2:2)

Contents

Bereshit/Genesis

Contents

Shemot/Exodus

Contents

Bemidbar/Numbers

Devarim/Deuteronomy

Vayikra/Leviticus

Index by Contributor

Introduction

When I mentioned the idea of a modern men's Torah commentary to a friend, he was more than slightly amused. "A men's Torah commentary?" he laughed. "You mean that the ancient Rabbis, Rashi, Ramban, Ibn Ezra, Maimonides, Samson Raphael Hirsch [the founder of modern Orthodoxy and classic Torah commentator], and Rabbi Gunther Plaut [the author of the modern Reform Torah commentary] weren't men? Not to mention all those obscure sages who have written countless commentaries on every text imaginable—books that line the shelves of seminary libraries and Jewish bookstores? To paraphrase the rock group Devo, 'Are they not men?'"

True, those commentaries were all written by men. Up until the modern age, Judaism was mostly produced, taught, and learned by men. But it isn't true enough. Because the whole notion of gender consciousness is remarkably modern, those commentators and authors didn't deal with the issues with which many modern men struggle—issues like relationships, sexuality, ambition, work and career, body image, aging, and life passages. Or if they did, you had to try to pull those insights out of the texts—a difficult, though exhilarating task. In collaboration with Jewish Lights, I wanted to create a Torah commentary that would open men up to the life of Torah and teach them how the life of Torah intersects with their own lives. I wanted to get men back to the life of Torah, and I am hoping that this book will show them how they can do precisely that.

"Whoa!" said another friend. "Think twice about this. There are many new Torah commentaries written from the perspective of women that have been published over the last few years.[1] Those worthwhile projects have done a great job reversing some of the Jewish tradition's misogyny. Won't such a 'male' commentary be seen as being 'retro' and even anti-feminist?"

Quite the opposite. Feminism has given the world countless psychological, political, sociological, spiritual, and literary gifts. It has single-handedly reminded us that we view our lives through many lenses, and not the least of those is the lens of gender. In fact, many early feminists hoped that the liberation of women would ultimately lead to the liberation of men from their narrow, constricting roles.

The Modern Men's Torah Commentary doesn't want to diminish the importance of the new canon of women's insights into Torah and Judaism any more than a call to re-engage men in synagogue life is a call to *disengage* women from the places that they have fought for and deservedly won. Rather, it seeks to add to the canon. It is an homage—in its truest, literary sense—to those feminist commentaries that have preceded it.

The Modern Men's Torah Commentary is a collection of insights into the weekly Torah portion, all written by Jewish men. And what a collection of men! In these pages you will find rabbis, cantors and Jewish synagogue composers, journalists, media figures, Jewish educators, professors, authors, Jewish communal leaders and professionals, even a well-known Jewish rock musician. They are Reform, Conservative, Reconstructionist, Orthodox, Jewish Renewal, and "just Jewish." They live in every region of the United States, Canada, England, Germany, and Israel. They are single, married, widowed, divorced, straight, and gay. They have children, and they are childless. They range in age from their late twenties to their mid-eighties.

They are a remarkable and eclectic collection of Jewish men, and their voices and insights are sacred and precious. Many of them stretched their minds and souls in order to look deeply into the text, in ways that they had never done before. In reclaiming their own stories, they allow us—men and women alike—to hear our own stories in a different way. I am deeply grateful to them, and for their insights. Editing their words became an act of love. Indeed, there were times that certain passages illuminated my soul or (metaphorically) struck me on the side of the head, in ways that made me say, "Thanks, I needed that insight." I am happy to say that many friendships began, grew, or were revived as a result of this project.

What issues in Jewish masculinity will you encounter as you read this book? A few among many:

- What it means to be a father, son, husband, partner, lover
- The Jewish man as celebrant and as mourner
- Balancing work, career, community, and family; avoiding burnout
- Men's spiritual nurturing
- Having—and being—a mentor
- How to handle aggression
- The meaning of self-sacrifice as a man
- How to reclaim the virtue of masculine patience in a hurried world
- The meaning of materialism in our lives as men
- Ethical struggles in interpersonal relationships
- Men's health issues
- Sexuality of all kinds
- The special challenges of being a father in Israel
- Moral responsibility for violence against women
- Body image
- Aging
- Dealing with fragility, death, and mortality as a man

What might Jewish men learn from all this?

Among other things, Jewish men might come to realize that authentic Jewish masculinity differs, somewhat, from the traditional American/Western version. "Men don't cry." "Take it like a man." Tell that to Abraham, who weeps when Sarah dies; or to Jacob, who weeps when he meets Rachel; or to Esau, the biblical prototype of a non-Jewish kind of toughness, who weeps when Jacob deceives him. His tears are so copious that one tradition says the Messiah will not come until all his tears have dried up.

Jewish history has its collection of warriors—King David, the Maccabees, the zealots of Masada, the Warsaw and Vilna ghetto fighters—but we remember David's psalms more than his battles. The judge Samson was strong but his brute power turned out to be blind and suicidal. As for the Maccabees, the ancient Rabbis chose to understand their victory over the Hellenists as being a spiritual victory rather than as the military success that it really was. The prophet Zechariah thundered, "Not by military might and not by power, but by God's spirit" (Zechariah 4:6). After the destruction of the Second Temple, Rabbinic tradition de-emphasized armed struggle, favoring the life of the mind and heart. For generations, Jewish men found their "macho" in mastery of Torah, in heartfelt worship, and in feats of loving-kindness and charity. True Jewish masculine power was, and is, not a fist but an open heart and open hand.

The Torah is the story of men meeting God at mountains: Noah's ark resting upon Ararat; Abraham and Isaac at Moriah; Jacob at a ladder (which is a good mountain substitute); Moses at Sinai. The mountain represents the heights of human experience, the ability to rise up.

But the Torah would be incomplete without its *wells*. Each patriarch digs or re-digs wells (Abraham and Isaac), or meets his beloved at a well (Jacob and Moses). We find God, therefore, not only in the heights of experience, but in its depths; not only in going up, but in going in.

So why is this volume needed at this time?

As virtually every top contemporary Jewish sociologist has noted, the great, often unspoken crisis facing modern liberal Judaism is the disengagement of its men. While we do not in any way mourn the passing of the exclusively male *minyan*, it is unfortunate that men are increasingly distancing themselves from Jewish religious life—as worshipers, as students of Torah, and as synagogue leaders. Just a short time ago, Jewish women were disconnected from Judaism. Today, it is Jewish men who seem to be disconnected. Let the record note: It's not Jewish *women* who are causing this. It may not even be fair to blame Jewish men themselves. It may simply be a sign of the times. But that doesn't make it better, easier, or something to ignore.

Consider contemporary Jewish worship. In a recent study, Brandeis University professor Sylvia Barack Fishman and Daniel Parmer noted that "nationally, girls and women outnumber men in weekly non-Orthodox worship services."[2] Based on my own experience of almost three decades in the Reform congregational rabbinate, the observation rings true. I have often found that at festival morning services, as much as 90 percent of the worshipers are women over age seventy. Many are primarily there for the *yizkor* (memorial) section of the service, which begs the question: don't Jewish men also have loved ones whom they need to mourn and remember?

Consider contemporary Jewish learning. While there are no firm statistics, anecdotal evidence abounds: The overwhelming majority of the audience for adult Jewish study appears to be female. At a recent ceremony in a synagogue that honored adult learners, all but two honorees were women. For many years, the organized Reform movement held summer *kallot* (study and spirituality retreats) that were extremely popular—but not with men. It was estimated that about 60 to 70 percent of the participants were women, and the men who came were, typically, accompanying their wives.

Consider conversion to Judaism and outreach. As Fishman and Parmer noted, "Men in general are far less likely to convert into another religion than women."[3] Many rabbis can testify to the frequent apathy of Jewish men when they join their gentile partners at "Introduction to Judaism" classes as a prelude to conversion. Jewish men seem to want their gentile (or, about-to-become-Jewish) partners to help raise Jewish children, but they seem to be offering a decreasing amount of input into that religious nurturing. Women, in fact, are more likely than men to see religion as a necessary component of their children's upbringing. And they are equally likely to be resentful of their husbands' religious apathy: "I don't get it. He demanded that we raise our children as Jews. I went along with that, even though it meant hurting my own Christian parents. The least he could do is help."

Consider Jewish youth education. On every imaginable scale of behaviors, male Jewish teenagers exhibit far less intense connections to Judaism than do their female peers. After bar/bat mitzvah, Jewish girls are far more likely to continue their Jewish education than boys. Synagogue youth groups are increasingly filled with young Jewish women craning their necks and wondering, in the words of one teenaged girl from Long Island, New York, "Where are all the guys?" The same is true of Jewish summer camps and teen leadership programs. And when they graduate from high school and go on to the world of the university, Jewish women undergraduates are far more likely to be involved in Hillel than their male counterparts (with the exception of Orthodox Jewish men).

These are more than simply anecdotal impressions. In their study, Fishman and Parmer alluded to the "feminization of liberal Judaism." In almost every venue of contemporary Jewish life, Jewish men demonstrate far less interest in Judaism than women do—from school age through adulthood. The current situation, they wrote, "contradicts thousands of years of Jewish history, during which men were the public and signifying Jews—and during which women were often marginalized or shut out of organized intellectual activities and public Judaism."

> Jewish men rank lower than Jewish women in secular ethnic, social, family, or peoplehood connections as well.... Jewish men have measurably lower rates of ethnic and religious social capital than Jewish women.... Men are less likely to value Jewishness in the United States and worldwide as a distinctive culture, and less likely to visit Israel. Jewish women more than Jewish men have mostly Jewish friends and describe themselves as affiliated with one of the wings of American Judaism ... and far more men than Jewish women call themselves "secular, cultural," or "just Jewish." Men invest less of their human capital into Jewishness.[4]

We can take some comfort in the fact that Jews are not alone in confronting this problem. Men are increasingly absent in the Catholic Church, both at the altars (the number of men entering the priesthood continues to drop) and in the pews. The need to engage men in the Church has led to a grassroots Catholic men's movement that sponsors a network of retreats and ministries across America. For many men, the evangelical Promise Keepers push all the right buttons, feeding the hunger for spirit and fellowship, addressing the emotional gap in families, calling for sexual discipline within marriage, and for men to be there for their wives and children. Seeking to "re-masculinize" the churches, the Promise Keepers charge men to become active advocates of their pastors and their faith.

The burning question is: Why? And while it is tempting to "round up the usual suspects," there are no easy answers.

How can we get Jewish men back into serious, engaging religious life?

It's not as if synagogues want to exclude men; that is hardly the case. Women were able to articulate what they wanted—what they *demanded*—out of Jewish life. Men must do the same thing, and vigorously.

For their part, the traditional Jewish men's organizations have hardly been sleeping during this crisis. In many ways, they have done a wonderful job of re-imagining their missions and revamping their efforts.

"We're sending signals to men that we care about them," says Doug Barden, executive director of Men of Reform Judaism. Men of Reform Judaism has created health awareness programs, Jewish literacy courses, and retreats dealing with such male-oriented issues as divorce, becoming unemployed, and taking care of elderly parents. They have created men's Seders and ways for men to become more involved with the Jewish festival and holiday cycle.

So, too, the Federation of Jewish Men's Clubs (Conservative), led by executive director Rabbi Charles Simon, has engaged in serious theological work with men. It instituted "Hearing Men's Voices," in which men were encouraged to share their own spiritual journeys. It has reconsidered not only the content of its programming but the venues, offering theology discussions in local pubs and "Monday Night Football" get-togethers, featuring discussions on sexual issues from a Jewish vantage point.

This is all good, and Jewish men need more. They need more and different entryways into Jewish study. Hence, this volume.

May *The Modern Men's Torah Commentary* contribute to your inner Jewish journey, and may it deepen the wells of your own authentic Jewish spirit. May it help show you the sources of inspiration and meaning that you may not have known even existed.

How to Use This Book

The Modern Men's Torah Commentary is simply that—a Torah commentary. It is arranged according to the weekly Torah portion or *parashah* (sometimes also called a *sedra*, a place in the *seder* [order] of the weekly Torah readings). Each commentator has chosen a verse or series of passages upon which to base his commentary. He then engages his own analysis of the text, raising up and elucidating those issues in the text that seem particularly salient to Jewish men's spiritual issues.

A word on the Torah texts themselves. The standard translation for the Torah passages has been the Jewish Publication Society's *Tanakh*, most recently republished in 1999. Sometimes our authors want to deviate from that translation. When that happens, we make such changes explicit by indicating that it is the author's own translation. In keeping with a commitment to Jewish pluralism and diversity, we have respected the predilections of various authors and maintained their preference for "Adonai," "G-d" or "*Ha-shem*" as the Divine Name. Likewise, we have respected the wishes and/or grammatical predilections of our various authors who have chosen to refer to God in the third person with the pronoun "He," while we simultaneously recognize the awkwardness of using any pronoun to refer to a God Who transcends gender.

So, too, our authors make liberal use of various Rabbinic and classic commentators, as well as many modern commentators and literary figures. To save you time and trouble, we have included a list of those sources in the back of the book. In addition, in an attempt to make this book as user-friendly as possible, we have tried to define as many Jewish, Hebrew, and Yiddish terms as possible, either in the body of the text or in a separate glossary at the back of the book.

It is our sincere hope that *The Modern Men's Torah Commentary* will become a source of great learning and inspiration.

Acknowledgments

As always, I am grateful to Stuart M. Matlins, publisher and editor in chief of Jewish Lights Publishing, for his vision and support of this project. I particularly value Stuart's unfailing courage; he suspected, all along, that this project might prove to be more than a little controversial. And yet, in his characteristic way, he urged me to push on, feeling that, as the leading publisher of Jewish feminist books, this focus on *modern* men's needs gave balance to the resources Jewish Lights provides to help people lead a Jewish life. So, too, I am grateful to Emily Wichland, vice president of Editorial and Production, for her skillful navigation of the byways of this project, as well as her almost saintly patience.

I am grateful as well to the many students whom I have taught in recent years—both in Atlanta and in various communities around North America. The ideas in this book found ready audiences and willing hearts in members of synagogue Brotherhoods and Men's Clubs around the country, and I have been moved by the utter willingness on the part of many Jewish men to re-imagine their Jewish lives and the work of their organizations.

Finally, I am profoundly grateful to my beloved, Sheila Shuster. She has encouraged me to see myself, and my manhood, as more than simply a reflection of what I do, but of what I am. For those insights—insights that I myself once taught, but needed to re-learn—I am deeply grateful.

Bereshit/
Genesis

בראשית

Bereshit

Where Are Your Brothers?

RABBI SHELDON ZIMMERMAN

The Lord said to Cain, "Where is your brother Abel?"
And he said, "I do not know. Am I my brother's keeper?"
(Genesis 4:9)

Bereshit contains the first question in the Torah directed to God by a human being. After Cain's offering receives no attention from God, Cain and Abel are out in the field and Cain kills his brother. "The Lord said to Cain, 'Where is your brother Abel?' And he said, 'I do not know. Am I my brother's keeper [*ha-shomer achi anochi*]?" (Genesis 4:9).

This is the first question directed to God in the entire Torah, and yet it remains unanswered. Punishment is meted out to Cain, but in no place surrounding this story is there an answer. In fact, in no place in the Torah is God seen as giving a direct answer to this question.

For many years I was troubled by the silence of the Torah in response to this question. I have come to believe, however, through

RABBI SHELDON ZIMMERMAN is rabbi of the Jewish Center of the Hamptons in East Hampton, New York. He has served as rabbi at Central Synagogue in New York City and Temple Emanu-El of Dallas, Texas. He is past president of Hebrew Union College–Jewish Institute of Religion; executive vice president of birthright israel North America, and vice president for Jewish Renaissance and Renewal of the United Jewish Communities. He was president of the Central Conference of American Rabbis (CCAR). He is one of the founders of Jewish Alcoholics, Chemically Dependent Persons, and Significant Others (JACS).

hints in the Book of Genesis and viewing the text as a structured whole, that this question is answered, that the answer is built through the narrative and is finally answered toward the end of the book itself. Only then does the Torah leave the stories of individual personalities, so much a part of Genesis, and move to the story of the beginning of our becoming a people in Exodus.

We can read Cain's answer not only as the *p'shat* (literal meaning) of the text but as a challenge about being his brother's keeper. In its literal sense it reads, "I do not know. Am I my brother's keeper?" We can read it, "I did not know [that] I was my brother's keeper." We can picture Cain as saying to God, "You never told me. You never explained to me that siblings bear a responsibility for each other. How could I know?" In fact, one of the interwoven themes throughout the text is "Who will be *shomer achi* [my brother's keeper]?" As the text evolves, we learn that certain brothers were their brothers' keepers, and that, in these cases, the brother we least expected to play this role does so.

We know very little about the relationship between Terah's sons, Abram, Nahor, and Haran. Haran dies, and Abram takes Haran's son Lot with him to the land of Canaan. Both Abram and Lot have flocks, herds, and tents. A quarrel breaks out between the herdsmen of Abram's cattle and those of Lot's cattle, because the land is inadequate for their grazing. Abram says to Lot, "Let there be no strife between you and me, between my herdsmen and yours, for we are kinsmen [*ki anashim achim anachnu*]" (Genesis 13:8). The word for "kinsmen" is *achim*, which can also be translated as "brothers."[1] Although no answer is given here to Cain's question, it is clear that in Abram's mind kinsmen bear some relationship of concern for and peace with each other. They separate, each going to a different geographical location (Genesis 13:11–12). In other narratives of brothers, a fuller answer will develop.

The relationship between Abraham's two sons, Isaac and Ishmael, takes us to yet greater understanding. When Sarah is unable to conceive, she gives her servant Hagar to Abraham as a concubine. After Hagar becomes pregnant, she acts badly toward

Sarah, and Sarah treats her harshly. Hagar runs away. An angel of Adonai finds her by a spring of water. The angel tells her to return to Sarah and submit to her harsh treatment. He tells her she will have a son and is to call him Ishmael. Hagar calls God *El Ro'i* ("God saw me"), and the well is named Beer-lahai-roi (Genesis 16:14). After Ishmael turns thirteen, Sarah becomes pregnant and bears Isaac. When Sarah witnesses Ishmael playing with Isaac, she is so distressed that Abraham sends Hagar and Ishmael away (Genesis 21:14).[2] Ishmael and his mother are cast out. We hear nothing more about Isaac and Ishmael together until a clue is given later in the text.

After the *Akedah*, the binding of Isaac on Mount Moriah, Abraham comes down the mountain alone. We hear nothing about Isaac. Where is he?[3] He is not present at his mother's burial and his father's mourning period for her. He is never mentioned being with his father during Abraham's lifetime.[4] Yet when Abraham's servant brings Rebekah to be Isaac's wife, the text indicates, "Isaac had just come back from the vicinity of Beer-lahai-roi, for he was settled in the land of the Negeb" (Genesis 24:62). Could it be that after his near-death experience, Isaac fled from both his father and mother (for perhaps in Isaac's view she also might have known about his father's actions)? Could it be that he ran away to the one person whom he remembered and who loved him when he was an infant, to Ishmael—to the vicinity of Beer-lahai-roi, the place identified with Hagar and where Ishmael's name was presented to her? The text will continue that after Abraham's death his sons Isaac and Ishmael bury him. They are together (Genesis 25:9). The Torah continues: "And Isaac settled near Beer-lahai-roi" (Genesis 25:11). The brothers settle together. The cast-out brother serves as a refuge for the almost sacrificed brother. "Am I my brother's keeper?" The cast-out brother answers, "Yes." He is there for Isaac when Isaac is most broken, most alone, most distrustful.

Isaac and Rebekah marry and have two sons, Esau and Jacob. We are well acquainted with how Jacob acquires the birthright and the blessing from Esau and how later he deceives Isaac (with Rebekah's help) and takes the blessing intended for Esau. Esau is so angered about the loss of both the birthright and the blessing that he threatens to kill Jacob when Isaac is dead. Feeling bereft of his parents' love, Esau even tries to gain their approval by marrying not a Canaanite, but rather the daughter of Ishmael, his first cousin. Esau is certainly cut off by his own mother and has to cry out to be blessed, even minimally, by his father (see Genesis 25:19–28:9).

Jacob flees to stay with his uncle Laban (Rebekah's brother). After many years, Jacob returns with his wives Leah and Rachel, his concubines, children, and great wealth. He learns that Esau is coming to greet him with a retinue of four hundred men. Jacob quickly devises a strategy for survival, first by trying to "buy" Esau's favor with gifts, then through prayer, and finally by dividing the camp into two parts so that at least one part might survive (Genesis 33:1–2).

Jacob approaches tentatively and bows low. Esau, however, runs to meet him and embrace him, falling on Jacob's neck and kissing him (Genesis 33:3–4).[5] What genuine and caring actions! After all these years and his own agony and sense of betrayal, Esau has come prepared to embrace his brother Jacob and Jacob's family. To the Rabbinic commentators, it seems so incredible and impossible, but not for a brother intent on forgiveness and reconciliation. Esau turns down the gifts with these memorable words: "I have enough, *achi* [my brother]" (Genesis 33:9). We hear the whisper of "*ha-shomer achi anochi*"! Esau is indicating that "I am the keeper of *achi*—my brother's keeper." How can we miss it?[6] Esau continues, "Let what you have remain yours" (Genesis 33:9). He seems to say, "I have my own blessings now. Whatever you have gained by your actions and even by what you took from me is yours; I cannot do to you what you did to me."

Yet, Esau permits himself to be pressed by Jacob, and he finally accepts. Perhaps Jacob fears that Esau will later regret this positive feeling. Perhaps Esau desires some payback. Or perhaps we need to read this as simply, "I have enough." Clearly, though, Esau sees himself as Jacob's *shomer*, "guardian" or "keeper." He even offers to send some of his men to watch over Jacob. But Jacob, still fearful and perhaps still Jacob and not yet truly Israel (although he has just received his new name), cannot accept his brother Esau's love and care. Jacob does arrive safely (*shalem*) in Shechem (Genesis 33:18), testimony to the change that has occurred in Esau. Later, when their father Isaac dies, the text tells us that his sons, Esau and Jacob, bury him together (Genesis 35:29), which is similar to what occurs with Isaac and Ishmael when their father, Abraham, dies (Genesis 25:9). Both pairs of brothers, called the sons of their fathers in the text, reconcile to and with each other, and they bury their fathers together. Yet, we still have not arrived at the complete answer to "*Ha-shomer achi anochi*—am I my brother's keeper?"

The stories of Joseph and his brothers are well known. Jacob loves Rachel, Joseph's mother, far more than he loves Leah. For the rest of her life, Leah remains the less-loved wife and mother. How difficult it must have been for the sons of Leah to witness their father's greater love for their aunt, and not their mother! How much harder, yet, to witness and experience their father's favoring of Joseph! His dreams only increase their enmity and hatred. When Joseph is sent by Jacob to check on his brothers' welfare, we can sense what awaits. Joseph says, "I am looking for my brothers" (Genesis 37:16). Sadly, he doesn't find his brothers to be his keepers, but rather to be those who would cast him into a pit, threaten to kill him, and then sell him into slavery. Reuben and Judah save him from death. But it is Judah whose words call us to attention: "Come, let us sell him to the Ishmaelites, but let us not do away with him ourselves. After all he is our *brother*, our own flesh [*ki achinu v'sareinu hu*]" (Genesis 37:27) Judah, slowly, rises to the task.

The Joseph story continues with Joseph's rise to power in Egypt, and as it moves to its closure, Jacob and his sons' provisions have run low. The sons must return to Egypt again. Jacob is reminded that the only way they can regain the freedom of their brother Simeon (now incarcerated by Joseph) and survive themselves is to bring Benjamin with them as the required proof of their sincerity. Reuben is willing to put up his two sons as security if Benjamin does not return. If Benjamin does not return, he says, "You may kill my two sons" (Genesis 42:37). However, they are his sons, not Reuben himself. Cain's question remains: "Am I [*anochi*] my brother's keeper?" Jacob is not moved to send Benjamin with the brothers.

The famine continues and deepens. The family's food is diminished further. The sons must return to Egypt. Judah comes forward. He tells his father that Joseph has said that they can only return if "your brother is with you [*achichem itchem*]" (Genesis 43:3).[7] The text practically calls out for our attention; by reporting Joseph's words verbatim, Judah is now affirming that Benjamin is "our brother."

Judah then says, "Send the boy in *my* care [*iti*] ... I myself [*anochi*] will be surety for him; you may hold *me* responsible: if I do not bring him back to you and set him before you, I shall stand guilty before you forever" (Genesis 43:8–9). Jacob heeds the meaning of the words. Judah is saying, "*Anochi shomer achi*—I am my brother's keeper." Jacob accedes and sends them on to Egypt.

When Judah confronts Joseph, the former recalls that Judah's mother, Leah, was his father's less-loved wife. He recalls hearing Jacob say, "My wife bore me two sons. But one is gone.... If you take this one from me, too, and he meets with disaster, you will send my white head down to Sheol in sorrow" (Genesis 44:27–29). How must Judah feel? His mother was the less-loved wife. He is the son of the less-loved wife, and his father loves him less than he loves Joseph and Benjamin. Yet, Judah stands up to Joseph. He overcomes his hurt, his pain, and his emptiness—and he repeats the promise that he made to Jacob: "When [my father] sees that the boy is not with us, he will die.... Now your servant has pledged himself for the boy to my father, saying, 'If I do not bring him back to you, I shall stand guilty before my father forever.' Therefore, please let your servant remain as a slave to my lord instead of the boy, and let the boy go back with his brothers. For how can I go back to my father unless the boy is with me? Let me not be witness to the woe that would overtake my father!" (Genesis 44:31–34). *I am my brother's keeper. I am my father's guardian.*

Judah, the less-loved wife's son and the less-loved son of his father, and Joseph, the brother cast out by his brothers, together give us the answer: "I am my brother's keeper." Joseph can no longer withhold himself and his feelings. He now reveals himself to his brothers. The story moves to the next level. All of them, including Jacob, come to Egypt—and there they will be nurtured, fed, cared for, and loved. Joseph will not only be their keeper; he will also be their father's guardian.

It is not always the most popular, loved, and admired who becomes the most caring. Sometimes it is the less-loved brother who rises through his pain, loss, and grief to embrace in love and care. The less loved can become the more loving. The less favored can become the most caring. The one who suffered more can become the one who loves more.

Cain's question is answered by brothers who are transformed through pain and remorse, and yet who are able to love and care. They are broken, but renewed; hurt, but reborn. "I am my brother's keeper—I am my *brothers'* keeper." Only now can the story move on to become the story of the Jewish people. We are all our brothers' keepers. We are forever responsible one for the other. Hope remains that what was once our reality can be transformed into a new reality of trust, love, and care.

The Curse of Solitude

Rabbi David J. Wolpe

It is not good for man to be alone. (Genesis 2:18)

What is the first statement about human nature in the Bible? "It is
not good for man to be alone." This is a pronouncement about loneliness, but it is also more than that. In his commentary to the
midrash *Pirkei d'Rabbi Eliezer*, Rabbi David Luria notes that a literal
reading yields: "It is not good for *a* man to be alone." In other words,
it may be teaching us something about single men. Single men commit more crimes, cause far more social disruption, are vastly over-
represented in jails. As men we need partners to moderate us.

Do not be alone, the Bible teaches. It is not good for you or for
society.

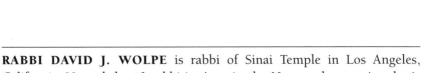

RABBI DAVID J. WOLPE is rabbi of Sinai Temple in Los Angeles,
California. Named the #1 rabbi in America by *Newsweek* magazine, he is
author of seven books, including *Why Faith Matters*. In addition to his
pulpit and communal responsibilities, he teaches modern Jewish thought
at University of California, Los Angeles.

Noach

What Kind of Father Was Lamech?

RABBI JOHN MOSCOWITZ

Noah was a righteous man; he was blameless in his age.

(Genesis 6:9)

At the birth of his son, Lamech predicts: "This one will provide us relief from our work and from the toil of our hands, out of the very soil which the Lord placed under a curse" (Genesis 5:29). Noah's name, Noach, heralds comfort for a beleaguered world. His great accomplishment—the saving of humanity—will inspire *Midrash Tanchuma* to acclaim, "Before Noah's birth, what was reaped was not what had been sewn. Where wheat or barley was sewn, thorns and thistles were reaped. But after Noah was born, the earth returned to orderly growth. What was sewn was reaped...."[1]

Such eloquent testimony aside, Lamech's announcement is worrisome. What is promised is more daunting than restoring nature's

RABBI JOHN MOSCOWITZ is senior rabbi of Holy Blossom Temple, Toronto, and a rabbinic fellow at the Shalom Hartman Institute, Jerusalem. Ordained at Hebrew Union College–Jewish Institute of Religion in 1982, he later studied history at the University of California, Los Angeles. He served as associate rabbi at Holy Blossom Temple until 2000, when he became senior rabbi. His areas of interest include the relationship between space and spirit in the making of religious community. His areas of intellectual interest include rabbinics and the dilemmas of Jewish modernity. Rabbi Moscowitz has served on the boards of various communal organizations.

11

harmony, more far-reaching than righting the order made wrong by human beings; Noah is, in effect, enlisted to rearrange the very nature of humanity. As Karen Armstrong puts it, he is charged to do nothing less than "… reverse the curse of Adam's sin and bring relief to both humanity and the afflicted earth."[2]

Unfazed, endowed with decency and attuned to God's will, Noah augurs hope as devastation looms. His father appears prescient.

Once the flood rampages and the waters recede, God, relenting of His promise to destroy the world, renews life through Noah and his sons, Shem, Ham, and Japheth. Now Noah can finally do what his name actually suggests: rest. (The etymology is askew; *Noach* more properly means "rest," not "relief" or "comfort" as Lamech's naming implies. This is only a curiosity and not yet an agitation. After all, Noah has indeed provided comfort and relief and is justified in unwinding inside his tent.)

Still—startlingly—as Noah rescues humanity, he cannot save himself. Once inside that tent, Noah becomes undone: "Noah, the tiller of the soil, was the first to plant a vineyard. He drank of the wine and became drunk, and he uncovered himself within his tent" (Genesis 9:20–21). Whatever "uncovered" means—the speculations abound—Noah is done, spent morally and physically, his impressive resumé in shambles. Why could Noah save humanity, but not himself? Why does he unravel so quickly, unbound from any moral compass or psychological core to hold himself at bay?

Is it, as Rashi and others hint, that while Noah is more decent and less corrupt than his peers, he is more ordinary than he appears—at ease following God's instructions, yet ill equipped to internalize the implications?

Or, does his personal undoing (mirrored in the telling actions of his son Ham, who deliberately stares at and then almost gleefully tells of his father's uncovered nakedness), in fact, belong at Lamech's feet—or, more precisely, with his fathering? Perhaps the undone son possesses insufficient internal paternal ballast to buoy himself when storm tossed and adrift. Maybe too much is expected of a son, by a father who provides too little.

Regarding fathers and sons, most especially what fathers do for sons, we begin not with Noah, but rather with Freud. And not with Freudian analysis, but rather with the childhood story Freud often told about himself and his father:

> And now, for the first time, I happened upon the youthful experience which even to-day still expresses its power in all these emotions and dreams. I might have been ten or twelve years old when my father began to take me with him on his walks, and in his conversation to reveal his views on the things of this world.
>
> Thus it was that he once told me the following incident, in order to show me that I had been born into happier times than he: "When I was a young man, I was walking one Saturday along the street in the village where you were born; I was well-dressed, with a new fur cap on my head. Up comes a Christian, who knocks my cap into the mud, and shouts, 'Jew, get off the pavement!'" "And what did you do?" "I went into the street and picked up the cap," he calmly replied.
>
> That did not seem heroic on the part of the big, strong man who was leading me, a little fellow, by the hand. I contrasted this situation, which did not please me, with another, more in harmony with my sentiments—the scene in which Hannibal's father, Hamilcar Barcas, made his son swear before the household altar to take vengeance on the Romans. Ever since then Hannibal has had a place in my phantasies.[3]

No wonder that Freud—by then in his seventies and summing things up in *Civilization and Its Discontents*—would observe, "I cannot think of any need in childhood as strong as a need for a father's protection."[4]

We know of Jacob Freud's parental inadequacies from his son's observations. Yet, how can we claim that Lamech, likewise, cannot be a "big strong man," holding his son firmly hand in hand?

While the biblical text is mute on Lamech's paternal ways, Leon Kass, an astute contemporary observer of biblical personalities and events, paints a picture of Noah. He sees Noah as a son without a proper father, and as a father who, in coming unglued in front of his sons, can no longer claim paternal authority.

> Noah's drunkenness robs [him] of his dignity, his parental authority, and his very humanity. Prostrate rather than upright, this newly established master of the earth has, in the space of one verse, utterly lost his standing. Worse, instead of escaping from his origins, Noah in fact returns to the shameful naked condition of the aboriginal state: "he was uncovered in his tent." Stripped of his clothing, naked, exposed and vulnerable to disgrace, he appears merely as a male, not as a father—not even as a humanized, rational animal. Noah will not be the last man who degrades and unfathers himself as a result of drink. Paternal authority and respectability are precarious, indeed.[5]

So there it is: Noah, stripped of any patina of civility, shorn of any claim to the mantel of fatherhood, is reduced to his animal self. Flat on his back, Noah is back to the origins he cannot escape—his father and his father's ways.

Who, then, was Lamech, and how might the son be like the father?

While the Bible is circumspect on Lamech, the Rabbis, perhaps intuiting in the son's eventual undoing something of the ways of the father, are not. Noting Genesis 4:19 ("Lamech took to himself two wives"), they remark on the male ways of that generation. Men would invariably take two wives at a time—making of the first almost a widow, while turning the second into something of a harlot.[6] In other words, Lamech literally turns his back on one wife and uses the second one, more or less, for sexual pleasure alone. So Lamech was no standup man—not for his women, not for his son. Given what Noah observed at home as a young man, need we wonder more about his moral compass?

This doesn't mean, however, that Lamech is without a certain kind of discernment. As fathers often do, he knows his son well. He understands, specifically, that Noah has the stuff inside to be counted on, to bear any burden out in the larger world—and, indeed, he will become the protecting father to the mass of humanity. Nonetheless, the father, knowing something about himself, is well aware that his son—this world-class hero-to-be—is possessed of an internal hollowness. As great as Noah will be in the world, he will be just as suspect at home.

So, indeed, Noah is no standup father to his own sons, and eventually he becomes a first-class fool at home. Perhaps Lamech was prescient; he sensed that Noah could be heroic, kind, and decent for all the world to see, and, yet, inside his tent for none but his own sons to know, his son will be unable to stand up straight—neither as a man nor as a father.

Lamech, knowing himself to be a bit crooked with his women, also knows he cannot be straight with his son. He therefore deliberately twists his son's name: Noah is the one who can never rest (and will be always taunted by having a name that suggests that he is restful, perhaps the very reason he becomes twisted); but Noah can be the one to bring relief and comfort for all humanity. Indeed, this is no misnaming at all; rest is about stability, normality, and continuity—achievements for which Noah lays the foundation by saving humanity. Nevertheless, these are accomplishments beyond the reach of his character, yet they are not necessarily beyond the double meaning of his name.

לך לך

Lech Lecha

More Than Bread and Wine

RABBI MORDECAI FINLEY, PhD

And King Melchizedek of Salem brought out bread and wine; he was a priest of God Most High. He blessed him saying,

> *"Blessed be Abram of God Most High,*
> *Creator of heaven and earth.*
> *And blessed be God Most High,*
> *Who has delivered your foes into your hand."*

(Genesis 14:18–20)

I do a fair amount of spiritual counseling in my work, more with men than with women, men who have known God and want to know what to do next; men who barely know themselves, and want to know what to do next. It often begins with: "What do I do about my father, mother, wife, son, daughter, sibling, work?" Or: "How do I handle my envy, sadness, rage, depression, death, or confusion?" Wherever it starts, at some point it gets to: "Who am I? What virtue or value ought I stand for right now? How do I discipline my thoughts and emotions and hold my ground here? How do I shape my own destiny? Do I lead my life, or does my life lead me?"

RABBI MORDECAI FINLEY, PhD, is rabbi of Ohr HaTorah congregation in Los Angeles, California. He a professor of liturgy, mysticism, and professional skills at the Academy for Jewish Religion, California campus, and served in the United States Marine Corps.

Some consolation comes from knowing that we all have feelings of exile and alienation—at least those of us who examine our lives, contemplate our paths, and feel our feelings. The things that pain us constitute some of the crucial steps in the hero's journey of the consciously lived life.

The wisdom for this journey comes from many places, but mostly from spiritual guides who have traversed these treacherous slopes. Spiritual guides rooted in the Jewish tradition learn how to map our journeys on the archetypal study of Torah. The surface of the Torah is a placeholder for deep patterns of meaning and experience that rumble underneath. The excavating of those myths is called midrash (the Hebrew word *midrash* literally means "seeking out, demanding"). The books of midrashim written by the ancient and not-so-ancient rabbis are filled with penetrating psychological and spiritual insights.

The spiritual guide today who is enriched by the Jewish tradition studies Torah and midrash and weaves a teaching woven from these ancient sources, but applied to people today. Let's take a few verses of Torah, enriched by some of the ancient midrashim, and share a narrative that speaks to men seeking spiritual growth.

First, the story: In the beginning of the Torah portion *Lech Lecha*, God calls to Abram to go from his land, from his birthplace, and from his father's house, to a land that God would show him. God does not name the land and does not say why Abram must go. The ancient midrashim fill in the details, and they tell us that Abram had thought his way out of the trap of polytheism and idol worship into the apprehension of the One God. He was told to go *physically* because he had already left *spiritually*. God was commanding him, in essence, to follow his heart out.

In commanding him out, God promises that God will make him a great nation, bless him, make his name great, and make him into a blessing. So, Abram leaves. With him are his nephew Lot, his wife Sarai, their wealth, and the persons they had acquired, and they all head for Canaan. (The Hebrew word root for the place name "Canaan" can mean "submission." It's the place where Abram will turn his life over to God.)

Abram arrives there, and things fall apart. A famine breaks out, so he goes to Egypt. He tells his wife to pretend that she is his sister, so that people won't kill him in order to take her. Pharaoh takes his wife from him, and Abram becomes wealthy in terms of herd animals and female slaves, but Abram is probably thinking that this was not exactly what God had in mind when God promised him blessings. Pharaoh releases Sarai because of the plagues that God sends upon him, and the Egyptian king rages at Abram: "Why did you not tell me that she was your wife?" (Genesis 12:18). Abram's response isn't recorded.

The family returns to Canaan, and Abram has a quarrel with his nephew Lot. They part ways: Abram stays in Canaan, and Lot goes to the plain, near Sodom, a place of "very wicked sinners" (Genesis 14:13). Again, God promises the land to Abram and his descendants—but Abram and Sarai have no descendants. Abram and his nephew are no longer speaking, and Lot has fallen in with a bad crowd. Abram is a childless old man who fights with his family and makes money in an unsavory fashion.

Then, in Genesis 14, a war breaks out. Four warlords make war on five other warlords, and Abram's nephew Lot is swept up in the fighting and is captured. Abram decides to intervene. He musters his militia of 318 fighting men and pursues the heretofore victorious "gang of four." He catches up with them outside of Damascus, wins the battle, and brings back the loot and the captives, including Lot.

Let us pause and consider: Abram thinks the blessing has come true. He has been victorious in war; he is now the de facto chief warlord over not only the four defeated ones, but the five warlords whom he has rescued. The booty and people are his. He can do what he wants. He now owns the land. He is great, wealthy, and famous and, with all these female captives, sure to be able to produce an heir. He is at the top of his game.

On his way back home, an odd thing happens. As he passes the city that will become Jerusalem, flush with victory, he meets a certain person named Melchizedek.

And King Melchizedek of Salem brought out bread and wine;
he was a priest of God Most High. He blessed him saying,
"Blessed be Abram of God Most High,
Creator of heaven and earth.
And blessed be God Most High,
Who has delivered your foes into your hand."
(Genesis 14:18–20)

Right after this blessing, the king of Sodom, one of the five warlords whom Abram had rescued, tries to extricate himself from his powerless position as a rescued captive. As if he has any leverage, he makes the following offer to Abram: "Give me the persons, and take the possessions for yourself" (Genesis 14:21). Astonishingly, Abram—master and commander of his world—tells this humiliated warlord that he won't take as much as thread or a sandal strap: "You shall not say, 'It is I who made Abram rich'" (Genesis 14:23). Abram asks him to pay his men and his allies for their efforts, but he takes nothing for himself.

What did Melchizedek say to Abram to make him renounce the bounty, fame, and power at hand? Did Abram suddenly "get religion"? What happened here? Who was Melchizedek? Let's hear from the midrash, but let's listen to it slowly.

First, the Bible has a very detailed chronology, but since scholars doubt its veracity, we don't pay much attention to it today. The ancient Rabbis took it seriously, and there are several important points that help us figure out who Melchizedek was and what he said to Abram. There are ten generations from Adam to Noah, but people lived a long time in the Bible—far beyond their own generations. Adam's grandson Seth was still alive when Noah was born. Methuselah, who was born about midway through Adam's life of 930 years, was alive when Shem, the son of Noah, was born. Shem, then, knew people who knew Adam.

A midrash (*Bereshit Rabbah* 36:8) tells us that Shem, the son of Noah, and his own great-grandson Eber had an academy in which they taught the knowledge of God. The source of this midrashic tradition seems to be Genesis 9:26, "Blessed be the Lord, the God of Shem," and the subsequent verse is interpreted to mean that God will "dwell in the tents of Shem" (Genesis 9:27). We find, for example, in the Talmud (*Makkot* 23b) that the Holy Spirit dwelt in three places: the tents of Shem, the court of the prophet Samuel, and the court of King Solomon. The academy of Shem was truly a place that taught the knowledge of God.

We further read (in the midrash *Bemidbar Rabbah* 4:8) that Adam was the world's first *kohen*, or priest. The coat of animal skin that God made for Adam after the expulsion from Eden was made out of the skin of the serpent in the Garden of Eden; that coat became Adam's priestly garment. Seth inherited both the priestly role and the garment; they were then passed on to Methuselah, and then to Noah, and then to Shem. According to a midrash, Shem's title was *Malki Tzedek*, "the King of Righteousness," or Melchizedek. So, Melchizedek was really Shem, the son of Noah. It was Shem/Melchizedek who came out to meet Abram, wearing the cloak of priesthood that God had created and that Adam had worn. Recall that Shem had founded the academy in which the Torah of God was taught. We should note, however, that the Hebrew word *Torah* means "instruction." When we say that Shem taught Torah, it's not the same Torah as the Five Books of Moses, but rather, it was some other vessel of instruction that gave expression to God's wisdom.

On the day after the battle, but before Abram spoke to the king of Sodom, Shem taught Abram Torah, and the midrashic tradition fills this out even more. Shem/Melchizedek brought "bread and wine" to Abram (Genesis 14:18). The midrash calls us to look at Proverbs 9:1–6:

> *Wisdom has built her house,*
> *She has hewn her seven pillars.*
> *She has prepared the feast,*
> *Mixed the wine,*
> *And also set the table.*
> *She has sent out her maids to announce*

On the heights of the town,
"Let the simple enter here";
To those devoid of sense she says,
"Come, eat my food
And drink the wine that I have mixed;
Give up simpleness and live,
Walk in the ways of understanding."

"Bread and wine," according to the midrash, is a metaphor for wisdom. The midrash tells us that when the Book of Genesis says that Shem/Melchizedek offered Abram bread and wine, he was really offering him the seven pillars of wisdom.

Shem was speaking to Abram with a kind of urgency. Shem knew how badly men (as well as some women) had been getting it wrong since the beginning of time. When the serpent seduced Eve, Adam knew better. Eve got the rules from Adam, but Adam got them directly from God, and he chose to rebel and eat from the fruit of the tree that had been forbidden him. Shem had been alive during the generation before the Flood, and he saw that vortex of venality that finally brought the mighty Flood onto the earth. Shem saw the Tower of Babel being built by people trying to protect themselves from God's judgment. Shem knew that God had chosen Abram to try to save humanity again, through a covenant of teaching, so that Abram would "instruct his children and his posterity to keep the way of the Lord by doing what is just and right" (Genesis 18:19).

This is what I think Shem/Melchizedek said to Abram as he returned from battle—victorious, flush with plunder and the shedding of blood: "What are you doing? What are you working for? *Whom* are you working for?" I can imagine Abram's answer: "I'm fighting a war and saving my kin." "Why?" Shem asks. "For the glory, the money, the power?" Shem knows: if those are the ultimate criteria by which we live—if this is what you, Abram, will teach—then civilization is doomed again.

"Are you working for him?" Shem asks, pointing to the scruffy warlord who has just offered to make Abram rich. "If not, then for whom?" Abram knows; he is working for God, for some idea of truth and justice. He saved his nephew, and the other people, because it was right.

His name, the power, the money, the fame: if he were going to acquire them, it would not be like this. And maybe the blessing wasn't about material blessing, anyway. Maybe when God said, "You will be blessed" and "You will be a blessing," God meant something else.

When Shem saw that Abram understood this and that he was now committed not only to the idea that there is One God, but to study and live by the wisdom of that One God, Shem gave the primordial, Eden-created, holy, priestly, serpent-skin robes to Abram.

Abram didn't know that the righteousness created in that moment would ripple through history. Once rescued, Lot foolishly stayed in Sodom until it was destroyed, escaping with his two daughters. The lasses thought that the entire world had been destroyed (memories of the Flood still abounded), and they each lay with their father, in order to produce progeny that would repopulate a devastated world. Two sons were born; one was named Moab. Generations later, the Moabites would produce Ruth, who was the ancestor of David, who is the ancestor of the Messiah. Maybe Abram never really knew why he saved Lot, but he finally knew for sure it wasn't about the loot.

Some ancient wisdom, rooted in Adam, passed painfully through the ages down to Shem, and it was then passed down to Abraham. Once he learned (and continued learning; there is a tradition that he studied for years in the academy of Shem, as did Isaac and Jacob, and maybe even Esau), he taught this to his own people. Some of this is written, and some of this is oral, and some of the oral tradition is only now being committed to writing. When you, the reader, are committed to learning that wisdom (for example, at the time of bar/bat mitzvah), at least metaphorically, you are putting on the *tallit* (the memory of the priestly robes passed down from Adam to Abram). When you put on that *tallit*, you link yourself back to Abram, to Shem, to Noah, to Methuselah—all the way back to Adam. You find your humanity.

And the blessing that Abram was to become? Whenever you go to synagogue and rise for the *Amidah* (the standing, statutory prayer), you will notice that the first blessing acknowledges God as *magen Avraham*, "the shield of Abraham" (and, nowadays, "help of Sarah"). We, the Jewish people, have helped God keep God's promise, creating a blessing named after Abraham that we recite every time we daven the *Amidah*. More deeply, every time we recite that blessing, we recall the spiritual journey of Abraham, and we link his journey to our own.

‏וירא

Vayera

The Joy of Waiting

DR. SANDER L. GILMAN

Then Abraham said to his servants, "You stay here with the ass. The boy and I will go up there; we will worship and we will return to you." ... Abraham then returned to his servants, and they departed together for Beer-sheba; and Abraham stayed in Beer-sheba.
(Genesis 22:5, 22:19)

Fleeing from the Nazis to Istanbul in 1935, the German-Jewish literary scholar Erich Auerbach came to examine the great divide between the Greeks and the Hebrews in their means of representing the world. The dichotomy between Hebrews and Hellenes, between Jews and Greeks, as the embodiment of the antithesis of cultures, had

---

DR. SANDER L. GILMAN is a distinguished professor of the liberal arts and sciences as well as professor of psychiatry at Emory University, where he is director of the Program in Psychoanalysis and the Health Sciences Humanities Initiative. He previously taught at Cornell University, the University of Chicago, and the University of Illinois at Chicago. A cultural and literary historian, he is author or editor of eighty books. He has been a visiting professor at numerous universities in North America, South Africa, the United Kingdom, Germany, and New Zealand, and served as president of the Modern Language Association. He has been awarded a doctor of laws (*honoris causa*) at the University of Toronto, elected an honorary professor of the Free University in Berlin, and elected an honorary member of the American Psychoanalytic Association.

haunted the nineteenth century from G. W. F. Hegel to Heinrich Heine to Matthew Arnold.

In his classic study *Mimesis* (eventually published in 1946), Auerbach sees the Hellenistic textual representation of the world as embodied in Homer's depiction of Odysseus's scar. For him, it is "fully externalized description, uniform illustration, uninterrupted connection, free expression, all events in the foreground, displaying unmistakable meanings." In the *Akedah*, the "binding of Isaac," Auerbach sees "certain parts brought into high relief, others left obscure, abruptness, suggestive influence of the unexpressed, 'background' quality, multiplicity of meanings and the need for interpretation, universal-historical claims, development of the concept of the historically becoming, and preoccupation with the problematic."[1] The former exemplifies the Greeks' tendency for realism; the latter, the skeletal and evocative nature of Jewish texts, demanding the necessary interpretation and reinterpretation so present in the millennia of readings of this central text.

But there is a level of detail often overlooked, including by Auerbach. Let us examine the other figures in this tale, in addition to Abraham and Isaac:

> So early next morning, Abraham saddled his ass and took with him two of his servants and his son Isaac.... Then Abraham said to his servants, "You stay here with the ass. The boy and I will go up there; we will worship and we will return to you." ... Abraham then returned to his servants, and they departed together for Beer-sheba; and Abraham stayed in Beer-sheba. (Genesis 22:3, 22:5, 22:19)

These two servants, most probably men, are stock figures. They reappear, as nameless figures, over and over again in the Hebrew Bible. While our eyes follow the central figures in the drama (Abraham and his son Isaac), these two figures recede from our attention (Islamic readings have it that the son is Ishmael rather than Isaac [Qur'an 37:101–13]).

Indeed, the focus of all biblical tales is only on the protagonists, from Abraham to Daniel. We focus on the actors, not the extras; we listen to the speaking roles, not the mute ones. The servants, from those armed by Abram in Genesis 14:14 to the one who mediates between Isaac and Rebekah in Genesis 24:65, remain anonymous, faceless. And they are often truly players off the stage of the action, as when Samuel turns to admonish Saul but first orders Saul to "tell the servant to walk ahead of us" (1 Samuel 9:27). The experience of the servant is to wait and to vanish quietly.

Yet one of the great complaints about our modern world is that we have all been reduced to such anonymous, faceless extras. Men especially, it is claimed, have had their powerful, socially (or divinely) defined role altered. Men have become mere cogs in a machine that robs them of individuality and thus of power and status. Charlie Chaplin's awful image of the mechanized world in *Modern Times* (1936), in which all human beings are interchangeable parts, is part of our male self-image. It is a commonplace of the post-Enlightenment world that men are no longer shapers of their own destiny, as opposed to a time when men were "really" men, as perhaps in the Hebrew Bible.

Where are the Abrahams and the Isaacs today? Where are the players on the divine stage, who were so present in the world that God took notice of them? As both Auerbach and the eleventh-century Iberian sage Yona ibn Janach imply (compare the midrash *Bereshit Rabbah* 56:12), these players symbolize something much greater. Perhaps, as Rabbi Joseph B. Soloveitchik wrote, they are surrogates for all religious human beings: "The chosen of the nation, from the moment that they revealed God, occupied themselves in a continual act of sacrifice."[2] Perhaps, as Lippman Bodoff argues in *The Binding of Isaac, Religious Murders & Kabbalah*, they represent a real father who never would actually sacrifice his son, since God could never ask such a thing.[3] We wonder: would a real father have gladly sacrificed his sons, as the World War I British poet Wilfred Owen implies in his extraordinary poem on the *Akedah*: "When lo! an angel called him out of heaven, Saying, Lay not thy hand upon the lad, … But the old man would not so, but slew his son, And half the seed of Europe, one by one."[4] Did the account of Abraham and Isaac defy the social conventions of Abraham's time about child sacrifice, as J. H. Hertz argued in his commentary? These, however, are not our questions.

Our question is about our inability to be center stage in today's world. Why does it seem that we are no longer able to shape our destinies or even to be a major player in the drama of our own lives; why have we been reduced to waiting for others to act? Why are men perpetually cast in the role of Hamlet's friends Rosencrantz and Guildenstern, or perhaps better their most famous offspring, Samuel Beckett's Vladimir and Estragon, as players off stage, while the real action takes place elsewhere—action that we are only vaguely aware of and that we can neither alter nor even respond to in our passive and dependent role? Where, in other words, have all of the real men gone; why are we, in our modern world, so beyond any awareness—never mind of revelation, but of any ability, actually, to act? Why are we perpetually "waiting for Godot," while others seem to meet him?

What is striking when we sit and wait with the servants while Abraham takes Isaac off into the distance, where the silhouette of Mount Moriah looms, is the boredom of everyday life, the very unmanliness of inaction, the small talk that passes for conversation, while others are acting, while others hear and answer the Divine: "An angel of the Lord called to him from heaven: 'Abraham! Abraham!' And he answered, 'Here I am'" (Genesis 22:11). Only at the very end, only after the action has passed, an action of which we have no knowledge, sitting and waiting—only then are we summoned to return with the actors, to return to that place from whence we had come. No one calls us; we never answer, "Here I am," because we are always there waiting; our here is indefinite and endless, our lives reduced to the role that we play in a divine script that we have never seen and the acts of which we will inhabit always on the margins.

But of course, it is that awareness of waiting that seems to define the role of all human beings in life. After Martin Heidegger's

Conversations of a Country Path about Thinking (1966), Western philosophy could speak of "waiting" as the state that enables us to move
from merely imagining the world to true "meditative thinking that
thinks the truth of being." In Heidegger's text, his "teacher" speaks
of "waiting, all right; but never awaiting. For awaiting already links
itself with re-presenting and what is re-presented." And his
"scholar" responds: "Waiting, however, lets go of that; or rather
I should say that waiting lets re-representing entirely alone." [5] In
waiting, we move from that desiccated thinking that seems to understand and know the world to an emotional response that is "appro-
priated" by "be-ing itself" and that, therefore, has turned toward
"be-ing itself." Heidegger says that simply being aware of waiting
makes waiting something very different; it makes waiting the very
essence of living. Life is neither active nor passive, neither being
center stage nor in the wings, but rather it is living unaware that
makes it so.

But this self-consciousness of waiting has been, at least since the
shaping of Rabbinic Judaism, *the* Jewish preoccupation. In many
ways, waiting for the Messiah defines being Jewish. And it is not
waiting center stage, but always on the margins. There is an old
cliché that being Jewish in the modern age is simply being modern,
and that being modern is simply being a Jew—that all of the anxi-
eties that modern man experiences, from alienation from the world
to the sense of impotence of action, defines both states. In other
words, today's Jew is not Abraham who hears the voice of the Divine,
but rather Woody Allen, who worries in *Without Feathers* (1975):
"What if nothing exists and we're all in somebody's dream? Or
what's worse, what if only that fat guy in the third row exists?"[6] And
the anonymous fat guy in the third row is very much like the servants waiting for Abraham. They seem to miss the action; they have
only to wait for the drama on center stage.

And yet that waiting is productive waiting, as long as one is consciously aware that one waits. That is what defines a Jewish life. It is
the stillness of such waiting that enables us to understand that we
are not the central players of our own existence—that "off stage" is

everywhere. That waiting for Godot, waiting for the Messiah, is the state that enables Jews to deal with the minutiae of daily existence as that which is important to defining our lives as human beings. The tasks of the quotidian life take on meaning only if we imagine waiting as that state that enables us to think about the importance of such mundane tasks. The 613 mitzvot are the articulation of the awareness of self-conscious waiting. (Indeed, if we follow Abraham ibn Ezra in *Yesod Mora*, "there is no end to the number of mitzvot.") It is not even the seemingly pedestrian task of splitting the firewood for the sacrifice that is ours, but rather, that of waiting with the ass. Such waiting is life—and it is the moment of that awareness that makes it possible to wait for the Messiah without doubt and hesitation. The act of waiting, for Jews, is not being impotent or passive; it is engaging in the meaningful activities of daily life, those so often dismissed as the activities done to pass the time.

Here we come to another understanding of a Jewish masculine identity—the ability to wait. Not in the negative sense of the alienation of modernity, but in the sense that not being a central player—being unable to comprehend the world as it is—is a role to be embraced. Being Jewish is waiting productively by acting self-consciously in the world, as if we were Abraham's servants. For remember that Maimonides states in *Sefer Ha-mitzvot* that the 497th mitzvah is to "help others load their beast" (Deuteronomy 22:4).

Come On In!

DR. RON WOLFSON

**Looking up, he saw three men standing near him. As
soon as he saw them, he ran from the entrance of the
tent to greet them....** (Genesis 18:2)

Our *parashah* begins with the classic text illustrating the mitzvah of
hachnasat orchim, "the welcoming of guests"—one of the most
important spiritual imperatives in Judaism. It is interesting to note
that it is a man who is at the center of the story. Three strangers walk
by his tent, and Abraham initiates the hospitality—in a hurry. The
key to understanding the text and the underlying message of the
story are the verbs used to describe Abraham's actions: he ran, he
rushed, he hastened. "Quick!" he cajoles Sarah. The Hebrew verbs
are even more dramatic: *vayaratz, vayimaheir, mahari!* The word for
"run" is used twice, "rushed" three times, and "fetch" four times
(Genesis 18:2–8).

DR. RON WOLFSON is Fingerhut Professor of Education at the
American Jewish University, president of Synagogue 3000, and author of
*The Spirituality of Welcoming: How to Tranform Your Congregation into a
Sacred Community*; *God's To-Do List: 103 Ways to Be an Angel and Do God's
Work on Earth*; *The Seven Questions You're Asked in Heaven: Reviewing and
Renewing Your Life on Earth*; as well as *The Art of Jewish Living* series, fam-
ily guides for preparing for and celebrating spiritual celebrations (all
Jewish Lights).

The biblical commentators have a field day with the story. What was Abraham's situation as he sat in the heat of the day at the entrance of his tent? Turn back to the end of the previous *parashah*, and we learn that Abraham had just circumcised himself at the age of ninety-nine! Moreover, Abraham was occupied with another visitor: "The Lord appeared to him ..." (Genesis 18:1). Rashi, the great medieval commentator, points out that Abraham was healing; hence, the imperative of *bikkur cholim*, "visiting the sick." Other commentators imagine that Abraham was either studying, the way we hear God's voice, or praying, the way we talk to God. And yet, when the three strangers come into view, we imagine Abraham turning to God and saying, "Excuse me, Lord, gotta go!" and rushing to greet them.

One further observation: Abraham has no idea who these strangers are; he has no clue that they are "angels of God" sent to announce that Abraham will, at long last, have an heir. To Abraham, they are simply sojourners in need of respite, and he implores them to enjoy the hospitality of his (and Sarah's) tent. From this example, the Talmud teaches this remarkable lesson: "Welcoming strangers [*hachnasat orchim*] is a greater mitzvah than welcoming the *Shechinah* [God's presence]" (*Shabbat* 127a).

I have often wondered why men seem to have lost the spiritual practice of hospitality. On airplanes, in elevators, even walking down the street, we rarely engage the stranger. Perhaps the Jewish DNA for hospitality has been dulled from centuries of persecution and fear of the stranger. For some, it's not easy to approach unfamiliar people. And yet, the simple act of smiling, extending a hand, sharing a word of welcome can be the first step in a new relationship—between man and his fellow man [*bein adam l'chaveiro*]. For each of us individually, and for us to create sacred communities of welcome, we would be well served to emulate the model of Abraham, the greatest greeter in the Torah.

חיי שרה

Chayei Sarah

The Grace of Mourning

RABBI ROBERT N. LEVINE, DD

Abraham proceeded to mourn for Sarah and to bewail her. (Genesis 23:2)

Chayei Sarah begins with Abraham losing a precious family member. His wife Sarah dies in the land of Canaan, and remarkably, the Torah records: "Abraham proceeded to mourn for Sarah and to bewail her" (Genesis 23:2). Then, he gets up from his mourning to negotiate a burial plot in the Promised Land.

Students of Torah know that the text rarely spends time describing the emotional state of its characters. In fact, this is the only Torah portion that shares details of mourning for a woman. Abraham's tears for his wife here are quite unexpected, and in order to understand their power, we have to understand their context.

Though I usually resent any broad generalizations that all men behave in a certain manner, it does seem clear that when they suffer a death, a strong majority of men are less comfortable expressing their feelings and more comfortable springing into action. We are good at making the arrangements, at picking people up at the air-

---

RABBI ROBERT N. LEVINE, DD, is rabbi of Congregation Rodeph Sholom on Manhattan's Upper West Side. He is also author of *Where Are You When I Need You? Befriending God When Life Hurts*; *There Is No Messiah and You're It: The Stunning Transformation of Judaism's Most Provocative Idea* (Jewish Lights), and *What God Can Do for You Now: For Seekers Who Want to Believe*.

port. We show our love less by heartfelt expression than by demonstrable deeds.

In his book *Fatherloss: How Sons of All Ages Come to Terms with the Deaths of Their Dads* (New York: Hyperion, 2001), Neil Chethik underscores the problems most men experience when faced with the loss of a loved one. In his view there are four distinct styles of mourning among men. One in five men can be labeled as "Dashers," those who speed through mourning and quickly rationalize their loss; one in five can be categorized as "Delayers," men who display little emotion at the time of death, but sometime later, often after feeling community support or understanding themselves better, experience mourning symptoms; one in five are "Displayers," those who are often overwhelmed and who cannot control their outburst, even if they hope to suppress them publicly. By far the largest category of mourners, according to Chethik, are the "Doers," those who tend to be less devastated by their emotion and who deal with their loss by staying busy up until, and after, the burial rites.

In my family, my mother's emotions flowed freely. My father, who was warm and genial, was much more of a schmoozer and quipster than a heartfelt communicator. Our conversations often turned to sports, which was comfortable terrain for both of us. Neither one of us talked freely about matters of the heart with each other. My father's love, in fact, was demonstrated by action. Dad shared his love by showing up. He would give the shirt off his back—not only for members of his family, but for anyone and everyone. He was the classic "Doer."

My father's own father never taught him to express emotions. Our patriarch Abraham never learns to share feelings during his formative years either. In fact, we know nothing about his mother, and all we know about his father, Terah, is that he took Abraham and other members of the family and went forth with them from Ur of the Chaldees. Abraham learns from his father that if there is something you must do, someplace you must go, you simply have to get up and get going. So, Abraham is well primed to answer God's call and journey to the land that God would show him.

Ironically, the man who becomes the father of many nations actually loses more people than he gains. No sooner does his entourage arrive in Canaan than famine strikes, and he is on his way to Egypt with his wife Sarah. Afraid that he will be killed because they will covet his beautiful wife, he convinces Sarah to pretend she is his sister. He is prepared to dispense with Sarah for his own protection. Her anger may never have abated. Then, he negotiates a separation from his nephew Lot, with whom he had traveled from "the old country."

Now lacking descendants, he and Sarah are unable to conceive a child. Oblivious to her pain and shame, he dutifully fathers a child with Sarah's handmaid and brings him into the covenant with a joyous *brit milah*.

This child, Ishmael, seems to drive a further wedge between Abraham and his wife. They seem to be in the habit of exchanging few words, as when the three angels come to tell them that Sarah, too, would finally have a child. She is skeptical about having a child at her advanced age, but she is excited about the impending sexual contact with her husband: "Now that I am withered, am I to have [sexual] enjoyment—with my husband so old?" (Genesis 18:12). Clearly such an encounter is so infrequent as to be newsworthy. Sarah's demeanor displays heartfelt emotion, while Abraham's affect is totally flat.

The birth of Isaac prompts Sarah to say, "God has brought me laughter; everyone who hears will laugh with me" (Genesis 21:6). Abraham's expression of feeling remains missing in action. When Sarah can't take the competitive presence of Ishmael after Isaac is grown, the situation grieves Abraham greatly, but he continues to suffer in silence. He neither protests to God nor battles with Sarah for the sake of his firstborn son.

Author Debra Tannen (*You Just Don't Understand: Women and Men in Conversation* [New York: William Morrow, 1990], p. 229) believes that men use silence to exercise power over women. Perhaps she is right, because when Abraham faces the ultimate test of offering his and Sarah's son, Isaac, on Mount Moriah as a burnt offering, he shares nothing of this ordeal with Sarah. The silence that pervades Abraham and Isaac's three-day walk up the mountain is as painful for the reader as it probably was for the participants.

Isaac is not only his father's beloved, last remaining son; he is also the repository of God's covenantal promise that Abraham would set the history and destiny of multiple civilizations in motion. Slaughtering Isaac also will spell the death of Abraham's considerable ambition and his potent legacy.

So, the Torah again leaves it to the reader to discern the intensity of emotion Abraham feels as he lifts the knife over his bound son. The midrash overcomes the text's inhibitions with powerful testimony:

> He then placed Isaac on the altar. Abraham's eyes gazed into Isaac's, and Isaac's eyes were lifted to the highest heavens. Tears gushed forth from Abraham's eyes until his whole body swam in them. "My son," he cried out, "since you are in anguish that your blood has to be shed, may your Creator provide you with another sacrifice in your stead." A heart-rending cry of agony burst from his throat; his eyes tremulously looked to the *Shechinah* [the divine presence]; he raised his voice and cried, "I will lift up mine eyes to the mountains; from whence shall my help come?" (*Yalkut Shimoni* 1:101)

Suffering in silence, Abraham, who endures the disappearance of one precious person after another from his life, will take it no more. According to the midrash, the emotional floodgates finally open, and he comes to realize the price he has paid for his silence and for his ambition to fulfill the human and divine expectations inherent in covenant. Personal vulnerability pierces his severe demeanor, and although he doesn't have to plunge the knife into his son, in a very real sense he still loses Isaac. The Torah hardly pictures them walking arm-in-arm down the mountain. Quite the contrary: Abraham returns alone. He will never truly have Isaac in his life again, and he can no longer deal passively with his loss.

Our text teaches, "And Abraham proceeded to mourn for Sarah and to bewail her" (Genesis 23:2). But the text literally says, "And

Abraham came to bewail her" (*vayavo Avraham lispod l'Sarah*). Where, in fact, was he coming from?

The Rabbis in the midrash speculate: "Rabbi Levi said: 'He was coming from his father's funeral.' Rabbi Jose said: 'He came straight from Mount Moriah'" (*Bereshit Rabbah* 58:5). Wherever he was, he wasn't present for his wife's death. Another precious person has departed, and he can no longer show Sarah the new Abraham—the one who not only feels emotions, but expresses what he is feeling. So he cries over the death of his wife who permitted him to live out his grandiose dreams. He cries for the corpses, real and metaphorical, that litter the path to his covenantal ambitions. He cries, because the Abraham who now has developed a "feminine" side will not be able to share this with the woman who would appreciate that side the most.

I witnessed much more of my father's emotional side later in his life. He said, "I love you" more freely; he hugged more openly. As his Alzheimer's disease progressed, he showed anger much more, but also much love. When I would see him, he would tell me how much he wanted to come back to Congregation Rodeph Sholom, the synagogue I serve as rabbi. I took that as a sign that even in his decline, even when he could not remember my name, he desperately wanted to be with me. That is a gift I will always cherish.

Abraham, too, expresses the emotion he so long repressed, but now he rises up to ensure that his wife would be buried in the land promised to them by God. Abraham resolves further to find a wife for his son Isaac who will help his son fulfill his ambitions and covenantal responsibilities—perhaps a woman with whom Isaac can share the feelings Abraham never could express to Sarah.

When the servant Eliezer brings Rebekah from "the old country," the Torah tells us that "Isaac then brought her into the tent of his mother Sarah, and he took Rebekah as his wife. Isaac loved her, and thus found comfort after his mother's death" (Genesis 24:67).

It must have been a great comfort to Abraham to see his son able to express love to Rebekah. Abraham is now a man who is more able not only to feel emotions, but to express them more completely. As men often do, Abraham will reconnect quickly, taking on another wife named Keturah. They will have six more children together, and obviously a deep marital bond.

Ultimately, Abraham provides a most useful model for men's grieving. His journey shows a way that the "Dasher" or "Delayer" can easily become a "Displayer," then a "Doer"—not someone running away from feelings, but a more emotionally mature man who uses his painful experience to become a more sensitive, directed member of a family and community. He will bury his wife with dignity in the land of their shared dreams and ensure that their legacy and the covenant will live on through their progeny.

The Torah finally says that God blessed Abraham *ba-kol*, "in all things" (Genesis 24:1). Among the most precious blessings he is able to enjoy in his satisfying later years are his ability to be more present as a man, husband, and father, as well as his ability to express what he feels and to act on his convictions. Abraham's odyssey can be instructive to every man who suffers a loss and seeks to learn and grow from his grief journey.

תולדות
Toldot

Twin Sons, Twin Destinies

RABBI PETER S. KNOBEL

This is the story of Isaac, son of Abraham. Abraham begot Isaac. Isaac was forty years old when he took to wife Rebekah, daughter of Bethuel the Aramean of Paddan-aram, sister of Laban the Aramean. Isaac pleaded with the Eternal on behalf of his wife, because she was barren; and the Eternal responded to his plea, and his wife Rebekah conceived. But the children struggled in her womb, and she said, "If so, why do I exist?" She went to inquire of the Eternal and the Eternal answered her:

> *"Two nations are in your womb,*
> *Two separate peoples shall issue from your body;*
> *One people shall be mightier than the other,*
> *And the older shall serve the younger."*

(Genesis 25:19–23)

Parashat Toldot details the struggle between Jacob and Esau. But this story is about far more than simply sibling rivalry. It is about different

---

RABBI PETER S. KNOBEL is senior rabbi of Beth Emet the Free Synagogue in Evanston, Illinois, and served as president of the Central Conference of American Rabbis (CCAR). He chaired the CCAR Siddur Editorial Committee that produced *Mishkhan T'filah*, the new Reform Jewish prayer book.

visions of the future. Those competing visions of the future will provide us with a template for understanding not only the two brothers, and not only the destiny of the Jewish people, but ourselves as well.

Rebekah is barren, and Isaac prayerfully intervenes on her behalf. Her pregnancy is so difficult that Rebekah asks God to explain what is happening to her and in a remarkable passage God answers her. Interesting to note: Both Rebekah and Isaac have access to God, but in some ways (and ironic, for a male-oriented tradition), her access to the Divine seems deeper and even more effective. While God grants Isaac's prayer for children, God seems to "favor" Rebekah by revealing the future of the sons to her, and not to Isaac.

Perhaps the relative strength of Rebekah stems not only from her strength, but from Isaac's weakness. True, Isaac has inherited the covenant from his father Abraham, but the *Akedah*, his near-sacrifice at the hand of his father, has left him vulnerable and traumatized. It is clear that Rebekah is in charge of carrying out God's plan and that her wisdom is necessary to guarantee that the proper son inherits the covenant.

According to a midrash, when Rebekah passed the legendary academy of Shem and Eber, Jacob tried to exit the womb so he could study Torah, and when she passed a tavern, Esau struggled to exit the womb so he could "party." The moral future of the two sons seems to have been ordained, even from the womb. From the very moment of his birth, Esau demonstrates physicality and a particular appetite for the sensuous. Jacob, who will ultimately prevail, is born grasping the heel of his brother, Esau. From the very moment of *his* birth, he is the usurper. It is ironic that while the text here emphasizes Jacob's lack of physicality, later in Genesis (32:23–33), when Jacob wrestles with a mysterious stranger who might be either an angel or his brother (among many distinct possiblities), the supposedly unphysical Jacob demonstrates his physical strength. Jacob matures; he uses both his mind and his physical strength. Maturity is about wholeness, the integration of human talents and abilities.

Key to understanding this portion is both the difference between the brothers and the place they hold in their parents' affection.

> When the boys grew up, Esau became a skillful hunter, a man
> of the outdoors; but Jacob was a mild man who stayed in
> camp. Isaac favored Esau because he had a taste for game; but
> Rebekah favored Jacob. (Genesis 25:27–28)

Why does Isaac favor the son who is the hunter, a man who lives
passionately and recklessly spurns his birthright? Once again, the
Akedah (the binding and near-sacrifice of Isaac) returns to the story
as a haunting presence. Isaac admires Esau's strength because it is
his way of responding to his own sense of vulnerability. Unable to
protect himself from his father and his father's God, he yearns for the
power to defend himself. Like a victim of a bully, he fantasizes about
being able to defeat the bully, and he invests his hope for the future
in his firstborn, who has the physical prowess to protect himself and
his family. The key to Isaac's love of Esau is that Esau represents the
powerful man that Isaac never was, but nevertheless wishes he had
been.

Isaac's own weakness blinds him to Jacob's strengths. Jacob has
no interest in hunting; his skills are mostly in the (stereotypically
unmasculine) domestic arts, and Isaac must have seen this as a sign
of weakness. The truth is that Jacob has learned intellectual survival
skills from his mother, Rebekah, but Isaac cannot appreciate that.

> Once when Jacob was cooking a stew, Esau came in from the
> open, famished. And Esau said to Jacob, "Give me some of
> that red stuff to gulp down, for I am famished"—which is
> why he was named Edom. Jacob said, "First sell me your
> birthright." And Esau said, "I am at the point of death, so of
> what use is my birthright to me?" But Jacob said, "Swear to
> me first." So he swore to him, and sold his birthright to Jacob.
> (Genesis 25:29–33)

Esau can think only about his momentary needs and desires, and
not about the future. By contrast, Jacob is cunning and calculating.
He takes advantage of the situation. We tend to denigrate these
traits, but they are also examples of the traits that are necessary for

leadership. Jacob perceives that his brother will squander the family legacy. If Jacob is going to protect that legacy, he needs to act decisively. His goals are the long-term survival of the family and its relationship to God and its destiny.

At the end of Isaac's life he is blind, and the time comes for him to bless the son who will ultimately become his heir. He sends Esau out to hunt game and to prepare a savory meal for him. Let us imagine how Isaac must have anticipated that meal! In Isaac's mind, it was to be more than a meal; it was to be a male bonding ritual. Father and son will share a moment of great intimacy, united in sharing the bounty of the hunt. The meal will strengthen the blind old man and make the blessing more powerful and effective.

How telling, then, that some commentators suggest that Isaac's blindness is far more than a physical disability. Isaac is blind—that is, oblivious—to the consequences of following the ancient and honored principle of letting the firstborn inherit. Isaac's love blinds him to the reality that his firstborn is unfit to head the family, because he lives only in the present and has no concept of the future.

But this glorious culinary moment of male bonding is not to be. Rebekah overhears Isaac tell Esau to go hunting and to prepare a savory meal so that he may bless him. Rebekah now prepares a reluctant Jacob for what will be a fateful moment. She cooks a savory dish disguised as game, and she wraps Jacob's arms in lambskin so that when the blind Isaac touches him he will believe that Jacob is, in fact, the hairy Esau. She is clear as to which son must inherit the covenant, and her clarity stands in stark contrast to her husband Isaac's blindness.

Jacob now appears before his father with the dish his mother has prepared. The swiftness of his arrival convinces Isaac that God must have blessed the hunt. It is a sign that he is about to do the right thing—that his favorite son Esau will, indeed, be his heir. The "natural" order will be restored; the "expected" order will be, in fact, the correct order. But birth order is not to be confused with destiny. God's plan is different. Each son is to be judged by his fitness, and not by the accident of birth.

When Jacob presents himself, Isaac has some doubts: Is this *really* Esau?

> So Jacob drew close to his father Isaac, who felt him and wondered. "The voice is the voice of Jacob, yet the hands are the hands of Esau." (Genesis 27:22)

Does Isaac know that he is being deceived? Is it possible that he knows that in spite of his love for Esau, Jacob must be his heir? The voice is the voice of the one who will use intelligence—some would say guile—to succeed, but the hands are the hands of the man who acts, but does not necessarily think.

Therein lie all the richness and complexity in this story. On some level, Jacob is not an admirable character. He will learn his lesson; he will pay for his treatment of his brother and father by being tricked by his uncle Laban. He will learn the lesson the hard way, but in the end he will be successful and God will bless him. The text teaches us that sometimes decisive action is necessary, but painful. Sometimes it means hurting others, even the members of our own family. Short-term pain may be necessary for long-term gain. This is not a pleasant or comforting message, but difficult circumstances sometimes conspire to make it painfully realistic.

And yet, in spite of apparently promising everything to Jacob, Isaac does reserve a blessing for Esau.

> *"See, your abode shall enjoy the fat of the earth*
> *And the dew of heaven above.*
> *Yet by your sword you shall live,*
> *And you shall serve your brother;*
> *But when you grow restive,*
> *You shall break his yoke from your neck."*
> (Genesis 27:39–40)

Ultimately, Esau will prosper. His military prowess will serve him well. In finding the appropriate blessing for Esau, Isaac recognizes his son's nature and strengths—and he develops a fuller understanding of both his sons' human qualities.

Rabbi Samuel Karff, a Reform rabbi from Houston, Texas, reminds us in *The Torah: A Modern Commentary*:

> Apparently even God must select imperfect instruments to fulfill His purposes. He must choose between Jacob—a man who desires the birthright so deeply he will cheat to secure it—and Esau who so lightly esteems it that he forfeits the birthright for a bowl of lentils. Jacob's calculated cunning must be weighed against Esau's undisciplined craving for immediate self-gratification. Working with "human material" involved God in a difficult but inescapable choice, and God decides: It is better to care too much than too little.[1]

This is, fortunately, not the end of the story. True, Jacob and Esau live separated from each other. They mature and become successful—each in his own right, each in his own way, each one living up to their father's blessing. Years later, they will meet again. Esau, the one who has been deceived and deprived of the blessing he thought he wanted, embraces his brother, Jacob.

Sometimes the bruising sibling rivalry of youth becomes the crucible for finding one's own way, and in that way, a new kind of relationship becomes possible.

ויצא

Vayetzei

Night School

RABBI KERRY M. OLITZKY

Early in the morning, Laban kissed his sons and daughters and bade them good-by; then Laban left on his journey homeward. Jacob went on his way, and angels of God encountered him. When he saw them, Jacob said, "This is God's camp." So he named that place Mahanaim. (Genesis 32:1–3)

While the entire Book of Genesis provides us with a woman's lens on the Jewish people throughout its early history (since women navigate the world through relationships, and most of Genesis is about family relationships and not the rules and regulations, which is the stuff out of which men make their lives), this Torah portion is

---

RABBI KERRY M. OLITZKY is executive director of the Jewish Outreach Institute, the only national independent organization dedicated to bringing Judaism to interfaith families and the unaffiliated. Named one of the fifty most influential rabbis by *Newsweek* magazine, he is author of many books, including *Life's Daily Blessings: Inspiring Reflections on Gratitude and Joy for Every Day, Based on Jewish Wisdom; Grief in Our Seasons: A Mourner's Kaddish Companion; 100 Blessings Every Day: Daily Twelve Step Recovery Affirmations, Exercises for Personal Growth and Renewal Reflecting Seasons of the Jewish Year;* and *Twelve Jewish Steps to Recovery: A Personal Guide to Turning from Alcoholism and Other Addictions—Drugs, Food, Gambling, Sex…* (all Jewish Lights).

focused on the spiritual journey of the later patriarch, Jacob. So we might expect to be able to use a primarily male lens as a vehicle through which to view Jacob's life and this portion of our sacred text. At the end of *Vayetzei*, we encounter Jacob as he prepares to meet his brother Esau, having left him behind many years earlier after unfairly seizing his entitlement as eldest son to an extra (double) portion of their father's inheritance. The position that he arrogates to himself is that of the primogenitor. This scheming nature of Jacob seems to be part of his personality.

As is noted in the beginning of the portion, in Genesis 28, Jacob stops for the night. He falls into a deep sleep and dreams—a common interpretative motif for the Bible. Whenever dreams appear, the reader is invited, beckoned, drawn, enticed to interpret the vision. But Jacob's dream is not a simple one whose meaning is readily apparent, either to the reader or to the dreamer himself. Rather, this dream reflects Jacob's spiritual struggle—what social gerontologists might call a mini–life review, and those who are more spiritually inclined would label a *cheshbon ha-nefesh* (literally, "an accounting of the soul"). In the middle of his life, at this important crossroads, it is time for Jacob to take stock, perhaps so that he can make some adjustments on the path that he has chosen for his journey before it is too late. In doing so, Jacob is suggesting by his example (an unusual approach for most males who prefer the more didactic approach) that other men do the same thing—at various points along their life journeys.

Jacob is weary—a profound weariness that emerges from a place far deeper than travel fatigue. It is a weariness that threatens his very being. Jacob is weary from his entire life's journey—only parts of which are shared in the Torah text, but with which readers can readily identify. Our jobs are tough. Our families make demands on us. And our bodies just "ain't what they used to be." So, Jacob demonstrates for us what is necessary. He is clearly trying to discern the path that brought him to this moment in his life. He is trying to discern the impact that his prior decisions—such as the trickery with which he deceived his brother and father—have made on his present situation, so that he might redirect his future life course. His whole life has been about the nature of journey, about going from place to place in order to succeed and achieve a measure of greatness—something that would become his legacy, something that would last beyond his years on this earth.

Unlike his future encounters of articulated struggle (such as in Genesis 32, when Jacob will wrestle with himself once again—in that episode Jacob's hidden self will be personified by an angel), this segment of Jacob's life features the well-known dream sequence symbolically identified as "Jacob's ladder." But this portion's narrative features a struggle of no less significance, even if it is not quite as explicit. It, too, is a struggle with self—a struggle with his manhood, perhaps a direct contrast with the way our own contemporary culture defines masculinity. And it is this struggle that manifests itself in various ways throughout Jacob's life, as it does throughout the lives of many men today.

Jacob lays his head on a stone—no soft feather pillow for this suddenly tough guy!—and dreams of angels ascending and descending on a ladder that reaches from the earth into the heavens. Note that the "earth to heaven" direction is not one that we would expect of angels. God appears to Jacob and promises him a secure future. God promises Jacob that he will return to the Land of Israel, which is a foreshadowing indicating that he will leave and that he will return, an assurance that we all crave.

It is now four chapters and many years later. As Jacob anticipates meeting Esau, what does he reveal to the reader? He is obviously concerned with his family's well-being, for which he holds himself responsible. So he divides his possessions—all that he owns—into two equal camps, just in case his attempt at reconciliation doesn't work. He may be a dreamer, but he is also a realist. Rather than anticipating that their well-worn and familiar childhood script will be replayed in this encounter, that he will prevail and deceive his brother once again, this time Jacob feels particularly vulnerable and fearful. The perspective of age—and the wisdom of experience that can come with it, but only when we learn from the events of the past—cause him to be anxious and afraid. It is important to note the complexity of this context. Here we encounter the human dimension of wisdom—learned from human experience—in the midst of the divinely revealed text of the Torah, revelation. Jacob now understands the ramification of his childhood acts. He fears that his brother will take advantage of the upper hand that he has always held, for Esau was always stronger, and that he will retaliate for what Jacob did to him when they were children and young men.

The reader of the text must consider: will his strategy serve to mitigate his brother Esau's brute strength, which frightens him? When men encounter one another, it is all too often in the context of the challenge of physical strength. Who is stronger than the other? "Feel my muscle. Punch me in the stomach and see how hard it is. Go ahead, I can take it." "Let's arm wrestle," my own brothers suggest whenever we get together, even after all these years. And I admit that I tend to do the same with my sons, as well, in a feeble attempt to prove that age has not robbed me of my strength and therefore my masculinity. Jacob even tries to soften up his brother by sending him gifts, hoping that the gesture will mitigate the events of a childhood that Jacob refuses to relinquish and assign to the past.

We return to Genesis 28, to the mysterious night vision of the ladder. Jacob awakens from his slumber, and he realizes that during the night he has somehow encountered divinity. In a profoundly insightful and spiritual moment, he exclaims, "God was *with me* in this place and I, I did not know [emphasis mine]" (Genesis 28:16). The redundant "I" tells us that he has learned something about himself in the night, and it is related to the preparation that he will need to make, years later, for the encounter with his brother.

What is it that he learned about himself during that night? Is it simply that he didn't really know himself previously, that he is someone other than who he thought he was? It seems that he has learned the important lesson that he was never alone, that he never had to depend on his strength alone, that God was with him throughout his journey. While he thought he was always acting alone, that he was a master of his own life, he comes to understand that God was

47

involved in all that took place. For a man, this is a difficult lesson to learn—that there is something or someone beyond the self, more powerful, that has control over our lives.

Some will suggest that this Torah portion is an example of what the Hasidim call *devekut* (cleaving) and *hitlahavut* (ecstasy). While Jacob never fully abdicates his ego (here is where this episode comes into direct conflict with those interested in Zen Buddhism, which suggests the positive inclination in such a position), he comes as close as possible to merging ecstatically with God. This is indicated in the statement "God is in this place and I, I did not know," the generally accepted translation of the verse, slightly different than the one that I suggested in the last paragraph. This is not easy for men. It demands intimacy and a surrender of one's self, as well as one's self-control—none of which are easy for men to do. And this is precisely why this portion is so instructive. For Jacob is not only a patriarch; he also represents the entire people of Israel.

But this portion teaches us that if we are able to pursue intimacy with God, then we can learn intimacy with others as well. Jewish theologian Martin Buber stated it differently. He argued that all of our human interactions should reflect the "I-Thou" interaction that we pursue with God. The contemporary Jewish theologian Dr. Eugene B. Borowitz suggests that we should live our lives as reflections of the covenantal relationship we seek with God.

This is a profound kind of intimacy that the text is suggesting—much more than the daily experience of humans, which usually finds itself in the form of a loving and mutually supportive sexual relationship. It is still limited by the human dimension. By attaching it to the Divine, as this portion is suggesting, we can transcend its human dimension and raise it heavenward. Then, the angels will indeed start at earth and climb heavenward—and bring us along on their way.

When this notion of being in control of our own life and its direction gets out of control, it becomes manifest as an addiction. This is why those in recovery force themselves to "turn it over" to God. Their poison of choice forces them to recognize that they are not in control. Rather, it was the addiction (to drugs or alcohol or compulsive behavior [sex, gambling, food]) that was controlling them. In order to regain control of their lives, they have to give up their control. This is the counterintuitive nature of spirituality as well.

Late in the portion, we see that Jacob fully understands the path that he has traveled. Even after his uncle Laban tricks him (clearly, poetic irony and a replay of/repay for his own trickery of his brother Esau), he understands the lesson of the dream. Perhaps he has learned these lessons in a dream because he was not able to learn them in his waking hours. Jacob readily sees the presence of God in the actions that surrounded him—something that he would have missed previously, something that men readily miss. "Early in the morning, Laban kissed his sons and daughters and bade them good-bye; then Laban left on his journey homeward. Jacob went on his way, and angels of God encountered him. When he saw them, Jacob said, 'This is God's camp.' So he named that place Mahanaim" (Genesis 32:1–3). Jacob has found a place for God in his life and, in so doing, a place for himself as well.

וישלח
Vayishlach

A Time to Embrace

Dr. Norman J. Cohen

Esau ran to greet him. He embraced him and, falling on his neck, he kissed him; and they wept. (Genesis 33:4)

Jacob sits on his camel for a long time, watching as Esau and his entourage make their way southeastward toward the mountains of Seir (Genesis 33:16–17).[1] He thinks to himself, "How could Esau really have believed that the two of them could dwell together after so much had happened between them?" Yes, they had found a way to make peace with each other after all the jealousy, strife, and bitterness of twenty years before, but Jacob knows that their basic differences would not allow them to live in proximity to each other. So as he sees Esau's caravan disappear over the faraway hills, he motions to his family to follow him as he turns west in the direction of Succoth.

DR. NORMAN J. COHEN is provost of Hebrew Union College–Jewish Institute of Religion, where he is also professor of midrash. He lectures frequently to audiences of many faiths, and participated in Bill Moyers' *Genesis: A Living Conversation* series on PBS. His books include *Self, Struggle and Change: Family Conflict Stories in Genesis and Their Healing Insights for Our Lives*; *Voices from Genesis: Guiding Us through the Stages of Life*; *The Way Into Torah*; *Hineini in our Lives: Learning How to Respond to Others through 14 Biblical Texts and Personal Stories*; and *Moses and the Journey to Leadership: Timeless Lessons of Effective Management from the Bible and Today's Leadership* (all Jewish Lights).

But were Jacob and Esau destined to live apart, just as they had to separate from the womb? When God tells Rebekah that she will give birth to twins, God emphasizes the word *yipparedu*, meaning "[they] shall be separated" (Genesis 25:23), indicating perhaps that her sons would always be in conflict.[2] Are we, like the sons of Isaac and Rebekah, so different from our own brothers that we are relegated to living at a distance from one another? Can we never overcome the chasm that may exist between us?

The tension between the two was exacerbated by the way in which their parents related to them. Isaac, grown old, was dependent upon Esau, the hunter, to provide him with food, and as a result, we are told that Isaac loved Esau, while Rebekah loved Jacob (Genesis 25:27–28). Is this so different from our own families in which an aging parent is dependent upon one child for his or her care and sustenance, which can adversely affect the relationship both between that child and his or her siblings, and between the parent and the other children? This is especially true in the case of brothers in need of their father's affection and recognition.

In the biblical saga, the tension between them reaches a fevered pitch when Jacob usurps the blessing intended for Esau, the firstborn, with the help of their mother (Genesis 27). Esau's pain, at having been rejected by his father and victimized by his brother, is palpable. When he hears from his father that it is Jacob who received the blessing—the legacy handed down from his grandfather Abraham—he bursts into wild and bitter sobbing and says to Isaac, "Bless me too, Father!" (Genesis 27:34–38). Esau's very human response not only elicits our sympathy; if we're honest with ourselves, it also causes us to identify with him. We recall those moments when we did not receive needed stroking or anticipated reward from our father, only to witness our brother being treated in what we perceived to be an undeserved fashion. Or perhaps it was even worse: we knew in our hearts that he tried to undermine our relationship with our father! Yes, Esau's painful words are our words; we have thought them, we have uttered them.

With Esau's rage so evident, Jacob has no choice but to listen to his mother Rebekah's insistence that he flee to her brother Laban's house in Haran (Genesis 27:41–45), for surely Esau would have killed him once Isaac died. The two brothers would not only live a great distance apart during the next two decades, but we can only surmise what impact the intervening years might have had upon their feelings toward each other.

However wide the chasm, a score of years pass, and Jacob finds himself on a journey homeward—a journey that involves confronting Esau. As he approaches his destination, he is met by a band of angels and thinks to himself, "This is God's camp" (*machaneh Elohim*). And yet, he names the place *Machanaim*, "two camps" (Genesis 32:2). Why does he choose the name "two camps" and not "God's camp"?

There are indeed two camps—Jacob and Esau—and Jacob himself makes the symbolism clear to us, when he implores God just a bit later, "And now I have become two camps. Deliver me, I pray, from the hand of my brother, from the hand of Esau" (Genesis 32:11–12). As he is about to confront his brother, what choices does Jacob have? Why should we expect him to be any different than we are? When a sibling with whom we struggle confronts us, we are quite adept at erecting protective defenses.

And so, Jacob first "sends messengers ahead of him to [greet] his brother Esau," calling him "my lord" and referring to himself as his brother's servant (Genesis 32:4–5). It is his hope to gain his brother's favor, though he clearly does not mean any of it. But it is of no avail, since he learns that his brother is marching toward him with a band of four hundred men. He, therefore, must prepare for the worst. He divides his entourage into two separate camps, thinking that if Esau attacks, one camp will be able to escape (Genesis 32:8–9). Often when we confront our own brothers, we do not expect to solve difficult long-standing conflicts, but only hope to move beyond them with as little damage as possible. Finally, as Esau draws closer and Jacob becomes even more desperate, he realizes that if he can, he has to appease his brother. We, ourselves, know the tactic well; by giving in to the other just a bit, by feeding our shadow, we hope that the conflict will disappear. Jacob sends large numbers from his herds in droves to his brother, instructing his servants to tell Esau that the herds are gifts from Jacob, who is following behind (Genesis 32:14–19). Jacob does not understand that Esau will not be appeased by gifts. If we are to reconcile with our brother, it will only happen if we are willing to embrace him. He will not be bought off!

Jacob, however, no longer will have the luxury of insulating himself from the confrontation with Esau. For all of his defensive strategy, Jacob finds himself alone on the bank of the Jabbok River, having sent his entire family across during the night. And it is there, at *Maavar Yabbok*, at the point of crossing the river, whose letters are simply an inversion of his own name, Yaakov, that his struggle for reconciliation with his brother actually begins.

A man (an *ish*) suddenly appears who attacks him (Genesis 32:25). Perhaps it is only a dream, or maybe Esau has, indeed, forded the river, taking advantage of his brother's vulnerability. Jacob and Esau wrestle in the mud on the riverbank, reenacting their struggle in their mother's womb (Genesis 25:22).[3]

They fight through the night, until the first rays of sunlight usher in a new day—perhaps a new beginning for the brothers. When the *ish*, the man—Esau—pleads with Jacob to let him go, he responds, "I will not let you go, unless you bless me" (Genesis 32:27). Jacob had already received Esau's blessing, yet he seems to still need it. We, like Jacob, may have gotten much recognition from those we have loved, including our parents. Yet, deep down, what we need most is the recognition of those whom we have hurt, especially our brother(s) with whom we may have struggled. And in the end, Jacob receives the blessing he seeks (Genesis 32:28–30), for when the *ish* takes leave of him, the Hebrew reads *vayivarech* (Genesis 32:30), which though customarily translated as "he left," clearly means "he blessed [him]," because the verb root *berech* implies blessing.

As the sun rises in the eastern sky, Jacob can be seen limping away from his night encounter, having been wounded in the struggle at the Yabbok (Genesis 32:32). He raises his eyes and sees Esau approaching from a distance, accompanied by the band of men his messengers have reported. In anticipation, he once again divides his retinue, but this time, he does not take up the rear, protecting himself. Rather, he himself goes on ahead, even though he may still fear for his life. Perhaps for the first time, Jacob is willing to face his brother openly. As he moves toward Esau, he bows low to the ground seven times, finally willing to humble himself and pay his older brother the respect he deserves (Genesis 33:1–3).

How do brothers greet each other after twenty years of estrangement? Who would be willing to take the first step, to utter the first words? How to even find the words? And in that instant when we first look at our sibling, we feel the pain/joy of the moment of reunion. After Jacob bows before him, Esau runs to greet him. How can he hold back? He has thought for a long time about this moment and wondered how he would react. But now, there are no feelings of hatred, jealousy, or revenge. Instead of striking his brother, Esau embraces him (Genesis 33:5)—the same brother with whom he had wrestled from the beginning, in real life and in their dreams. They had struggled in their mother's womb; now they are holding each other with arms open wide.[4] It is, indeed, possible for brothers to move from conflict to unity, from struggle to embrace. The similiarity in sound between the roots *avak* (struggle or wrestle) and the operative word here, *chabak* (embrace), underscores this point.

We can only overcome the distance we feel from our brothers by giving up the insulated defensive postures that we habitually assume and reaching out to find acceptance. Jacob has to be ready to truly give of himself—to sacrifice a part of his ego—if he and Esau are to reconcile. And he does. He implores Esau to take the gift (*minchah*) he has brought so that Esau will find favor (*chen*) with him. In anticipation of his meeting with his brother, Jacob had divided his retinue into two armed camps (*machanaim*), yet now he offers Esau his *minchah* (gift)—a sign of affection and love (Genesis 33:9–10).[5]

But Jacob knows what he must truly give up if he is to repair his relationship with his brother. He must return that which he stole from him twenty years before—Esau's rightful blessing. And the text comes full circle as Jacob begs Esau, "Please accept my present [*bir-*

chati]" (Genesis 33:11). His *minchah*, his gift to his brother, is his *b'rachah*, the "blessing" he possesses, the one he is guilty of taking.

Jacob has grown enough to want Esau to have the *b'rachah* that rightfully belongs to him. And after much urging, Esau accepts it. In so doing, Esau is able to let go of the anger he has harbored and the pain that he has borne alone. He can finally embrace the brother whom he saw as the favored of their parents, and Jacob responds by saying, "You received me favorably [*va-tirtzeni*]" (Genesis 33:10).[6]

The solidification of the relationship between the brothers seems to be achieved, and Esau, for his part, is ready to ride off together with Jacob and begin their lives anew. Believing they can once again live in close proximity in Seir, where he has settled, Esau says to Jacob, "Let us [then] start on our journey [together]" (Genesis 33:12). But Jacob seems to understand that as much as the hunter and the shepherd may care for each other, they can never really live together. But how can he explain this to Esau, without hurting him? Similarly, how can we say to our brother that as much as it is nice to spend time together and have our children get to know their cousins, it really isn't feasible for us to spend the summer together, as if we were still kids in Mom and Dad's house?

So when Esau starts on his journey to Seir, though Jacob promises to follow him, Jacob turns toward Succoth and Shechem. One can only surmise what is going through Esau's mind as he glances back at his brother. Does he notice, at all, that Jacob's entourage has begun to turn slightly westward, and not east to Seir? Or is he oblivious to the reality of who they are and how their destinies are different? Maybe in his naïveté or perhaps in his optimism, Esau believes, or tries to convince himself, that Jacob will arrive in Seir.

Like Jacob and Esau, we, too, hopefully achieve a rapprochement with our brothers—yet that moment of understanding and healing will not necessarily last forever. Reconciliation between brothers does not always mean closeness, at least in a world that is not yet Eden.

וישב

Vayeshev

Every Family Has a Joseph

PROF. JULIUS LESTER

Now Israel loved Joseph best of all his sons, for he was the child of his old age; and he had made him an ornamented tunic. (Genesis 37:3)

Of the fifty chapters that compose the Book of Genesis, exactly half—twenty-five—are about Jacob and his family. Of those twenty-five, thirteen are devoted to Joseph, Jacob's favorite son. Genesis devotes more space to Joseph's story than anyone else's, and at the heart of this narrative is Joseph's relationship with his father.

Of the three patriarchs, Jacob is more human than his austere, forbidding grandfather, Abraham, or his silent and remote father, Isaac. Jacob is a man of the world who does not hesitate to use deceit to get what he wants.

He deceives his father so he can receive the blessing that should have gone to his twin brother, Esau. He deceives his father-in-law, Laban, to escape from the peonage under which he has been living.

PROF. JULIUS LESTER is professor emeritus of Judaic and Near Eastern Studies at the University of Massachusetts at Amherst. He is author of many books, including *Lovesong: Becoming a Jew*; *When the Beginning Began*, a book of midrashim; and *The Autobiography of God*, a novel. For fourteen years he was lay leader of Beth El Synagogue in St. Johnsbury, Vermont. He lives in western Massachusetts with his wife, two cats, and more books than he can ever read.

When Jacob meets Esau after many years apart, he deceives him by promising that the two will travel together the next day. Instead, Jacob goes in the opposite direction to avoid his brother.

Worst of all, according to Torah commentators, Jacob does something no parent should do; he does not hide the fact that Joseph is his favorite son, leading the Rabbis to say that a father should not single out one child among his other children (Talmud, *Shabbat* 10b).

However, it is significant that when the Torah states that Joseph was loved more than the other eleven sons, it is not Jacob but *Israel* who "loved Joseph best of all his sons" (Genesis 27:3)—Israel, the name that Jacob received after he wrestled all night with the angel. The Stone edition of the *Chumash* quotes Rav Bachya, an eleventh-century Spanish commentator, as explaining that when the Torah refers to Jacob by the name "Israel," it is referring to his "higher nature." Thus "Jacob-as-Israel" singled out Joseph because he recognized his son's potential spiritual greatness.

The simple fact is that many parents do have favorites among their children. Some try to hide this; others don't. But children always know which one of them is mother's favorite, which one is father's, and which one simply does not belong.

Although a father loves all of his children, it is only human for him to have more affection for that child who is most like him, or for that child who shares his interests, or for that child in whom he sees something of himself.

But can a father justify being as flagrant as Jacob was about his love for Joseph? Isn't it wrong for a father to flaunt his love for the favorite in front of the other children? Doing so accomplishes nothing, except create resentment of the father and hatred of the favored one.

Joseph's behavior does not help matters. The Torah describes him as a *naar*, a "youth" (Genesis 37:3), but he is seventeen years old when the Torah begins his story. At that time, a male at this age was considered a man. A midrash says that Joseph "painted his eyes, dressed his hair carefully, and walked with a mincing step" (*Bereshit Rabbah* 84:7). If this isn't bad enough, Joseph is a tattletale who runs to tell his father when his brothers are doing things Jacob disapproves of. Finally, and worst of all, Joseph tells his brothers and father the dreams in which his father and brothers are subservient to him.

But I understand Joseph. I was the Joseph in my family; my father was Jacob.

I was born in 1939, at a time when racial segregation was the accepted norm. I grew up in the black community of Kansas City, Kansas, which was so separate from white communities that my only contact with whites came in stores. Up to the age of fourteen, I can recall having spoken with only one white person—my piano teacher—for a brief period.

Segregation gave white people an almost absolute power over black lives. Though we lived in fear of that power, we also believed that one day things would be different, and when that day came, we had to be prepared.

I do not know what it was my father and my teachers saw in me, but they saw something and chose me as one of those they would arm to do battle with white society's oppressive power.

"You're going to be somebody when you grow up," my father and teachers repeatedly told me. That sentence was spoken as if it were a command. From the time I entered kindergarten, I understood that I was being prepared to enter a world none of us could imagine then, but we had faith that world was coming. When the world of racial segregation was destroyed, we had to be prepared to demonstrate that we were the equals of any white person.

My father was a Methodist minister. I had one sibling—a brother, nine years my senior. I don't know how it is now, but then, preachers' children carried the burden of goodness. We didn't need to be told that how we acted reflected on our fathers. We had to be better than other children. I could not play marbles for keeps because that was gambling. I could not go to the movies on Sundays, which was the day all the kids went, because that was a sin. I could not fight, and a teacher once spanked me for striking back at a boy who hit me first. "I know he hit you first, but you're Reverend Lester's son. You know better," the teacher explained. Last, but surely not least, we were expected to know more about the Bible than other children. In short, we were expected to be miniature versions of our fathers.

Preachers' kids reacted to these expectations in one of two ways: they either rebeled, or they conformed. My brother rebelled and never stopped rebelling until the day of his death at age fifty-eight. He stayed out late partying; he came to church smelling of liquor; he gambled; he loved women, and they loved him back. And I, like Joseph, told my father every bad thing I could find out about my brother, which I learned from listening on the extension phone to his conversations with girls.

My father's mantra throughout my childhood and adolescence was: "Don't be like your brother. You're going to be somebody!" It was evident in our household that my brother was my mother's favorite and that I was my father's. If my brother could have sold me to passing traders, he probably would have. But he joined the military when I was eight years old, and from that time until his death I saw him (perhaps) ten times.

In recounting this, I am aware that my brother is the more sympathetic figure in my family story. As the favored one, I get no sympathy—and certainly none is extended to my father, who comes across as being little more than cruel.

But if a child has been favored with unique gifts of intelligence and creativity, if a child has been chosen to be somebody, is it not the father's responsibility to protect that child and those gifts, to lavish love on that child, even if it means being cruel to the other children?

Israel sees that this son loves to hear the stories about his great-grandfather and grandfather. (I loved listening to my father's stories about how he and his parents survived a time even crueler than the racial segregation of my youth.) Israel sees how Joseph's eyes brighten when he talks of this God they worship, a God no one else acknowledges, a God no one can see. (I loved it when my father quizzed me about the Bible). Israel sees that Joseph feels the presence of that God about whom he tells stories, and he also sees the other brothers roll their eyes. (My brother rolled his eyes when

Daddy would talk about the ways God had intervened in his life. My eyes shone with wonder.)

The souls of Israel and Joseph are one, and the father does everything he can to strengthen the boy's bond with him, to make the boy's bond with their God even stronger. At the same time, he protects this child from the ways and the values of the ten sons who slaughtered all the men of the town of Shechem because one of them wanted to marry their sister Dinah (Genesis 34).

Israel, with his own hands, makes Joseph a tunic of the finest wool. Picture Israel at a spinning wheel, transforming sheep's wool into threads—and then, sitting at a loom and weaving the threads into a garment for this son. When Joseph puts on the garment, he is wrapping himself in his father.

Because Jacob did everything to strengthen his bond with Joseph, Joseph was prepared when he underwent trials more extensive than any endured by Abraham, Isaac, or Jacob—being sold into slavery in Egypt by his brothers; being accused of attempting to rape his master's wife and spending two years in an Egyptian prison for the alleged offense. Of all the figures in the Torah, for me Joseph is the most remarkable, because for twenty-two years he lived in Egypt, then rose to a place of power second only to that of Pharaoh. Yet he retained the religion of his father. And he did this alone—without the support of a community, without the support of a family.

A midrash says that when Potiphar's wife tried to seduce Joseph, he was about to relent when an image of his father's face came to his mind, and that was what gave him the strength to resist (*Bereshit Rabbah* 87:9). If Jacob had not favored Joseph with his love, if Jacob had not clothed Joseph in himself, if Jacob had not bound Joseph's soul to his, Joseph would have assimilated into Egyptian religion.

One of the real ironies of my life is that I, the son of a Methodist minister, was able to convert to Judaism in 1982—precisely because I was the favorite son of my minister-father. His cruel love estranged me from my brother—and yet, my brother's antipathy, together with my bond to my father, enabled me to withstand the loneliness of the year I studied for conversion, which was perhaps the loneliest year of my life. It was the heat of my brother's antipathy and the protection of my father's love that enabled me to withstand the withering disapproval of my conversion that came from segments of black America.

We may not like Jacob for singling Joseph out as he did, but a father who cares overly much about being liked by his children is not necessarily the best father. A father must risk being disliked—even hated by his other children, even by his wife—if it means assuming the spiritual responsibility of nurturing and protecting the soul of a child on whom God has bestowed a special gift.

For there is no greater burden than being chosen by God.

מקץ
Miketz

(Re-)Dressing Up

JOEL LURIE GRISHAVER

Thereupon Pharaoh sent for Joseph, and he was rushed from the dungeon. He had his hair cut and changed his clothes, and he appeared before Pharaoh. (Genesis 41:14)

There are a few basic axioms in the Torah of Men. We all know the big ones, like men don't ask for directions. Men never cry in public except in dark movie theaters. Men talk a lot in public but have nothing to say when alone with their spouses. But the biggest issue that plays out in all of this literature is the "alpha dog" issue. Men's life is all about finding a place in the pecking order and trying to keep far from shame. Masculinity is a big issue in the Joseph story and plays out specifically in *Miketz*.

Let's start our exploration outside of the biblical text and move backward into it. In his book *Man Enough: Fathers, Sons, and the Search for Masculinity*, Frank Pittman says, "Boys without models are likely to overdo the masculinity, like a masculine impersonator."[1] But he goes further and talks about boys raised by mothers:

JOEL LURIE GRISHAVER is a Jewish writer, teacher, cartoonist, and storyteller. In 1981, he and two friends started Torah Aura Productions, a leading publisher of educational Judaica. Joel is an internationally known activist for Jewish educational innovation, a consultant to the Consortium for the Jewish Family, the author of many books, and a winner of the Covenant Award.

The mother must teach her son how to respect and how to follow the rules. She must teach him how to find a woman to take care of him and finish the job she began training him how to live in a family. But, no matter how good a job a woman does in teaching a boy how to be a man, he knows that she is not the real thing, and so he tends to exaggerate the differences between men and the woman she embodies.[2]

We have already seen in previous passages that Joseph struggles with masculinity. His proclamation of others bowing down to him is a clear exaggeration, in timing if not in fact. But, more frequently, we see him in a different role. He is really good at being a favorite. He is a perfect number two to the alpha dog. In sequence, he serves his father, Potiphar, the jailer, and Pharaoh. He becomes the trusted servant. In every place, except at home, "everything was put in his hands" and "he succeeded because the Eternal was with him." But, Joseph never succeeds at becoming a peer to his pack of brothers. He has no idea how to be number one and has no experience being an equal. His story is that of using the power and protection of others.

Joseph is raised by Bilhah, his mother's servant woman, because his mother, Rachel, the favorite wife, had died. He is not good at working with his brothers, and he is kept at home. He is both a favorite child and a picked-on child. Both the midrash and the literary tradition challenge his masculinity. In Genesis 39:6, we read, "Now Joseph was well built and handsome" (*y'feh toar viy'feh mareh*). Because the Hebrew is similar to Genesis 29:17—"Rachel was shapely and beautiful"—the midrash suggests that he looked like his mother. Rashi takes the verse and goes further: "Once Joseph saw that he was in charge, he began to eat and drink and curl his hair." In his epic novel *Joseph and His Brothers*, Thomas Mann suggests that Joseph's "coat of many colors" was made from one of his mother's garments. These commentaries present Joseph as the first metrosexual who is really good at getting powerful men to trust him.

All this is background to our *parashah*. Our text opens with Pharaoh dreaming two dreams, and no one can tell him what they mean. Only then (after two years) does the wine steward remember Joseph, and he tells Pharaoh about him. The steward has not been in debt to Joseph. He had not been waiting for the right moment; rather, he sees a chance to improve his status by using Joseph to solve Pharaoh's problem. One of those "men truths" revealed in all the gender literature is that while women use the gift of "empathy" and become the person in need's equal, men use the gift of "a solution." Solving a problem raises one's status in the pecking order. So Joseph preens again—this time, in Genesis 41:14: "He had his hair cut and changed his clothes, and he appeared before Pharaoh."

This is the moment when the tradition marks his transformation; he leaves being Joseph the egotist and becomes Joseph the *tzaddik*, the righteous man. To see why, we need to see the details of the text. Joseph begins by suggesting that interpreting dreams is beyond him: "God will see to Pharaoh's welfare" (Genesis 41:16); "Pharaoh's dreams are one and the same: God has told Pharaoh what He is about to do" (Genesis 41:25); "As for Pharaoh having had the same dream twice, it means that the matter has been determined by God, and that God will soon carry it out" (Genesis 41:32).

We learn two big lessons from this last verse. One lesson is about Joseph, and one lesson is about the nature of the whole Torah. Many things in the Torah happen twice, or even more times than that. In the Joseph story we have the following sets of repetitions: three sets of two dreams; Joseph is "in the pit" twice; and Joseph becomes his master's lead servant three times, or perhaps even four. The lesson here is that when a thing happens twice, it can serve as proof. Joseph's being in and out of the pit (a mini-Egypt) and his getting into and out of jail (another slavery) become proof (like the traditional two witnesses that are necessary in a rabbinical court) that Israel will survive its time in Egypt and be able to leave. Joseph's life is a rehearsal for his final role as Pharaoh's number two, through which he saves his family and feeds the world. Later, he will tell his brothers, "God has sent me ahead of you to ensure your survival on earth, and to save your lives in an extraordinary deliverance" (Genesis 45:7). Abraham's and Jacob's survival in Egypt and their successful return to Canaan become proof that the Exodus will happen.

But the second truth is about Joseph and his role as the *tzaddik*. Joseph's role as Pharaoh's number two trains him to be God's number two. There is an ego death, a collapse of "me-ness" that allows him to admit that he is powerless and that without God his success and Israel's safety would never take place. Joseph's practice with Potiphar and the jailer prepares him to be a man of faith, serving God's needs. That is the beauty of the transformation. He is no longer a boy who rejoices at people bowing down to him. Instead, he becomes a man who credits God for his success.

All this sets us up for his final encounter with his brothers. The obvious reading is that the games played with gold and cups are a manipulation, an act of vengeance or perhaps a test. The midrash, in defense of Joseph, suggests that he is providing his brothers with a chance to do *teshuvah* (repentance)—to not do to Benjamin what they had done to him. Whatever the explanation, this much is true: Joseph is not yet ready to cry in front of his brothers. He cannot demonstrate his weakness because he is not yet secure enough in who he has become. Joseph is dressed in Egyptian "drag," pretending to be an Egyptian, acting with the power of Pharaoh, and Joseph needs to flee rather than to cry in front of his brothers. He is not yet secure enough to show his weakness in front of his brothers. There is still the past to overcome, but that will happen next week.

ויגש

Vayigash

Mensching Up

RABBI DANIEL F. POLISH

Joseph could no longer control himself before all his attendants, and he cried out.... So there was no one else about when Joseph made himself known to his brothers. His sobs were so loud that the Egyptians could hear, and so the news reached Pharaoh's palace. (Genesis 45:1–2)

There are parts of the Torah that apply to everyone, without regard to age or gender, such as "Honor your father and your mother" (Exodus 20:12). Other parts need some transposition before they can appropriately apply to men and women alike, such as "You shall not covet your neighbor's house: You shall not covet your neighbor's wife ..." (Exodus 20:14). And, yes, feminist critics are right: some parts of the Torah, such as "every male among you shall be circumcised at the age of eight days" (Genesis 17:12), clearly presume that the text is addressed to men. Some passages of the Torah are, indeed, profoundly patriarchal, and even misogynist. Today, we tend to ignore or gloss over those passages. In our time, we prefer to under-

---

RABBI DANIEL F. POLISH is rabbi of Congregation Shir Chadash of the Hudson Valley in Poughkeepsie, New York. He is author of *Bringing the Psalms to Life: How to Understand and Use the Book of Psalms*; *Keeping Faith with the Psalms: Deepen Your Relationship with God Using the Book of Psalms* (both Jewish Lights); and *Talking about God: Exploring the Meaning of Religious Life with Kierkegaard, Buber, Tillich and Heschel* (SkyLight Paths).

stand the biblical text in the most egalitarian light; men and women should learn equally from it.

But there are some parts of the Torah that raise concerns that are particular to men and that pertain to the uniqueness of men's experience.

In the familiar story of Joseph and his brothers—and his father and his "boss," Pharaoh—we encounter several issues that challenge how men might live their lives. Consider the scene in Genesis 45, which is one of the most emotionally intense chapters of the entire Torah. It is wonderfully staged, leading us to an emotional high point.

"Joseph could no longer control himself.... So there was no one else about when Joseph made himself known to his brothers" (Genesis 45:1). Then we read some of the deepest theological statements in the entire biblical text, as Joseph interprets what has happened to him as God's will.

But soon enough, we are back in the realm of emotions: "With that he embraced his brother Benjamin around the neck and wept.... He kissed all his brothers and wept upon them; only then were his brothers able to talk to him" (Genesis 45:14–15). It is a wonderful alternation between reason and emotion. Joseph is overcome with feeling. But first, he must instruct his brothers about the meaning of the experience. Then he goes back into his deeply emotional state, and then he can talk again.

This story reflects a uniquely male dilemma. Our society, and most likely ancient societies as well, endowed women with an abundance of emotions. Social norms allow women to surrender to the torrents of emotion that human circumstances can elicit. But society expects that men will remain vigilant against being overcome by their emotions. They must stand guard over unchecked feelings. And so, rather than display strong emotion in public, they process situations through their intellects; they "explain" events, and interpret what is going on. They must remain, or appear, impassive rather than express the waves of feelings coursing through them.

By the time we get to that momentous episode, Joseph has been dealing with his brothers over a long period of time. They knew him to be only an Egyptian official. At one point, they describe him to their father as "the man" (Genesis 43:3–7). I like to think that the term had the same meaning for them that it has on today's streets. Joseph had indeed been "the man." Now "the man" was about to tell them that he was the brother whom they thought—or assumed, or feared—they had killed so long ago.

You can understand how such a moment would fill Joseph with emotion. The brothers, for their part, are about to learn that "the man" who has the power of life or death over them is, in fact, the brother whom they so grievously wronged long ago. We can imagine the mixture of emotions that is about to erupt in them.

So we have a powerfully emotional scene. At the very beginning of the dramatic events, the text notes that Joseph has all his retainers leave, "so there was no one else about when Joseph made himself known to his brothers" (Genesis 45:1). Does he want no Egyptians present because of the enormity of the secret he is about to reveal? Or because he does not want his subordinates to see him overcome by the emotions that he knows are about to overwhelm him?

In Joseph, we see a struggle against men's conventional gender roles. Men are supposed to stay in control and keep their emotions under wraps. "Boys don't cry"; all the more so, men—especially powerful men. But here, finally, the emotions prevail.

This episode has stunning emotional power. Perhaps part of that power comes from the fact that it is a group of men standing and crying about the enormity of what they are going through. Would it have the same resonance if it were a group of women giving vent to their emotions? Does the conclusion of the Book of Ruth, with its volubly expressive Naomi and her cohort, stir us as much as this scene does?

In most cultures, it is the women who keen and wail. But, in this way, men tend to be stunted and diminished. Some have suggested that women cry and men get ulcers. Joseph teaches us that men can cry, too. Even powerful men (Joseph was second in power to the Pharaoh, who was himself the most powerful human being on the planet in his time) can live rich emotional lives and give expression to those emotions. Joseph cries. All his brothers cry.

Jacob is finally reunited with the son he loved so intensely and had assumed he'd lost. At that moment, he, too, "wept on his [Joseph's] neck a good while" (Genesis 46:29). We remember that we can also cry, and that we can give voice to the welter of emotions roiling within us.

Another momentous encounter directs our attention to another male issue. In all the years I have heard people pour out their hearts, I have never heard a woman speak of feeling inadequate in comparison to her mother. I have heard many tales of complicated and twisted relationships, but never this kind of competition.

But men? It is a common perception that men measure their success or failure against the reality or the image of their father. How many times do we read biographies or news stories about some public figure who is consumed by the sense of not living up to his father's real or imagined stature? Or the story of someone who pushes himself beyond his real capacities because of his desire to surpass his father? Fathers loom large in the emotional lives of their sons, and they provide the yardsticks by which sons evaluate themselves.

So we should not be surprised to encounter that human reality in this story as well. In Genesis 47, Joseph brings his father to meet the Pharaoh. The most powerful man in the world meets this little *yid* (Jew). Pharaoh asks Jacob his age (Genesis 47:8). We don't know why he does this; maybe he is making polite small talk, like a solicitous politician asking an elderly constituent: "How old are you, old man?"

But Jacob's answer is especially poignant. "The years of my sojourn [on earth] are one hundred and thirty. Few and hard have been the years of my life, nor do they come up to the life spans of my fathers during their sojourns" (Genesis 47:9). Is he being obsequious or humble? Or is he being bitter? His life has, in fact, not been easy. It has, indeed, been filled with sorrow. But even in his old age, it is striking to notice that Jacob is still measuring his worth against that of his fathers', and he finds himself wanting.

This ache is common, and it is sad and needlessly painful. We all have our own journeys and sojourns. We all walk our own paths, even if it is different from the one that our fathers trod. Can't that be good enough? When we are able to own our own path and treasure our own sojourn, then our lives will be more than "few and hard." Honor our fathers and our mothers? Absolutely. How can we not? But let us honor ourselves as well. That is a harder challenge for so many of us.

One final encounter brings us to the very core of what I believe the whole Joseph story is all about. It is actually the first encounter in the *parashah*. Beginning in Genesis 44:18, we find Judah pleading with the man whom he calls "my lord" to send Benjamin home with his brothers: "Therefore, please let your servant remain as a slave to my lord instead of the boy, and let the boy go back with his brothers. For how can I go back to my father unless the boy is with me? Let me not be witness to the woe that would overtake my father!" (Genesis 44:33–34).

Judah is willing to stay as a slave in Egypt (a powerful foreshadowing of the next chapter in biblical history) rather than let his father endure the pain of losing a son. This is a very different Judah from the angry youth who was willing to sell Joseph down to Egypt and then torment his father with Joseph's bloodstained garment. The earlier "version" of Judah—like all the brothers (including, from a different perspective, Joseph)—considered only himself and his happiness. The Judah we encounter here is able to put the happiness of others first, even above his own.

The story is about "mensching up." In the course of this saga, each brother becomes more of a mensch than he was at the beginning of the story. Of course, mensching up is not only for men. Women can mensch up, too. But conventional wisdom tells us that women, whether by virtue of different wiring or different socialization, are reflexively more empathetic than men and are more attuned to the moods and needs of others. Men, according to some observers, are more "inner directed," attuned to the moods and needs of themselves.

Here, in this very dramatic encounter, we see Judah discovering empathy. He cares now, as he did not before, about the feelings of his father and about how his own actions affect his father. He becomes a mensch. Only after Judah proves that he can grow will Joseph make himself "known to his brothers" (Genesis 45:1). Only after he sees that they have changed and that they care about the father they all share is he prepared to go from being "the man" to being their brother. The whole saga is about the lot of them—our fathers, our brothers—growing, becoming menschen. It is about them breaking out of the conventional male role and learning what women apparently know instinctively. Perhaps we need to hear their story in a way our sisters do not.

ויחי
Vayechi

Owning All Our Feelings

RABBI HAYIM HERRING, PHD

And Jacob called his sons and said, "Come together that I may tell you what is to befall you in days to come."
(Genesis 49:1)

In an episode from the sitcom *Frasier*, Marty, Frasier's father, explains to his psychiatrist-son how men should deal with their feelings. While not an exact quote from the script, I recall that Marty's advice was that men should tough it out and shove their feelings as far down inside of themselves as possible until they can no longer feel them anymore.

This is great advice, but only for those who want to increase their risks for poor physical and emotional health and leave a string of damaged relationships in their wake. Unfortunately, it is also the life path that our ancestor Jacob seems to follow, and one that he has bequeathed to many of his male descendants.

So let's linger on Jacob's past and observe how he handles life's lows, so that we can gain insight into how to enrich our own relationships with those who mean the most to us.

The Torah portion finds us at the very end of Jacob's life. His children are gathered around his deathbed, after being informed that

RABBI HAYIM HERRING, PHD, is executive director of STAR (Synagogues: Transformation and Renewal). He is a nationally known activist and thinker on synagogue life and on strengthening Jewish community.

their father appears ready to take his last breath. In a most realistic scene, Jacob rallies one more time to impart a prophetic word to each of his sons. What kind of word is it? Depending upon the child, it is either a curse, a blessing, or something in between. But whatever that last word is, Jacob leaves no opportunity for his children to respond. After offering this paternal projection of the future of his children, he immediately passes away.

With that in mind, let's take a look at the message he delivers to three of his sons: Reuben, Simeon, and Levi. Simeon and Levi are actually treated as one fraternal unit, because Jacob addresses them both simultaneously. Here's what he says to Reuben:

> *Reuben, you are my firstborn,*
> *My might and first fruit of my vigor,*
> *Exceeding in rank*
> *And exceeding in honor.*
> *Unstable as water, you shall excel no longer;*
> *For when you mounted your father's bed,*
> *You brought disgrace—my couch he mounted!*
> (Genesis 49:3–4)

Imagine that you are Reuben. For the first few moments when you hear your father speak, you believe that you are about to receive your entitlement—the blessing of the firstborn. (Jacob does seem to set that expectation for his eldest son.) But as your father completes his vision of your future fortune, he dashes those hopes, and, in fact, he humiliates you in front of your brothers. You are left with no recourse, no ability to defend yourself—just a deep feeling of disgrace.

To what incident is Jacob alluding when he refers to Reuben "mounting his couch"? After the rape of Dinah, Jacob's daughter, and the death of Rachel, his beloved wife, Jacob was challenged by yet another family trauma. His firstborn son, Reuben, made what appeared to be a power play for family leadership. He slept with his father's concubine, Bilhah, which some scholars suggest could symbolize Reuben's early claim to family leadership (Genesis 35:22).

The Torah states that Jacob learned about this grievous affront, but it does not provide his reaction. In fact, the physical layout of the Hebrew text appears with an intentional gap. The text literally says, "And Jacob heard" (Genesis 35:22), but that is all it says, almost pleading with us to fill in the gap.

As I interpret that incomplete sentence, I understand it as: "And Jacob heard what Reuben did, was filled with anger, and kept it to himself." He was deeply disturbed by this incident, but like some people who are unable to confront their own anger, he suppressed it. It continued to fester within him, until this ugly sore bursts open at Jacob's deathbed. Jacob knows that this is his final opportunity to express his feelings, and they erupt with the bitterness of many years.

The outcome is not much different for two other brothers, Simeon and Levi. Here is how Jacob envisions their future:

> Simeon and Levi are a pair;
> Their weapons are tools of lawlessness.
> Let not my person be included in their council,
> Let not my being be counted in their assembly.
> For when angry they slay men,
> And when pleased they maim oxen.
> Cursed be their anger so fierce,
> And their wrath so relentless.
> I will divide them in Jacob,
> Scatter them in Israel.
>   (Genesis 49:5–7)

While Reuben will lose his status as a firstborn, Jacob predicts that Simeon and Levi will lose their identities; in the unfolding narrative of the future nation of Israel, they will become indistinguishable. Again, these two brothers are unable to respond to this harsh, projected fate.

What, now, is the source of Jacob's anger? Jacob is referring to how Simeon and Levi responded to the rape of their sister, Dinah (Genesis 34). Dinah strayed from the family encampment and was forcibly taken and raped by Shechem, the son of Hamor, chief of the Hivite clan. When Jacob learned about it, his initial reaction was to wait until his sons returned home from shepherding their flocks. Dinah's brothers, Simeon and Levi, were especially outraged at the rape of their sister and at the inaction of their father in rescuing her, and they demanded retribution for the wrong that Shechem had inflicted on the family's honor.

Moved to act, Jacob's strategy was to pursue an alliance with Shechem's clan—on the condition that all their males would be circumcised, which would then enable Shechem to live honorably with Dinah. But Simeon and Levi had other notions of justice. When the Hivite males of the clan were weak and in pain because of their circumcision, Simeon and Levi slew all of the males as an act of vengeance. When Jacob learned what they had done, he reprimanded Simeon and Levi for giving Jacob's family a bad reputation among the locals and for putting them at risk. But that comment did not capture the depth of his anger toward them. Again, it is only years later, on his deathbed, that we fully feel the force of Jacob's fury.

A common thread connects these two different excerpts from Jacob's deathbed prophecy. In each case, Jacob experienced a traumatic family event, and in each case, Jacob does not reveal the full extent of his feelings or does not reveal them at all. So why does Jacob finally reveal his full emotions now, many years later, in a way that almost makes it feel like these events happened only yesterday? It is as if his feelings about these episodes have been simmering for all of those years, and they finally erupt. Jacob's insides are like a series of steam pipes without a release valve. Continuing this metaphor, his impending death is the catalyst that increases the pressure beyond what the pipes can bear, leading Jacob to explode so angrily.

Jacob's pattern of behavior is generally consistent. He experiences a painful event. If he responds, his response is like an iceberg: at best, we get only a partial glimpse of his feelings, with the larger part of them buried beneath the visible surface. In addition to these two episodes, we can find several other examples that exhibit this same pattern: his response to hearing about his son Joseph's dreams of family leadership (Genesis 37:11); his reaction to the death of his beloved wife, Rachel (Genesis 48:7); and, as noted earlier, his response to the rape of his daughter, Dinah (Genesis 34).

Jacob's response is more typical of men than of women. That statement may seem out of touch with our contemporary beliefs about the equality of men and women. But, in our just quest for gender equality, we must also honestly state some fundamental differences between men and women—as well as being skeptical of those who seek to generalize about such differences. There is still the real possibility that those who do so are motivated because they wish to bar women from having equal access to educational, professional, religious, and political opportunities.

Others may have less malicious agendas, but the result is the same. For example, a popular rationale articulated over a century ago (and still heard in some circles today) for limiting the Jewish religious expression of women has been framed as a "compliment" to women. The line of this "reasoning" is that because men are spiritually inferior to women, men need mitzvot in order to sensitize them to the divine rhythms of life. But women, because of their ability to bear children, are innately in tune with these rhythms. Therefore, it is unnecessary to require women to observe mitzvot because of their inherent spiritual superiority. Even well-intentioned generalized gender statements can support gender inequities!

Yet, scientific research suggests that our impressionistic observations about women having more emotional depth and greater facility with relationships than men are, in fact, correct. Michael Connor, an experienced medical and family psychologist, writes that, like Jacob, men tend to have a difficult time relating to their feelings. As a result, they may withdraw from situations that evoke these feelings or try to stabilize emotional situations by asserting power. Men often prefer actions to feelings, and solutions over emotions. While women pay attention both to solving problems and the process for arriving at resolutions, men focus more on the resolutions and can be inattentive to the process. Renato M. E. Sabbatini, who holds a doctorate in neurophysiology, says that some of these emotional differences may be tied to physiological distinctions between men and women, including the number of neurons that connect the two hemispheres of the brain and the differences in response to danger in their autonomic and sympathetic nervous systems.

While being held accountable for our claims, we need to be able to discuss gender differences within the Jewish community and in synagogues in particular. As Brandeis University professor Sylvia Barack Fishman shows in a recent study, the sighting of men in mainstream liberal synagogues is becoming increasingly rare, and that is clearly a problem for the Jewish community.

So we need to be able to surface these kinds of issues, even if they make men and women a little uncomfortable. We need to do so because this kind of honesty makes relationships more fulfilling. It helps to keep expectations realistic, and instead of having one of those "men are from Mars, women are from Venus" moments, men and women can label the differences that lead to them and then work on resolving them.

At the same time, we need to remember that in this case, biology is not destiny. Even if the tendency to repress feelings is more of a male issue, men can learn to better open up their deeper feelings instead of bottling them up. I observe in my male friends a willingness to speak more openly about their feelings than in the past. And, as I work with teenagers, I notice how much more comfortable they are in verbalizing their feelings than I certainly was at their age. While I still remember television shows and commercials that emphasized the rugged, silent male hero (the Marlboro Man, the Lone Ranger, and Superman), my son and his contemporaries speak naturally about their relationships and are much more at home with the notions of interdependence and collaboration.

But there is still some work to do, and I don't think that men can do it alone. It will take the encouragement of female and male role models who will lead the way. If Judaism teaches us anything, it is that we have the ability to make wise choices. If the anecdotal evidence about the next generation of men is any indication, there is reason to be hopeful for more men choosing to form healthy relationships based on more open communications.

Shemot/ Exodus

שמות
Shemot

The Making of Moses

RABBI JEFFREY K. SALKIN

**Some time after that, when Moses had grown up, he
went out to his kinsfolk and witnessed their labors.**

(Exodus 2:11)

Jewish men grow up hearing (at least) two distinctive messages
about masculinity. On the one hand, there's "Be a man." It's a command that often translates to: Be tough, determined, stoic, and com-
petent in all things. On the other hand, there's also (or there used to
be, when more people spoke Yiddish) *Zei a mensch*—which, while
we might be tempted to also translate as "Be a man," reveals a very
different sense of masculinity. It is a masculinity that appreciates

---

RABBI JEFFREY K. SALKIN, the editor of this volume, is author or editor of many books on Jewish spirituality and life, including *A Dream of
Zion: American Jews Reflect on Why Israel Matters to Them; Righteous
Gentiles in the Hebrew Bible: Ancient Role Models for Sacred Relationships;*
and *Being God's Partner: How to Find the Hidden Link between Spirituality
and Your Work* (all Jewish Lights). His articles, both popular and scholarly,
have appeared in numerous magazines and newspapers. He has been a congregational rabbi and an activist in the Reform movement. He currently
lives in Atlanta, Georgia, where he directs the work of Kol Echad: Making
Judaism Matter, a transdenominational adult study community, and
frequently lectures in synagogues, community centers, and universities
around North America. He is looking forward to sharing his life with Sheila
Shuster and their four children.

kindness, compassion, moral complexity, and the blessing of living in community. A Yiddish proverb sums it up: "A mensch is called a mensch because he struggles."

The process of sorting out all the discordant messages about manhood takes us right to this Torah portion—to the early life of Moses. When Jewish men ask the crucial question, "What does Judaism have to say to me about what it means to be a man?" we might choose to look no further than Moses—the quintessential Jew of the Bible, but also, perhaps, the quintessential Jewish man.

Let us open the pages of the text and search out the deeper meanings in Moses's journey to manhood. In particular, let us look at what we might call the "maturation" narrative—the verses in the Book of Exodus that speak of how Moses grows into adulthood:

> Some time after that, when Moses had grown up, he went out to his kinsfolk and witnessed their labors. He saw an Egyptian beating a Hebrew, one of his kinsmen. He turned this way and that and, seeing no one about [*ki ein ish*, literally, "there is no man"], he struck down the Egyptian and hid him in the sand. When he went out the next day, he found two Hebrews fighting; so he said to the offender, "Why do you strike your fellow?" He retorted, "Who made you chief and ruler over us? Do you mean to kill me as you killed the Egyptian?" Moses was frightened, and thought: Then the matter is known! When Pharaoh learned of the matter, he sought to kill Moses; but Moses fled from Pharaoh. He arrived in the land of Midian, and sat down beside a well. (Exodus 2:11–15)

The first step on Moses's journey to manhood is that he must recognize his people.

We wonder aloud: How does Moses know that the Israelites were his people? Did his adoptive mother, the daughter of Pharaoh (Bityah, as the Rabbis called her) tell him? Did his birth mother, Yocheved, tell him? When Moses sees"an Egyptian beating a Hebrew, one of his kinsmen," does he, in fact, know that the victim is one of his kinsmen? Or, it is possible that Moses does not know that these are his kinsfolk—that their identification as such is merely the literary device of an omniscient narrator of the biblical text?

Let us assume that Moses does, indeed, know that the Hebrews are his people. His act of striking down the Egyptian is a perfectly acceptable act of defense. In fact, Rashi, the medieval commentator, suggests that the Egyptian taskmaster had raped a Hebrew slave woman, and he was now finishing off the deed by beating her husband. Moses responds, therefore, to another man's "unmanning" by literally becoming a man. It's similar to the way the great Hebrew poet Chaim Nachman Bialik responded to the atrocities in Kishinev, Russia, in the early twentieth century. There, Jewish men had looked on passively as Cossacks raped their wives, and their only "response" was to ask the rabbinical authorities if their wives, having been violated by gentiles, were now permitted to them. "These are the heirs of the Maccabees?" Bialik asked, in horror.

Moreover, Moses responds in this quintessentially masculine way precisely because there is no one else there to defend the hapless Hebrew. His turning "this way and that" is not because he is avoiding detection; it is simply because, as the text tells us, *ki ein ish*, literally, "there was no man." In fact, Rashi explains that he is looking for other "men" who could adjudicate the struggle between the Egyptian and the Israelite. Moses isn't looking to see if there are any potential witnesses to his act of defense; he is looking to see if there are any other people around to whom he could make a moral appeal. But he is alone—radically alone. At this moment, Moses knows that he has to be the man, anticipating by a millennium the words of the sage Hillel, "In a place where there are no men, strive to be a man."

So, job one is to respond to the pain of your own people—with force, if necessary. Jewish history has borne this truth out. After centuries of "feminization" at the hands of the nations of the world, in which Jews were expected to be passive, the psychosexual theory of Zionism is that it was the remasculinization of the Jewish people.

I recall the observation of Martin Peretz, the publisher and editor of the *New Republic*, who was present at the Warsaw Ghetto memorial on the fiftieth anniversary of the uprising. A cadre of twelve Israeli paratroopers placed a wreath upon the memorial. Someone asked Peretz, "What is the significance of the twelve Israeli paratroopers? Could it be to symbolize the twelve tribes of ancient Israel?" To which Peretz replied, "No, that's not it at all. The presence of the twelve Israeli paratroopers at the Warsaw Ghetto memorial symbolizes something else. It says to the world: 'Don't ever _____ with us again.'" That might not be the "nicest," and certainly not the most elegant message that the Jews have to deliver to the world—but the tragic events of the last century have reminded us that it is, nevertheless, an essential message.

But the journey of the Jewish man cannot end with brute machismo, even if it is sometimes necessary. The next day, Moses sees two Hebrews fighting, and this time he doesn't respond with force. No, in fact, he responds in a way that is slightly more quintessentially Jewish. He identifies the offending party (how? we don't know) and rather than speaking with his fists, he speaks with his lips—and he asks a question: "Why do you strike your fellow?" (Exodus 2:13). Like all good Jewish questions, it starts with the interrogative "Why?" To be a Jewish man, then, is to ask good questions that go to the very heart of the matter at hand. Rashi suggests that the response of the fighters (in verse 14) is particularly cutting: "Who made you *a man* [*ish*]? You are still a boy!" There is no guarantee that we will like the answers to our questions; certainly, Moses does not like "getting lip" from the offender—a retort that can only be loosely translated as "Who died and left you boss?" Later in the wilderness, when Korach and his band mount a rebellion against his authority (Numbers 16), Moses will hear an echo of that first complaint in the complaint of Korach. It will sound vaguely familiar.

And so, Moses flees to Midian. There he finds himself in a third confrontation. He encounters the seven daughters of the priest of Midian (whom the text calls Reuel, but whom we also know as Jethro). Some shepherds are harassing them at the well, driving them away (the Hebrew word is *vay'garshum* [Exodus 2:17]; amazingly, when Moses's first son is born, he names him Gershom, which means "I have been a stranger in a strange land," but which carries the unmistakable echo of the incident at the well). The Midianite daughters tell their father, "An Egyptian rescued us from the shepherds" (Exodus 2:19). In fact, history will unfold so that the exact *opposite* will turn out to be true; a *shepherd* (Moses) will wind up rescuing the people from the *Egyptians*!

So, in this step of the journey, Moses intervenes once again. The text does not tell us exactly how Moses defends the women. But the point is that he does so and, in so doing, goes beyond the boundaries of his people and his gender. The first two interventions involved Jewish men; this one involves gentile women. In this step of the journey, Moses goes from the particular to the universal.

So, bonding yourself with your people, responding to their pain, questioning injustice, responding to the pain of those who are beyond the boundaries of your own people—these are all essential moments in the journey toward manhood.

But there is one more piece to Moses's journey to manhood. When Moses meets Reuel/Jethro and becomes his son-in-law, it is the beginning of probably the most beautiful relationship in the entire Torah. Reuel/Jethro becomes not only Moses's father-in-law, but his tutor, mentor, and advisor—the literary "ancestor" of such characters as Merlin, Falstaff, Yoda, and Obiwan.

Why is Moses so open to this gift of the love of an older man? Moses never knew his real father, Amram. Who's the only father figure in his life? Because Pharaoh's daughter had adopted Moses as an infant, the only other paternal presence would have been Pharaoh himself.

And yet, does Pharaoh offer him any paternal or grandfatherly love? No—not in the Bible, and not in the various midrashim and legends that surround Moses's life in Jewish lore. Recall the famous midrash about how Pharaoh's sorcerers tell him that the infant Moses in his court will someday try to depose him. In order to determine little Moses's loyalty, Pharaoh devises a plan. He sets both a golden vessel (in some versions of the story, it is Pharaoh's crown itself) and a blazing hot coal before the child to see which one he chooses. As we would expect from any child, Moses is attracted to the shiny golden vessel—a gesture that indicates that this child will, in fact, grow up to be a threat to Pharaoh's power. Therefore, the angel Gabriel invisibly comes down and moves Moses's hand to the coal. Moses touches the coal, which burns his fingers, forcing the infant to place his wounded fingers into his mouth—thus burning his tongue, and providing us with the etiology of Moses's fabled speech impediment (*Shemot Rabbah* 1:26).

So, in fact, Pharaoh's attitude toward this foundling in his palace bordered on the homicidal. "When Pharaoh learned of the matter [i.e., that Moses had killed the Egyptian], he sought to kill Moses" (Exodus 2:15). Or, to be brutally honest about it: Moses is a refugee from the murderous urges of his royal grandfather—an almost *akedah*, an updated binding of Isaac. With no loving, nurturing man in his life, it is no accident that Moses is drawn to Jethro—for men need mentors, teachers, older brothers, role models. Some biblical scholars have even gone so far as to surmise that there are entire layers of biblical religion that may, in fact, have originated in Midian.

Come to think of it—leave it to a fatherless man to teach the world how to love a "Father" God.

At the foot of Mount Sinai, when the Israelites wonder aloud about Moses's disappearance from their midst—a disappearance that ultimately leads to the construction of the Golden Calf—they mutter to themselves: "… for that man Moses [*ki zeh Moshe ha-ish*, literally, "for this Moses, the man"], who brought us from the land of Egypt—we do not know what has happened to him" (Exodus 32:1). They could have just as easily reflected on the disappearance of "Moses"; the words "the man" are almost superfluous.

But that is exactly what the text is saying. Moses is simply *ha-ish*—"the man." Not a god or even a god substitute. Just a man. And his people, despite their fantasies and their unconscious wish projections, know it as well.

With apologies to Tom Wolfe, Moses is "a man in full." His life example is there for Jewish men—and all men—from which to learn and from which to grow.

וארא

Va'era

My God Can Beat Up Your God!

RABBI RAMI SHAPIRO

**Then the Lord said to Moses, "You shall soon see what I
will do to Pharaoh: he shall let them go because of a
greater might; indeed, because of a greater might he
shall drive them from his land."** (Exodus 6:1)

"My dad can beat up your dad ..." "Cannot!" "Can too!" "Cannot!"
"Can too!" "Oh, yeah? Show me!" So much for the theology of *Va'era*.
  In today's vernacular, God says:

> Wait'll you see what I do to that fake god Pharaoh. I'm gonna
> kick his ass so hard he'll have to let My people go. Man, I'm
> gonna kick his ass so hard he will push the people out of
> Egypt. Just you wait and see.

I get this. Moses is angry: his people are enslaved, and he is powerless to do anything about it. It's no surprise that his God is a superhero; a strange being from another dimension with powers beyond
those of mortal men who, disguised as Creator of the universe and

---

RABBI RAMI SHAPIRO was ordained by Hebrew Union College–Jewish
Institute of Religion and holds a PhD in Jewish Studies from Union
Graduate School. An award-winning author, he is the author of *The Sacred
Art of Lovingkindness: Preparing to Practice*; *Recovery: The Twelve Steps as
Spiritual Practice* (both SkyLight Paths); and *Open Secrets*.

Chooser of the Jews, fights a never-ending battle for truth, justice, and the Israelite way. This is every Jewish boy's fantasy.

The Pharaoh in my life was a ten-year-old girl who lived in the house behind us on Woodlawn Street in Springfield, Massachusetts. She was big, tough, mean, and in no way charmed by my wimpish wit and servile attitude. She and her lackey, another girl from the neighborhood, taunted me mercilessly for being fat and incompetent at all the things that mattered like catching a ball and spitting. Each season had its own plague. In the winter, she would grab my hat, stuff it with snow, and slam it down on to my head so hard I thought my brain would freeze. In the summer, it had something to do with my Bermuda shorts, which I still refuse to wear lest she be lurking behind me even now. You get the idea.

Unlike Moses, however, I didn't kill her; but, like Moses, I did run away (my family moved to the next town); and, like him too, I dreamed of finding someone with the superpowers to kick her ass.

Lots of Torah is like this: boys' fantasies about smashing bad guys. You need a man-god for this. Sure, the She-Hulk could do it, but no little Jewish boy, trapped as he is in the wimpy body of Dr. Bruce Banner (in my case a fat Bruce Banner), is going to choose her over the original Hulk. That would be like asking your sister to fight for you. Not cool. Which is why Torah makes a big deal about Moses having a new name for God:

> I am the Lord. I appeared to Abraham, Isaac, and Jacob as El Shaddai, but I did not make Myself known to them by My name YHVH. (Exodus 6:2–3)

The new name is YHVH. What was wrong with the old name? Often translated as "God Almighty," El Shaddai hints of *shaddaim*, "breasts." This Almighty God used to be the Almighty Goddess, the Breasted One, and it was Her servants—the midwives Shifra and Puah, Moses's birth mother Yocheved, his sister Miriam, and his adopted mother, the Pharaoh's daughter—who have watched over and protected Moses so far. But now Moses needs a new god, a male god, someone for whom he can play stand-in: "The Lord replied to

Moses, 'See, I place you in the role of God to Pharaoh, with your brother as your prophet'" (Exodus 7:1).

But there is a problem. YHVH is just too powerful. He needs a weakness, something to keep the drama going to satisfy Moses's revenge fantasy. God needs Kryptonite, and without it the drama devolves into farce, like when the bank robbers in the 1950s *Superman* television show watch all their bullets bounce off the chest of the Man of Steel and then, obviously rendered stupid by the sight, throw their empty revolvers at him as if the guns might do what the bullets could not. True, Superman always ducks, which in and of itself makes no sense, but the problem is greater than that: If there is nothing that can stop Superman, then there is no drama. If there is nothing more powerful than God, there is no need to tell stories about God.

So what can Torah provide that will keep the God of Steel battling Pharaoh for more than a millisecond? Only one thing—God himself:

> You shall repeat all that I command you, and your brother Aaron shall speak to Pharaoh to let the Israelites depart from his land. But I will harden Pharaoh's heart, that I may multiply My signs and marvels in the land of Egypt. When Pharaoh does not heed you, I will lay My hand upon Egypt and deliver My ranks, My people the Israelites, from the land of Egypt with extraordinary chastisements. And the Egyptians shall know that I am YHVH, when I stretch out My hand over Egypt and bring out the Israelites from their midst." (Exodus 7:2–5)

Since Pharaoh himself can't stand up to God, God will prop him up so He can continue to beat him up. In other words, if there is to be a story at all, God will have to battle Himself. This is classic "Bizarro Superman."

"Bizarro Superman," created in October 1958 (*Superboy* #68) when Superboy was hit by a duplicating ray, is Superman's doppelganger. He has all of Superman's strength, but none of his wisdom. In Moses's fantasy, God is figuratively hit by a duplicating ray, powered by God's all too human need to prove to people that He is the Top God, and uses Pharaoh as His punching bag.

Just imagine a cartoon bolt of psychic energy flashing from God's head to Pharaoh's heart, hardening it against all reason and hope of repentance or surrender: ZZZZTTTT!!! You can see the thought bubble over the startled Pharaoh's head: "I ... can't ... stop ... enslaving these people! I want to ... but ... I ... can't! Something is controlling me!" Hard not to feel sorry for the guy, but, hey, we'll leave "love your enemies" to a later superhero, published by Brand X.

Anyway, God is going to harden Pharaoh's heart so Moses can slam those Egyptian bastards with ten plagues rather than have them fold after one. And then comes the opening confrontation. Moses and his sidekick Aaron confront the evil Pharaoh and his priestly minions. To demonstrate his power, Moses uses the magic staff given to him by God. He throws it to the ground, and it turns into a giant snake!

"Hah!" says Pharaoh. "Am I to be impressed by such weak magic? You and your puny God are no match for the might of Pharaoh! Priests! Show this slave the power of Egypt!" The priests and magicians grab their own magic staves and throw them to the ground. ZAPP!! More snakes hissing wickedly at the serpent of Moses. SSSSSSSSSSSS! "Fools!" cries Moses. "Do you think your magic equal to God's? Observe!" SSSLLLUUURRRPPP!! "Aaron's rod swallowed their rods. Yet Pharaoh's heart stiffened" (Exodus 7:12–13).

With all this snake slithering, rod swallowing, and heart stiffening, it is difficult not to see this as homoerotic metaphor. No wonder the Torah quickly moves on to the more manly art of bad-guy bashing.

Having out-snaked the priests of Egypt, Moses now turns the Nile to blood and then plagues the people and their livestock with frogs, vermin, insects, pestilence, boils, hail, and, in the following chapter, things far worse than that.

And why? God is not shy regarding motive:

> I will send all My plagues upon your person, and your courtiers, and your people, in order that you may know that there is none

> like Me in all the world.... I have spared you for this purpose: in
> order to show you My power, and in order that My fame may
> resound throughout the world. (Exodus 9:14, 9:16)

Whoa! Forget Jesus, Gandhi, and Martin Luther King Jr. This Guy
makes Jack Bauer look like a girlie-man. Imagine the scene: God,
pictured as some constantly shape-shifting flame, hovers over a
beaten Pharaoh, lying prostrate on the marble floor of his palace—
one arm propping up his broken body, the other raised defensively
against what is sure to be another blow. He wants to surrender. He
wants to free the Hebrew slaves. But every time he opens his mouth
to do so, a strange madness overtakes him and he commands the
opposite. God knows Pharaoh is beaten. God knows it is only His
Bizarro power that keeps the contest going, and God wants Pharaoh
to know this as well: "Puny Egyptian, you want to know why I keep
you alive? You live that I might torment you longer! You live that
through your torment the world know that YHVH is God Supreme!
HAHAHAHAHAHA!!"

Something has gone terribly wrong. God has become the very
thing He hates. To paraphrase Lord Acton: "All power corrupts, and
the All Powerful corrupts absolutely." God no longer needs a doppelganger. Bizarro Superman and Superman are one. Moses's original drama of liberation has devolved into a schizophrenic horror
story of cosmic proportions: "God and Mad God in a Battle of
Titans!! The Fate of the World Hangs in the Balance!! Don't Miss the
Next Exciting Issue!!!! Excelsior!"

This is not the first time we have seen the mad God of Torah.
God destroys almost all life in the story of the Flood (Genesis 6:9ff.).
He murders thousands in his decimation of Sodom and Gomorrah
(Genesis 19:23–26). The difference between those stories and ours
is that in neither of the earlier stories does the hero assist in the
madness: Noah ignores the morality of God's actions, and Abraham
actively resists it, but in our story Moses and God are interchangeable. God becomes man, and man becomes God, and both go mad.

What are we to make of all this? Let me suggest the following.

Before men are men, they are boys ruled by their mothers and enslaved by their fears. In the beginning, Mother protects us, guides us, and, in my case, dresses us in lime-green double-knit jeans that attract bullies like moths to a flame.

Before men are men, they dream of conquest. Sure, they have sexual fantasies, but at this age sticking their swords into the dragon's heart is way cooler than sticking their penises anywhere else.

Before men are men, they are tormented by not-yet-being-men and haunted by the fear that they may not measure up to manhood. And when at last they become men, they discover that, in some sense, they are still boys—wounded, fearful, but with just enough power to say "no lime-green jeans!"

Men need male heroes and male gods. They need to see themselves writ large, that they might know both the good and the evil of which they are capable. They need a Moses who climbs Mount Sinai—if not in a single bound, then at least without the wheezing of the average octogenarian. They need a hero almost killed as an infant, and again as an adult, and again as an old man, who perseveres and leads his people to freedom, and who is yet capable of slaughtering tens of thousands of them when they challenge his will and his god. They need to see the insanity of the powerful if they are to avoid the madness of power. They need Superman and Bizarro, for they are us.

In the end, the message is simple: Beware of gods, especially all-powerful ones. Beware that your lust for revenge doesn't make you a monster. Beware that your desire to right wrongs doesn't end up perpetuating them. Beware that even just ends are never used to justify unjust means and that the means themselves are always just— "Look! Up in the sky! It's a bird! It's a plane! No, it's a little boy setting his world right the only way he knows! Be careful!"

בא

Bo

The Inner Pharaoh

RABBI JOSEPH BLACK

Then the Lord said to Moses, "Go to Pharaoh. For I have hardened his heart and the hearts of his courtiers, in order that I may display these My signs among them, and that you may recount in the hearing of your sons and of your sons' sons how I made a mockery of the Egyptians and how I displayed My signs among them— in order that you may know that I am the Lord." So Moses and Aaron went to Pharaoh and said to him, "Thus says the Lord, the God of the Hebrews, 'How long will you refuse to humble yourself before Me? Let My people go that they may worship Me.'" (Exodus 10:1–3)

Denial isn't just a river in Egypt. That's how the saying goes. Maybe so, but the odyssey of Pharaoh's hardened heart, which takes place on the banks of the Nile and reaches its apex in *Parashat Bo*, teaches us a vital lesson about stubbornness, letting go, and confronting the danger inherent in refusing to acknowledge the truths in our lives.

RABBI JOSEPH BLACK is senior rabbi of Congregation Albert in Albuquerque, New Mexico. He is a nationally recognized singer/songwriter and poet who has shared his love of music with hundreds of communities around the country. Rabbi Black lives in Albuquerque with his wife, Sue, and their children, Elana and Ethan.

As the plagues progress, Pharaoh is clearly a man in denial. He refuses to see the truth of God's power displayed in front of him. Whether his inability to perceive his destiny comes about as a result of his own personality, a divine hand, or some combination of the two is a topic that has fascinated scholars for generations.

In Exodus 10:1–3 we find the following:

> Then the Lord said to Moses, "Go to Pharaoh. For I have hardened his heart and the hearts of his courtiers, in order that I may display My signs among them, and that you may recount in the hearing of your sons and of your sons' sons how I made a mockery of the Egyptians and how I displayed My signs among them—in order that you may know that I am the Lord." So Moses and Aaron went to Pharaoh and said to him, "Thus says the Lord, the God of the Hebrews, 'How long will you refuse to humble yourself before Me? Let My people go that they may worship Me.'"

Our *parashah* sets the stage for the final showdown between Pharaoh and God. The text teaches that God hardened Pharaoh's heart in order to make "a mockery" of him and his people. This seems to pose some sticky ethical problems. If Pharaoh's heart is deliberately hardened, then God seems to not be playing fair.

Many commentators have tried to explain away the ethical problem inherent in Pharaoh's hardened heart by noting that the hardening takes place over time—as a gradual process. At first, Pharaoh hardens it himself, ignoring the warnings of the plagues in a grand display of hubris and chutzpah (Exodus 7:13, 7:14, 7:22, 8:15, 8:28, 9:7). As the plagues continue and increase in both severity and consequence, however, Pharaoh's resistance appears to waver, giving Moses and the Israelites partial concessions so as to bargain for time and leniency (Exodus 8:4, 8:21–25, 9:27–28, 10:8, 10:16–17). But, as the immediate terror of the plagues fades into memory, Pharaoh's intransigence regroups and plunges him ever closer to the inevitable climax. From a traditional perspective, our Rabbis taught that in order to facilitate Pharaoh's downfall, God eventually steps in and completes the hardening process. God is merely "closing the deal"—thereby ensuring Pharaoh's humiliation and God's absolute victory.[1]

The plague narrative can be interpreted in many different ways. On a literal level, it is the story of how hubris can lead to destruction. Pharaoh, in our text, is the absolute ruler of Egypt. In his eyes and the eyes of his people, he is a god: infallible and unquestioning, the voice of authority, the source of life and death itself. Moses, on the other hand, at the beginning of his career, is a reluctant prophet. He is filled with self-doubt. "Why me?" he says when God calls to him out of the burning bush. "I'm just a shepherd. I have a speech impediment. Don't pick me!" (Exodus 3:11, 4:1, 4:10).

It's as though the Torah has deliberately placed these two different personalities opposite each other to highlight the lessons learned from Pharaoh's downfall and Moses's victory.

But upon closer analysis, we see that even Moses, the quintessential reluctant prophet, gets caught up in the posturing of the plagues narrative. In his last conversation with Pharaoh before the final plague, we find the following dialogue: Pharaoh said to him [Moses]: "Be gone from me! Take care not to see me again, for the moment you look upon my face you shall die." And Moses replied, "You have spoken rightly. I shall not see your face again!" (Exodus 10:28–29). In this terse prediction, Moses is showing his inner warrior. He is predicting Pharaoh's death, meeting him on his own territory, *mano a mano*.

Pharaoh represents the figure of a man who cannot admit failure and has to win at any cost. Every interaction becomes a challenge. He has to be right, and he will do whatever it takes to avoid looking foolish, fallible, or mortal. In his later years, Moses himself inherits this trait and pays dearly when, in *Parashat Chukat* (Numbers 20:2–13), he hits the rock at Meribah instead of speaking to it—disobeying God and sealing his own fate in the process. Whether acting out of anger, grief, fatigue, or hubris, Moses falls victim to the same demons that plagued Pharaoh: he could not allow himself to appear weak in front of his people.

Perhaps all of us have a little bit of Pharaoh in us. For too long, our society has taught us that winning is everything—and losing is paramount to disaster. Nowhere is this better observed than in our political system.

If an elected official's position on an issue shifts, evolves, or even changes, he or she is perceived as weak. There is no dialogue in our election process—only diatribe. The purpose of a political debate is not to share ideas with your opponent—it is to see who can shout the loudest, find loopholes, and claim victory.

Could you imagine what it would be like if, at some point in a political disagreement, one opponent turned to the other and said, "You know, you have a good point there. I think you've convinced me that I've been wrong and you are right. I'm going to change my mind." It could never happen. Such an admission would be political suicide. And that's too bad.

Do we really want our leaders to be delusional, hard-hearted partisans who make their decisions based exclusively on opinion polls and political platforms? Or do we want them to be able to carefully consider all sides of an issue—to question themselves and their advisors before acting and when, necessary, change their minds and work together for the greater good of society?

But we see these traits in ourselves, not only in our political system. How many times in our own lives—in work, in our friendships, with our spouses, partners, and children—have we found ourselves blindly holding onto the fantasy of our own infallibility and failing to read the writing on the wall until it is too late? For too long, masculinity has been defined in terms of machismo that sees failure as a sign of weakness.

We need to learn how to disagree—how to fail and how to learn from our failures. Nobody is always right. The drive to succeed at all costs has taken a terrible toll on families, friendships, and even personal health.

Heart disease is one of the biggest health problems affecting middle-aged men. While many of the factors that contribute to heart disease are hereditary, other factors include stress, improper diet, and lack of exercise. Perhaps hard-heartedness is connected to hardening of the arteries. Both can be fatal.

Gribbenes (*Parashat Bo*)

© Joe Black (Pesach, 5768)

This year, on Pesach, I ate my father's food:
Gribbenes, Gehachte Leber, and Gefilte Fish.
My Doctor tells me it hardens my arteries
But I think it softens my soul.

I wonder if Pharaoh ate gribbenes …
His heart hardened, melted, hardened, melted
Like schmaltz
Floating on the surface
With each successive reconstitution—
Thawing, cooling, thickening, slickening
Until, finally
It merges into the mixed multitude
of shredded leeks, onions, bones and flesh that gather
On the bottom of the pot.

Pharaoh, after some prodding, hardened his own heart.
It was he who chilled his veins, sinews and arteries.
It was he who refused to open his eyes to the greasy truth
That haunted him with each successive plague.

Night after sleepless night—he felt them:
The shortness of breath
The sharp pain that radiated
From the back of his neck to the tips of his fingers....

If only, godlike, he could have seen the blockage.
If only hearing, seeing, welcoming freedom's cry
Could somehow miraculously have melted away his stubbornness
Flowing effortlessly into the banks of the Nile.

But then, of course,
We would have no story.
Dayenu.

בשלח
Beshalach

The Real Birth of a Nation

CANTOR JEFF KLEPPER

In Your love You lead the people You redeemed;
In Your strength You guide them to Your holy abode.
(Exodus 15:13)

He not busy being born is busy dying.
(Bob Dylan, "It's Alright Ma [I'm Only Bleeding]" [copyright
©1965; renewed 1993, Special Rider Music])

Of all the experiences in my lifetime, few will ever match the awe,
the fear, the excitement, the love, and the joy of watching the birth
of my children. The power of childbirth lies in the struggle between
life and death. Lurking somewhere in our consciousness is the
knowledge that when we are gone, the child will serve as our
replacement on earth. Fighting through the pain, the sweat, the
blood, the screams, hearing the sound of baby's first cry is the music
of redemption, the victory of life over death.

The Book of Exodus begins with a portent of death. Pharaoh
attempts to solve his Jewish problem by drowning every Jewish male

CANTOR JEFF KLEPPER, a graduate of Hebrew Union College–Jewish
Institute of Religion, has served congregations in the United States and
Israel. He teaches future cantors at Hebrew College in Newton,
Massachusetts, and co-founded the Hava Nashira Songleader Workshop.
His songs are sung and performed around the world, most notably "*Shalom
Rav*" (co-written with Daniel Freelander, his partner in the group Kol
B'seder). He serves as cantor at Temple Sinai in Sharon, Massachusetts.

baby. As an epic narrative, it is brilliant. As the story of our own people, it is a nightmare. But it is a story we love to tell and retell. We act it out around the dinner table each year on Passover.

By the time we reach our portion, *Beshalach*, the plagues have taken their toll, and the Israelites have been released from Egypt. As Moses leads them into the desert, we know that danger lies ahead. Seeing the Egyptian army giving chase, the Israelites are convinced they have reached the end of the road. In voices dripping with irony they say to Moses, "Was it for want of graves in Egypt that you brought us to die in the wilderness?" Moses replies, "Have no fear" (Exodus 14:11–13). With God's intervention at the Sea of Reeds, it is Pharaoh's army who drowns in the very water that serves as our passage to freedom.

As suggested by the following midrash, the Rabbis are attracted to the metaphor of childbirth when discussing the Exodus. Egypt is understood as a womb, and the Sea of Reeds as the "water breaking," a symbolic birth canal through which we are reborn as a people.

> Rabbi Judah, attempting to startle a congregation of drowsy students, proclaimed, "One woman in Egypt brought forth six hundred thousand at a birth!" Challenged by Rabbi Ishmael, the teacher replied: "This was Yocheved—she bore Moses, who was counted as equal to six hundred thousand of Israel—for so it says, "Then sang Moses and the children of Israel!" (Exodus 15:1).[1]

When I first became a father, I quickly learned some necessary but painful truths. First, I realized that Mommy, Daddy, and baby are a triangle. If three's a crowd, then Daddy is the odd man out. When our baby was nursing, I would watch in wonderment, admittedly envious of the closeness of their relationship. As little Rachel was suckling, I would look into her happy drunken eyes with all the depth of my love, and there were times her eyes spoke back: "Aren't you the guy who hangs around Mommy?"

Then I came to appreciate what every mother instinctively knows. The physical attachment of mother and baby in nursing is more than a special bond. It is a sacred act, symbolic of our relationship to God.

I wonder: As the Israelites march deeper into the desert and the water runs out, does Moses feel a little like a new father? Moses quickly learns that only God can provide sustenance. In the first episode of complaining, at Marah, Moses gets off easy by following God's advice:

> And the people grumbled against Moses, saying, "What shall we drink?" So he cried out to the Lord, and the Lord showed him a piece of wood; he threw it into the water and the water became sweet. (Exodus 15:24–25)

A week or so later, Moses doesn't get off the hook so easily. The people are crying like hungry babies. Moses and Aaron are powerless; of course they are, because God is the provider. So, like a mother feeding her hungry babies, God feeds (her) children of Israel with manna, God's miracle food, which is soft, sweet, creamy, and plentiful, not unlike breast milk. (Just push the two n's of "manna" together and they spell "mama," but that trick only works in English.)

Of all the tasks that God assigns Moses, the hardest is serving as Israel's father figure. For most of us, fatherhood (or parenthood) is the hardest thing we will ever do. Many of the qualities necessary to be a good father (tenderness, compassion, patience, forgiveness) may not be ones valued in the workplace. Our impressive titles and take-home pay (beyond what's needed for shelter, food, and clothes) are of little importance to a child. Whether you are a mailman or a CEO, when you walk through the door you are just Dad.

We have all watched our children squabble and complain, or worse. Do we ever know what to say? Do we often blurt out words we later regret? As our frustration builds, do we sometimes imagine that hitting or spanking might "teach a lesson"? Or worse, do we fail to take a deep breath and rein in those feelings?

Like children in the back seat on a long car ride, the Israelites continue to complain: "'Give us water to drink,' they said; and

Moses replied to them, 'Why do you quarrel with me? Why do you try the Lord?'" (Exodus 17:2).

Looking to God for help yet again, Moses is instructed to take his magic staff and strike the side of Mount Horeb: "Take along the rod with which you struck the Nile, and set out. I will be standing there before you on the rock at Horeb. Strike the rock and water will issue from it, and the people will drink" (Exodus 17:5–6).

When God instructs Moses to hit the rock, there is more than one reason for doing so. God is not stupid. Moses is beside himself. God knows that a few good swings with the staff not only will produce the much-needed water, but will help Moses calm down. There are many times when going out for a run, or mowing the lawn, or doing something—anything—is the best we can do in that situation.

Near the end of *Beshalach*, we witness a tender scene that offers a rare glimpse of Moses's humanity. Joshua's army is locked in a ferocious battle with Amalek.

> Moses, Aaron, and Hur went up to the top of the hill. Then, whenever Moses held up his hand, Israel prevailed; but whenever he let down his hand, Amalek prevailed. But Moses's hands grew heavy; so they took a stone and put it under him and he sat on it, while Aaron and Hur, one on each side, supported his hands; thus his hands remained steady until the sun set. (Exodus 17:10–12)

As I have grown into adulthood and now, into my fifties, I have come to realize one great truth: People need each other. We cannot do it alone. We need each other's care, support, love, guidance, wisdom, and concern. Even the great Moses, who at eighty had to be a man of great stature, imposing presence, and superb physical condition to do the things he did, needed to rest. The text above does not tell us if Moses asked for help, or if Aaron and Hur offered it first. We don't have to do everything by ourselves. It's not a sign of weakness to ask for assistance. My guess is that Aaron, knowing Moses so well, sensed that something was wrong and stepped forward. By allowing his brother and friend to witness his vulnerability, Moses was able to shift the momentum of the battle, leading to victory.

Yet, the closing words of *Beshalach* are ominous: "The Lord will be at war with Amalek throughout the ages" (Exodus 17:16). I believe that there are two Amaleks. One would do us physical harm from without—against him, we fight for survival. The other is the Amalek who dwells within—the inner demons, fears, and doubts that would enslave us. Against him, we fight for our soul's redemption. It is a deeply personal struggle, but we need not face it alone.

Not Just for the Birds

Ari L. Goldman

**And Miriam chanted for them: "Sing to the Lord, for He
has triumphed gloriously...."** (Exodus 15:21)

The Shabbat on which we read *Beshalach* is also known as Shabbat
Shirah (the Shabbat of song) because of the triumphant Song of the
Sea that is recorded in that Torah portion. The Israelites, on seeing
their adversaries drowned in the Sea of Reeds, break into a song of
praise: "I will sing to the Lord, for He has triumphed gloriously; /
Horse and driver He has hurled into the sea" (Exodus 15:1).

When I was a little boy, this was a very special Shabbat for me.
Every year on Shabbat Shirah, my great-aunts, Minnie and Paulie,
who helped raise me after my parents were divorced, would take me
to Riverside Park near their Manhattan apartment so that we could
feed kasha to the birds. In so doing, they made an ancient story

ARI L. GOLDMAN spent twenty years as a reporter at the *New York Times*
before taking a position as a professor at the Graduate School of Journalism
at Columbia University. He is author of three books, including the best-
selling *The Search for God at Harvard*. He has been a Fulbright professor in
Israel, a fellow at the Oxford Centre for Hebrew and Jewish Studies in
England, and a visiting professor at Stern College for Women at Yeshiva
University. He also serves on the board of several Jewish organizations,
including the Covenant Foundation, the Jewish Book Council, and
Congregation Ramath Orah, an Orthodox synagogue in New York City.

come alive for a boy who loved both nature and kasha, which was, for me, the ultimate comfort food.

This was one of those folk customs that I never learned about in Jewish day school or read about in books. It was the custom of my elderly aunts, who were as intent on engaging my imagination as in observing any ritual.

I had almost forgotten about the kasha custom until I had children of my own and told them the story of my aunts. Just to check my memory, I went to my rabbi, Stephen Friedman. "Yes," he told me. "We do this on Shabbat Shirah to honor the birds, who every day bring music into our lives."

"And kasha?" I asked. "Why do we feed them kasha?"

"Kasha?" he responded with a chuckle. "I never heard of that part."

His response got me wondering. Was it really kasha that my aunts fed the birds? And do birds even like kasha? And do they like it cooked or raw?

Only one way to find out, I decided. I enlisted the help of my youngest son, Judah. We boiled up a big pot of kasha and took it along with a box of uncooked kasha and headed for the park.

And here is what we found: pigeons like it cooked and sparrows like it raw. And here's something else we found: my aunts knew what they were doing. They engaged my senses in a way that I would want to carry on the tradition and pass it on to my own son. I can only hope that he will someday do the same.

יתרו
Yitro

No Exodus from the Family!

RABBI DAN EHRENKRANTZ

Jethro, priest of Midian, Moses's father-in-law, heard all that God had done for Moses and for Israel His people.... (Exodus 18:1)

People who take on leadership roles often do so at the expense of their personal relationships. *Moshe rabbeinu*, "Moses our teacher," suffered this fate. For millennia, his people have loved him, but those to whom he was closest during his lifetime paid the price for his dedication.

Men and women today frequently search for the right balance between work and family. But balance is the wrong metaphor. It implies that by simply shifting our attention this way or that, we can fully satisfy all our obligations. If only life were that simple. The reality is that we often work to sustain our families. Sometimes if our work is slighted our families suffer. What's more, both arenas need and deserve our complete devotion. In short, it is impossible to achieve harmony by pursuing balance.

RABBI DAN EHRENKRANTZ is president of the Reconstructionist Rabbinical College (RRC) in Philadelphia, Pennsylvania, and is the first graduate of RRC to become its president. Named one of the fifty most influential rabbis by *Newsweek* magazine, Rabbi Ehrenkrantz previously served as the spiritual leader of Congregation Bnai Keshet, a Reconstructionist synagogue in Montclair, New Jersey.

Instead of balance, perhaps wisdom and spirit should be our goals. We need wisdom to know when to focus on our families and when to focus on our work, and we need spirit so that we can bring our best selves to every interaction and every task. If we cultivate spirit throughout our lives, our unavoidable absences will be easier, both for our families and for ourselves, to bear.

For all the attention the Torah gives Moses, we do not know much about his home life. We see Moses primarily through his work—as a leader, teacher, and prophet—for an unruly mob of freed slaves and their children. But before he takes on these responsibilities, we see glimpses of a different Moses:

> Now the priest of Midian had seven daughters. They came to draw water, and filled the troughs to water their father's flock; but shepherds came and drove them off. Moses rose to their defense, and he watered their flock. When they returned to their father Reuel, he said, "How is it that you have come back so soon today?" They answered, "An Egyptian rescued us from the shepherds; he even drew water for us and watered the flock." He said to his daughters, "Where is he then? Why did you leave the man? Ask him in to break bread." Moses consented to stay with the man, and he gave Moses his daughter Zipporah as wife. She bore a son whom he named Gershom, for he said, "I have been a stranger in a foreign land." (Exodus 2:16–22)

The question of Moses's kinship is an interesting one. Although when Moses arrives in Midian the daughters of the local priests consider him an Egyptian, an incident preceding this one reveals a different perspective. There Moses tries to defend the Hebrews by killing an Egyptian taskmaster, but the Hebrews reject this attempt at leadership and spread word of the murder until it reaches Pharaoh. Moses, now aligned with the Hebrews in the minds of the Egyptians, is forced to flee Egypt.

Inclined to protect those who are mistreated, as we have seen, Moses defends the women from the stronger and/or more numerous shepherds. In fact he is so successful that the women are able to complete their tasks unusually early. It is clear that Moses's care and concern are not limited to his own people; there is no "us and them" mentality based on ethnic divisions. Moses opposes injustice wherever he finds it.

Reuel, the priest of Midian whom the Torah later calls Jethro, also seems unconcerned with ethnic identity. He sees Moses as a person who stands up for those in need even when it puts him at risk and seems to offer no gain. Jethro sees Moses as the kind of man who would make a good husband for his daughter Zipporah.

The next time we see Zipporah, Moses is about to reenter Egypt for the first time since his exile. In a strange scene (Exodus 4:24–26), she performs a circumcision on Moses (or her son; the text is unclear) in order to ward off a mortal danger. Although the scene is shrouded in mystery, Zipporah's devotion to her family, as well as her courage and wisdom, are clear. How odd it is then that the very next time Zipporah appears we learn that Moses has banished her.

> Jethro, Moses's father-in-law, took Zipporah, Moses's wife, after she had been sent away [*shilucheha*; translation modified from JPS translation, which says "sent home" rather than "sent away"].... Jethro, Moses's father-in-law, brought Moses's sons and wife to him in the wilderness, where he was encamped at the mountain of God. (Exodus 18:2, 18:5)

Why was Zipporah "sent away"? Perhaps there is a hint in Deuteronomy 24:1: "A man takes a wife and possesses her. She fails to please him because he finds something obnoxious about her, and he writes her a bill of divorcement, hands it to her, and sends her away [*v'shilchah*] from his house."

Were Moses and Zipporah divorced? The Torah does not tell us, and it is unclear whether the connotation of formal divorce contained in the word *shilucheha* would have been clear to someone living in the ancient world. But even if Moses and Zipporah were not formally divorced, it seems safe to say that they were at least estranged.

What went on in their household that caused this estrangement? It is not too difficult to imagine that the demands of confronting Pharaoh, dealing with the failure of the early plagues, and balancing the uncompromising demands of God for leadership and the reality of a people reluctant to accept his direction—that all of this had taken a toll on Moses's intimate relationships.

For example, the Torah tells us nothing of the birth of Moses's second son, Eliezer. We meet him for the first time in Exodus 18, when we are told that his name means "The God of my father was my help, and He delivered me from the sword of Pharaoh" (Exodus 18:4). Somewhere between the plagues and the Exodus, Zipporah bore Moses a second child. The Torah misses this moment—and perhaps so did Moses. It is certainly hard to imagine him taking time from negotiating with Pharaoh to attend to the birth and infancy needs of his son. This alone might be enough to have caused a rift with his wife.

How painful it must have been for Jethro to watch his daughter and grandchildren suffer because of the very qualities that had commended Moses to him in the first place! Jethro hoped that Moses might yet turn out to be a good husband and father and undoubtedly wondered how he could get Moses to see the error of his ways. Direct confrontation was destined to fail, since a father-in-law must tread lightly when challenging his son-in-law. Jethro sets the stage very carefully, beginning by letting Moses know that his family is on the way: "Jethro, Moses's father-in-law, brought Moses's sons and wife to him in the wilderness, where he was encamped at the mountain of God. He sent word to Moses, 'I, your father-in-law Jethro, am coming to you, with your wife and her two sons'" (Exodus 18:5–6).

These verses emphasize Moses's family relationships—father-in-law, wife, sons. Jethro must have hoped that with the exodus from Egypt behind him, Moses would be ready to embrace his family.

> Moses went out to meet his father-in-law; he bowed low and kissed him; each asked after the other's welfare, and they went into the tent. Moses then recounted to his father-in-law every-

thing that the Lord had done to Pharaoh and to the Egyptians for Israel's sake, all the hardships that had befallen them on the way, and how the Lord had delivered them. (Exodus 18:7–8)

Jethro finds Moses more than willing to rekindle their relationship, but not in the way he had hoped. Moses is eager to talk about his work and accomplishments, his challenges and triumphs. But there is no mention of his wife and sons. Moses greets Jethro, but it appears that he does not greet the rest of his family, nor does he ask after their welfare or bring them into the tent, the ultimate symbol of family embrace and unity. Moses and his family remain estranged. Jethro notes this behavior but does not give up.

> And Jethro rejoiced over all the kindness that the Lord had shown Israel when He delivered them from the Egyptians. "Blessed be the Lord," Jethro said, "who delivered you from the Egyptians and from Pharaoh, and who delivered the people from under the hand of the Egyptians. Now I know that the Lord is greater than all gods, yes, by the result of their very schemes against [the people]." And Jethro, Moses's father-in-law, brought a burnt offering and sacrifices for God; and Aaron came with all the elders of Israel to partake of the meal before God with Moses's father-in-law. (Exodus 18:9–12)

Jethro understands that Moses is consumed by his role as leader of his people and that as long as he, Jethro, stands outside of the project that Moses has taken on, his influence with Moses will be limited. Jethro, a Midianite priest with his own rituals and deities, declares God's greatness and shares a religious meal with the elders of Israel. In this way, Jethro lets Moses know that he fully understands and respects the importance of his work. Jewish tradition imagines that Jethro converts to Judaism. What is important is that Jethro demonstrates his respect for Moses and his mission.

Before Jethro can have any influence upon Moses, he has to understand the constraints that Moses's role places on him. After watching Moses as he works, Jethro realizes that his son-in-law cannot possibly be the husband and father he should be while shouldering so many responsibilities:

> Next day, Moses sat as magistrate among the people, while the people stood about Moses from morning until evening. But when Moses's father-in-law saw how much he had to do for the people, he said, "What is this thing that you are doing to the people? Why do you act alone, while all the people stand about you from morning until evening?" (Exodus 18:13–14)

Seeing where Moses's devotion presently lies, Jethro cleverly points out that Moses is being unfair to his people by making them wait from morning until night to see him: "But Moses's father-in-law said to him, 'The thing you are doing is not right; you will surely wear yourself out, and these people as well. For the task is too heavy for you; you cannot do it alone'" (Exodus 18:17–18).

In short, Jethro sees that his daughter and grandchildren are being neglected, but rather than chastise Moses for being selfish and irresponsible, he expresses his respect for Moses's accomplishments, makes an effort to understand the challenges of his situation, and seeks to alleviate his burden. A more enlightened and supportive father-in-law would be hard to imagine.

Jethro suggests that Moses create a system of progressive courts. Only the most difficult matters need to be decided by Moses personally; capable people selected by Moses can handle the others. That way, Moses will be able to carry out his leadership responsibilities but will also have time to spend with his family.

Moses implements Jethro's suggestion. The Torah easily accepts that wisdom can come from a Midianite priest, that wisdom is welcome whatever its origin. All of us need help from time to time, and that help may come from family members, including enlightened in-laws.

Was Jethro successful in turning Moses's attention back to his family obligations? Here's what we are told: "Then Moses bade his father-in-law farewell, and he went his way to his own land" (Exodus 18:27).

When Jethro arrives at Moses's tent, his daughter and grandchildren are mentioned twice. When he leaves, not a word. Perhaps Jethro's warm family presence and his wise counsel helped reunite Moses with his wife and children. If so, the situation appears to have been short-lived. Moses's sons are never seen again. As for Zipporah, it is unclear whether she is mentioned again. In Numbers 12, Moses's family life is the subject of a discussion between Aaron and Miriam: "When they were in Hazeroth, Miriam and Aaron spoke against Moses because of the Cushite woman he had married: 'He married a Cushite woman!'" (Numbers 12:1).

Since Zipporah was a Midianite, not a Cushite, some commentators believe the woman referred to is a new wife. This reading suggests that Moses and Zipporah were divorced. Another possibility is that Moses took a wife in addition to Zipporah. Other commentators understand the reference to be to Zipporah herself. In any case, what is important is the subject of Aaron and Miriam's complaint. Some ancient Rabbis believed they were angry with Moses for choosing a life of celibacy rather than behaving like a proper husband. God quickly rises to Moses's defense, sharply criticizing Aaron and Miriam and even punishing Miriam with a skin ailment. If Aaron and Miriam are critical of Moses's behavior toward his immediate family, God does not seem to be, and he makes sure that Moses never hears his siblings' harsh words.

The Torah ends with Moses's death. In this beautiful scene, God personally attends to Moses's burial: "So Moses the servant of the Lord died there, in the land of Moab, at the command of the Lord. He buried him in the valley in the land of Moab, near Beth-peor; and no one knows his burial place to this day" (Deuteronomy 34:5–6).

The honor of being buried by God is perhaps an unfortunate necessity. Aaron and Miriam have died, Moses's sons are never mentioned after Jethro brings them to Moses, and Moses's home life was such that no wife is with him when his end comes. Moses has no family to attend his funeral. His grave can go unmarked because it will have no visitors.

Moses's life story tells us that taking on leadership roles in the community often comes at a high price. Moses was not immune to this danger; unable to tear himself away from the people, or from God, he dies alone. Despite his father-in-law's effort to help him conduct his business in a way that would yield time to build family relationships, Moses focuses all of his energy on being the leader of the Israelites. Still, who could fault Moses for getting lost in his work when the episode following Jethro's departure has Moses traveling up Mount Sinai to speak with God?

The difficulties of making a meaningful contribution to society while building and maintaining intimate relationships cannot be framed as an issue of balance. The issue for us, as well as Moses, is one of wisdom—of knowing when to pay attention to work and when to focus on family—and of spirit. Did Moses give his wife (wives?) and children the same quality of attention he gave his leadership tasks? Was he as engaged when he interacted with them as he was when he spoke with God? Only the people in a given relationship know what leads to estrangement. Perhaps there was no alternative for Moses; perhaps his unique role in the world made it impossible to sustain family relationships.

Unfortunately, the Torah's presentation of Moses's family life is an all too realistic portrait of many of our own lives. It is hard, perhaps impossible, to be completely successful in every sphere of life. Yet however demanding our professional lives may be, we can be thankful that our burdens are not as great as those shouldered by Moses. We know that while we might not be able to "have it all," if we cultivate wisdom and spirit we will be able to have enough—a close relationship with God, a warm circle of friends, a rich family life, and the ability to contribute to society while deriving satisfaction from our work.

Honor and Love

RABBI DAVID WOZNICA

Honor your father and your mother, that you may long endure on the land that the Lord your God is assigning to you. (Exodus 20:12)

The relationship between children and parents is often among life's most beautiful and most complicated. So significant is the commandment in the Torah to "Honor your father and your mother ..." that the Talmud teaches that when we show honor to our parents, we honor God. Indeed, by honoring our parents, we bring God into our homes; a home where parents are treated with respect and dignity is a home where God lives.

It is noteworthy that God does not command us to love our parents. Love is an emotion, and Judaism rarely mandates human emotion. After all, how can we be commanded to feel when we have little control over our most private thoughts and feelings? Judaism is primarily concerned with our actions. Although our feelings often drive our actions, Judaism wisely understands that how we act will ultimately shape our feelings.

Even in the best of child-parent relationships, there are moments of mixed emotions. In those trying moments, we can, however, act

RABBI DAVID WOZNICA serves as rabbi of Stephen S. Wise Temple in Los Angeles, California. Previously, he was the founding director of the 92nd Street Y Bronfman Center for Jewish Life in New York City.

honorably toward our parents. In fact, it is precisely at those times, we should remember that most parents want very much for their children to love them and that, in most cases, a parent's love for their child is deep and everlasting. As children, undoubtedly there were times when we caused our parents grief. Perhaps we were asserting newfound teenage independence or became preoccupied with friends or hobbies. Or as adults, we become so immersed in our work or families that we may find it difficult to make enough time for them.

The following examples illustrate the importance of expressing our love as well as choosing carefully the way we conclude conversations with our parents.

I heard a story about a funeral where a lone man stood by the graveside for a considerable time after the other mourners had left. The rabbi approached the man and gently suggested that it was time to go. The man responded, "You don't understand, I loved my wife." The rabbi waited for some time and then approached the husband once again. "You don't understand, Rabbi. I loved my wife."

"I have no doubt that you loved her very much, but it is getting late and it is time we should go," said the rabbi. He waited a short while longer and then approached the grieving husband for a third time.

"You don't understand, Rabbi, I loved my wife—and I hardly ever told her."

For those men who do not easily express their emotions, the lesson of this grieving husband may be particularly helpful.

When I was in college, a letter that appeared in the editorial section of our university newspaper struck me. It was from a young woman whose father had passed away suddenly and unexpectedly. What made the situation particularly heart wrenching was that their last conversation had been a terrible argument. The woman predicted that she would be haunted for the rest of her life by these last fighting words and implored the readers never to conclude conversations in such a way.

We all feel the anguish of the husband and the daughter who live with regret. For those blessed to have one or both parents alive, we can learn valuable lessons from these two examples of the importance of expressing our love to our parents. As we watch our parents age, how many of us wish we had spent more time with them, had asked them more about their lives before we were born, and talked frankly with them about their hopes and disappointments? If you have yet to ask these questions, this is the time to ask.

What if your mother and/or father is no longer living?

One of Judaism's greatest gifts is *Yizkor*, the service when we remember those who are no longer with us. While many Jews associate *Yizkor* exclusively with Yom Kippur, it is actually recited four times each year.

Whether in the context of a *Yizkor* service or, if you prefer, in a quiet private moment, take a few minutes to say the words to your parents that you never said, the words you always wanted to say. Close your eyes and in your mind reach out to take the hand of your mother or father and say the words in your heart. "Thank you for all that you did for me, for shaping my life, for feeding me, for helping me ..."

You might say: "I am sorry for the times that I hurt you." "I miss you." Or, in the hope of moving forward in your own life and letting go of the hurt and anger, "I forgive you. I forgive you for the times you were not a better mother or father." Tell them: "I love you. I wish I had told you or said so more often when you were here."

May those of you who have unsettled issues with a mother or father find the strength to reach out to your parent. And, if you have feelings of gratitude that you want to express, I encourage you to do so. Your words can leave you and your parents with a deep and beautiful memory, whether your parents are standing in front of you, hearing your voice across a telephone line, or patiently listening to you from the heavens above.

מִשְׁפָּטִים
Mishpatim

A Man in Public

Rabbi Donniel Hartman, PhD

**When you encounter your enemy's ox or ass wandering,
you must take it back to him.** (Exodus 23:4)

A central feature of biblical religiosity is that it is not determined by one's faith and ritual practices alone, but equally by one's moral character and behavior toward others. The aspiration of the Bible is to create out of the Jews a holy people, and as such, much of the legal code pertains to regulating people's interactions with one another, both in the private and public domain, in order to ensure peaceful coexistence and the protection of rights to self and property. It is within this context that one finds the vast majority of the laws that appear in *Parashat Mishpatim*.

In my analysis of the *parashah*, I will focus on the legal discussion around the moral responsibilities toward others in the public domain. In the Bible, the domain of public social life is primarily a masculine one, and the ethic of public social life is essentially a male ethic. As a result, one can read *Mishpatim* as outlining the essential characteristics of what it means to be a man in one's interactions with others.

RABBI DONNIEL HARTMAN, PhD, is codirector of the Shalom Hartman Institute in Jerusalem and is author of *The Boundaries of Judaism* and coeditor and contributor to *Judaism and the Challenges of Modern Life.*

116

One of the important features found in *Mishpatim* regarding the regulating of behavior in the public sphere is when it deals with those situations wherein there is a breakdown within the normal and expected realities that generally govern this sphere. Such a breakdown undermines peaceful coexistence between society's members. One such case, which will be the focus of this chapter, is that of lost property, that is, property not under the control of (literally, "under the hand of") its original owner. Under normal circumstances, ownership is recognized by possession. In the private domain, the private nature associates everything within it to the owner. Given the fact that the public domain is a shared one, ownership is recognized by the fact that the item is controlled by and in the possession of its owner. Associating property to one's owner is essential, for entering the public domain with one's property engenders certain responsibilities on the part of both the owner and others. The owner, for example, has to ensure that his property does not cause damage to other persons and property, and being owned by someone likewise requires that others refrain from damaging or appropriating it for themself.

Lost property is potentially an explosive situation, for the status of the property is not clear—a confusion that can lead to competing expectations on the part of the original owner and others who encounter the property. To whom does the lost property belong? Given the fact that the public domain is owned, or not owned equally by all, is this an opportunity for others to enhance their financial standing by appropriating the item for themselves, or does the original owner still maintain his ownership even though the property is not now in his possession?

Our *parashah*, incorporating classic biblical brevity, states as follows: "When you encounter your enemy's ox or ass wandering, you must take it back to him" (Exodus 23:4). In this regulation, three principles are set forth that outline our moral responsibilities to one another. First, ownership is not contingent on possession. A safe public space requires that we know that we can bring our property into that space and not lose ownership as a result of unforeseen and uncontrollable circumstances. A Jewish public space is safe and caring in the sense that it is not a place where fellow citizens come in search of benefiting from other's misfortunes.

Second, our responsibilities to others are not dependent on our feelings and prior relationships. In speaking of lost property, the Bible specifically states: "when you encounter your *enemy's* ox or ass." The public sphere must be governed by universally applied ethical norms that are not contingent on personal relationships and past history. When we enter the public domain and know that we are encountering friend and foe, we must be assured that all will treat us equally, and the purpose of the law is to regulate precisely such a code and standard.

Third, and in many ways most important, the Bible obligates us to return the lost property. Not only can one not appropriate the property for oneself, but equally, one cannot ignore it. The biblical ethic of moral responsibility is not exhausted by John Stuart Mill's "no-harm principle," that is, the responsibility to refrain from actively causing damage to others. Rather, the Torah requires proactive moral behavior: you must return it. The public domain and our interaction with others must not only not express a yearning to profit from others' misfortunes, but it must entail the creating of a caring and protecting environment in which fellow citizens recognize that it is their duty to assist and protect one another.

As is often the case in the Bible, laws in the Books of Exodus, Leviticus, and Numbers are repeated, expanded upon, and sometimes changed in the Book of Deuteronomy. The Deuteronomic parallel for the version of the law in Exodus states as follows:

> If you see your fellow's ox or sheep gone astray, do not ignore it;
> you must take it back to your fellow. If your fellow does not live
> near you, or if you do not know who he is, you shall bring it
> home and it shall remain with you until your fellow claims it;
> then you shall give it back to him. You shall do the same with
> his ass; you shall do the same with his garment; and so too shall
> you do with anything that your fellow loses and you find; you
> must not remain indifferent. (Deuteronomy 22:1–3)

The discussion in Deuteronomy offers a number of clarifications and additions, the most significant of which is the recognition that returning lost property is not simple, because the identity of the owner is not always immediately apparent. This additional burden, however, does not change the core responsibility toward one's fellow citizen. Following the proactive requirement of *Mishpatim*, Deuteronomy obligates us to not remain indifferent. It is indifference toward the needs of others that will change and ruin the type of public domain that the Bible is attempting to create.

As is the case with much of biblical law, the details beyond the core moral direction are absent and not elucidated by the text. Thus, for example, *Mishpatim* does not offer any guidance as to what to do if one doesn't know the identity of the owner, or how one distinguishes between lost and abandoned property, or whether there are limits to one's responsibility to return the property.

The expansion and development of biblical law is one of the core features of Rabbinic law. In our case, the above issues are dealt with in the Talmud in *Baba Metzia*, chapter 2. There, the Rabbis add two key conditions and stipulations. The first is that the duty to return lost property is contingent on whether the property is returnable, that is, there are distinguishing characteristics (*simanim*) that enable the owner to identify the property as his and that will provide proof of ownership and therefore guide the individual who finds the property in the process of returning it. Lost property without distinguishable characteristics is not simply temporarily ownerless, but permanently so, for it constitutes a condition that cannot be rectified. Consequently, such property can remain in the hands of any individual who finds it.

The second condition is that one's responsibility to lost property is contingent on an assessment of the original owner's desire toward this property and on whether he hopes and expects that the property will be returned. The factors that influence the owner's desire and expectation are numerous. For example: (1) Is there an identifiable sign enabling the property's return? The absence of such a sign would cause the owner to abandon any hope that the property would be returned. (2) How do we assess the value of the property, and in particular, the relationship to the effort and time it would take to collect it? The more valuable the property and the less effort it requires would result in extending the desire to have the property returned; the less valuable and greater effort entailed would make the property less desirable, and thus influence the original owner's intent. (3) Is the property durable, or not? A lack of durability would directly affect the assessment of the owner as to the status of his property and cause him to relinquish ownership, and thus allow the individual who finds it to keep it.

The unifying principle behind the three examples is that one's responsibility to others is shaped by the others' desires and intent. A person must not simply commit to moral activism, that is, to return and care for even one's enemy's property, but to becoming an expert in ascertaining one's fellow citizen's thought processes through the various artifacts and properties that one encounters.

Following this condition, one of the more beautiful and interesting additions to this law offered by the Rabbis in the second chapter of *Baba Metzia* pertains to property that is at present not in the possession of its owner and has no distinguishing characteristics, but that was clearly placed and not lost or abandoned. Such property, once taken into one's hands, would be fundamentally unreturnable, as there is no way to govern and regulate the future exchange. A person who finds such a property could see himself or herself as extremely lucky, benefiting as it were from a gift from God. Instead, the Rabbis add a third category. Not only is there property that must be returned and property that may be kept, there is also lost property that cannot be touched. The fact that it was clearly laid down in a specific place is evidence that the original owner intends on returning, and as such, one is bound to respect that intent and to leave the property alone. In this case, one's moral responsibility to others requires that one ignore the lost property.

In order to facilitate the return of the lost property, the Rabbis appointed Jerusalem, the place where all pilgrims come three times a year, as the national center where property is returned to its original owner. Around Pesach, Sukkot, and Shavuot, a central location was designated as the place where all who found property and all who lost it would come. One would declare what he or she had found; the other would declare the distinguishing characteristics and thus reclaim ownership. Jerusalem is the place where one comes not only to encounter God, but also to encounter one's fellow citizens and together give expression to our mutual care, loyalty, and responsibilities. A Jewish city—a Jewish public domain—is one where such a designated space can be found, and where it is found, it shapes and colors the nature, morality, decency, and caring that governs the people within that society.

In summation, the Torah is attempting to create men who, in their interactions with others, are governed by a sense of responsibility to act not in accordance with their own interests, but rather in accordance with the needs, hopes, and aspirations of the other. If Hillel (Talmud, *Shabbat* 31a) states that the fundamental principle governing our moral interactions is "what is hateful to you, do not do to others," the laws of lost property dictate and teach us that you are not the sole barometer of what is right and what is necessary, but, rather, the other person who is in need of your assistance. It is your responsibility to truly see the other—to be sensitive to their needs and desires and then to respond with moral activism.

The power associated with being a man is not a tool for self-interests alone, as in the Hobbesian state of nature, but a responsibility to create a public domain where one can expect that one's needs and vulnerabilities are responded to with care and concern. This is a Jewish public space. To live within this space and to help create it is what it means to be a Jewish man.

תרומה
Terumah

Gold for God?

RABBI PERRY NETTER

Tell the Israelite people to bring Me gifts; you shall accept gifts for Me from every person whose heart so moves him. (Exodus 25:1)

Terumah is the beginning of the end of the Book of Exodus, but it feels more like a beginning without end. For fifteen chapters, covering the last third of the book, the Torah obsesses about the details of the *mishkan*, the portable wilderness tent that served as the cultic center of the nascent Jewish people. That is a lot of parchment and ink, and a lot of Shabbat-morning Torah readings. But verbosity in the Torah does not necessarily translate into theological importance. After all, the creation of the world required only a single chapter to tell the story. The narrative of the revelation of Torah at Sinai required only two chapters. But the instructions governing the building of the *mishkan* take fifteen chapters! Construction, by and large, is a male pursuit, but even the most macho of builders tires quickly of this endless tale of construction. It is remarkable how swiftly eyes glaze over as this section of the Torah is read in the synagogue.

RABBI PERRY NETTER was ordained by the Jewish Theological Seminary in 1982, and has served congregations in Arcadia, Westwood, and Los Angeles, California. Author of *Divorce Is a Mitzvah: A Practical Guide to Finding Wholeness and Holiness When Your Marriage Dies* (Jewish Lights), he is a divorce mediator in Beverly Hills, California.

For fifteen chapters, we read of dimensions (so many cubits and so many handbreadths) and we read of furniture and ritual objects (the Ark with its *keruvim* [cherubim] and the seven-branched menorah and the altar and the inner and outer curtains and the lavers and tongs and fire-pans and bowls and jars and jugs and ladles). We read of materials—gold and silver and copper; blue, purple, and crimson yarns; fine linen, goats' hair, tanned ram skins, dolphin skins, and acacia wood; oil and spices.

We will leave aside the thorny question of where all these materials came from. Suffice it to say that many rabbis over the centuries have successfully dealt with this narrative challenge. But even if we can solve that textual problem, it seems to me there remains a more fundamental problem. Even if we can find an answer that explains how the Israelites came into possession of so much wealth, the more profound question is: What is all that gold and silver doing in the *mishkan* to begin with? For whom is this ostentatious display of wealth? Who needs all that glitter?

Does God need the gold? The books of biblical wisdom indicate that there are things of greater value than gold: *Tov pir'yi macharutz umipaz; ut'vuati mikesef nivchar*, "My fruit is better than gold, fine gold, / And my produce better than choice silver" (Proverbs 8:19). *Tov shem mishemen tov*, "A good name is better than fragrant oil" (Ecclesiastes 7:1). *Tov li torat picha me'alfei zahav v'chasef*, "I prefer the teaching You proclaimed, / to thousands of gold and silver pieces" (Psalm 119:72). Not unexpectedly, in the biblical worldview, gold is not especially high in God's taxonomy of values. Even still, God asks for gold and silver and copper to build the *mishkan*. Actually, to be more precise, God doesn't ask. The Torah makes it clear: God *demands* the gold.

Vayik'chu li terumah me'et kol ish asher yidvenu libo, tik'chu et terumati, "that they take Me a donation from every man, as his heart may urge him you shall take My donation" (Genesis 25:1; translation from Robert Alter, *The Five Books of Moses* [New York: Norton, 2008], p. 460). *Terumah* means a gift, a freewill offering with neither a minimum nor a maximum amount. Unlike the *maaser*, the yearly tithe that was a Temple tax of 10 percent of personal earnings, *terumah* is not quantified. In the case of *terumah*, the very act of giving has intrinsic value; the substance and the amount of the gift are, at best, secondary.

Many commentators ask, why didn't the Torah use the more appropriate verb *vayitnu*, "that they *give*," instead of *vayik'chu*, "that they *take*"? The internal contradiction between the act of taking and the nature of a freewill offering was not lost on many commentators.

As we might expect, there are many answers to this question, including the reference to the well-known theology of the Psalmist: *Ladonai haaretz um'lo'o*, "The earth is the Lord's, and all that it holds" (Psalm 24:1). God holds title to all there is; we are merely the stewards of the stuff in our possession. Our material things are not ours to give; God can certainly take back what belongs to God. Another popular idea suggests that the Torah uses the verb "to take" rather than "to give" because whenever we give *tzedakah*, the giver benefits more than the receiver. But these answers emerge from a homiletical tradition that reads the biblical narrative with an eye toward gleaning moral imperatives and ideals regarding character.

Let us be honest. The act of giving *tzedakah* is counterintuitive; it runs counter to the very nature of modern manhood—namely, to amass the symbols of success. This is the reason, it can be argued, why *tzedakah* is such an esteemed mitzvah. If giving of our resources was not a prestigious mitzvah, how many of us would part with our hard-earned shekels? More to the point is an even more difficult question, a question that requires rigorous honesty to answer: how many of us would give *tzedakah* if there was no tax deduction for charitable donations?

We work hard for our money. The things we buy with the money we earn—the gold, the silver, the copper; the large house in an exceptional neighborhood; the prestigious schools to which we send our kids; the designer clothes we wear; the cars we drive—are as much symbolic as they are functional. The purpose of a car is to transport us from point A to point B. Is driving a Lexus a symbol of success, or of excess?

In his seminal essay, "The Lonely Man of Faith," Talmudic scholar and religious leader Rabbi Joseph B. Soloveitchik reconciles the internal contradictions of the two biblical creation stories by crafting complementary typological portrayals of men, which he calls Adam the first and Adam the second. Adam the first, created in the image of God, is majestic man, dignified and glorious. He is a creative being, tasked with filling the earth and subduing it. Adam the first gains control of nature; he overpowers and manipulates his environment. He is a builder of ziggurats and cathedrals and skyscrapers. Adam the first displays his mastery over the world. Adam the second displays vulnerability and fragility.

Soloveitchik's reading of the two creation stories, which describes and defines two disparate parts of a unified personality, closely approximates the psychoanalytical theorist Carl Jung's notion of individuation. For Jung, the process of individuation is achieved when we attain wholeness by integrating all the various parts of the psyche—including the masculine (*animus*) and the feminine (*anima*) parts of our personalities.

The male part of our personality, the need to conquer and to build, to hunt and to gather, is dominant in adolescence and early adulthood. There is a script written for us from the moment we are born and the attending doctor, nurse, or midwife announces sight of the outer signs of our masculinity. It establishes the benchmark for measuring success or failure as a man. The essence of the script is earn, baby, earn.

One of the first questions a man is asked upon being introduced in a social situation is, "What do you do?" The question is not merely idle chatter. It is large talk. One of the first questions in a social situation is rarely, "How's your *neshamah* [soul]?" Rarely is it ever a question, period. For most of us, internality is transient and ephemeral, and difficult to capture. For a man, external factors determine existential reality and identity. In many ways, our work defines us.

Men pay an enormous psychological price for being born with a greater preponderance of testosterone than estrogen. Economic insecurity, the threat of poverty, the fear of failure—all are gender determined, all part of the XY chromosome. Men have an inbred fear that the book of life ends after chapter 11. Our primary responsibility in life as a man, *qua* man, is to provide for ourselves, our life partners, and our children. How well we provide economic stability, how much we earn, how much we conspicuously consume—all these determine our societal status. For American men, our bottom line value *is* the bottom line. Men labor under the tyranny of material gain—an unforgiving, unrelenting, and insatiable taskmaster. That is why men who go through divorce or bankruptcy or job loss or any of the myriad male adulthood challenges lose more than a marriage or a business or a job; they also lose the very symbols of success they worked so long and hard to amass. That is what men who suffer economic loss mean when they say they "need to start all over."

Knowing this, why would God ask for men to give up the gold? Perhaps this divine demand proves, once and for all, that God is a man. Perhaps the male deity also needed symbols of success to appear triumphant in the eyes of the other gods of ancient ethnic peoples. The God of Israel just could not be seen driving a Yugo.

Or, not.

I am sure there was a practical, aesthetic reason for the use of gold. We have to remember that the *mishkan* was built in a world devoid of electricity, which means candles provided the visible light. I used to think that the overuse of gold, as an element of interior design in Byzantine churches, made them gaudy and ostentatious, until I remembered that the interiors of churches were lit by candlelight. The gold on the icons reflected the light of the candles with radiant brilliance. It must have been an impressive sight to the penitent, instilling awe and piety in the worshipers. A similar phenomenon must have been operative within the *mishkan* as well.

Beyond aesthetic considerations, however, the command to take gold for the *mishkan* teaches an important moral lesson: gold is, well—just gold. It is nice to have; it is beautiful, valuable, and extraordinary. But parting with it is good for the soul. Our worth as men transcends material gain. We are not the sum total of what we own. The first line of the threefold priestly blessing (Numbers 6:24) reads: *Yevarechecha Adonai v'yishmerecha*, "May God bless you and protect you." My favorite homiletical rendering of these verses conveys a profound life lesson: "May God bless you with all the material success life has to offer, and protect you from your possessions ever possessing you."

Which leads to the final theological lesson, arguably the most important of all: God demanded the gold in order to teach men to learn how to say "enough"—and believe it when they say it. The *mishkan*, built to house God, must reflect the nature of the God whom is to be worshiped and adored. The God of Israel, the Creator of the world, the *Ein Sof* (the "One without end," the utterly unknowable aspect of God as described in Jewish mysticism) is a God who knows how to live within finitude. We learn this from the third-century sage Resh Lakish, who suggested that the origin of one of God's names, Shaddai, comes from the declaration *Ani hu she'amarti l'olam, dai*, "I am the one who said to the world, 'Enough!'" (Talmud, *Chagigah* 12a). In the beginning, God could have made the oceans endless. God could have made the universe infinite. But God didn't. At the end of the day, God said, "Enough. I don't need any more."

If we are to believe the Torah, the first Jewish fundraising campaign was a complete success. In the greatest internal threat to the veracity of the Torah, Moses tells the people to stop bringing stuff, which, no doubt, strains credulity. But if the Torah is to be believed, there was more than enough to finish the job (Exodus 36:4–7).

Let this, then, be the symbolism of the *mishkan* built for a God who knew how to say "Enough!" by a people who, for a fleeting moment, knew how to say "Enough!" After the liberation from Egyptian bondage, God provided liberation from the tyrannical pursuit of materialism. The men in the wilderness understood what God was asking, and they responded admirably. Would that their descendents understand this as well.

תצוה
Tetzaveh

The Audible Priest

RABBI AVRAHAM (AVI) WEISS

Aaron shall wear it [a golden bell] while officiating, so that the sound of it is heard when he comes into the sanctuary before the Lord and when he goes out—that he may not die. (Exodus 28:35)

This Torah portion presents us with the details of the garments that are to be worn by the High Priest. It tells us that bells will be sewn onto the hem of the priestly robe (ephod). As the priest enters the sanctuary with the bells on his robe, a voice will be heard—*v'nishma kolo* (Exodus 28:33–35). What is the significance of these bells? And whose voice is the Torah referring to?

On its simplest level, the voice refers to that of the bells. Among his many duties, the priest would offer atonement for his own sin. As it would be embarrassing for others to be present during this personal *teshuvah* (repentance) process, the bells signal that those present should leave, allowing the priest to have private moments with God.

RABBI AVRAHAM (AVI) WEISS is founder and president of Yeshivat Chovevei Torah—the modern and open Orthodox rabbinical school. He is the senior rabbi of the Hebrew Institute of Riverdale, a modern and open Orthodox congregation in New York. He is also national president of The Coalition for Jewish Concerns—AMCHA, a grassroots organization that speaks out for Jewish causes and Israel. He is author of *Spiritual Activism: A Jewish Guide to Leadership and Repairing the World* (Jewish Lights).

An important teaching emerges. There are times when we must allow others—even our most righteous and pious—personal space to grieve, to rejoice, or to reflect.

Another idea: With many people in the sanctuary, it was only fair that they know when the priest was entering, so that his entrance would not take them by surprise.

Here there is a significant lesson: Whenever one enters a room, in the spirit of the priestly bells, it's important to knock, protecting the privacy of those inside. Privacy is so important that Jewish law tells us that one should be careful to knock before entering anywhere— even one's own home or a child's room (Talmud, *Pesachim* 112a).

Yet another thought: If the small priestly bells could be heard, it tells us that the atmosphere of the holy sanctuary was serene—that there was a kind of decorum, the kind of quiet that is necessary for reflection. In a place of holy worship, it is important to maintain a level of silence in order for people to dialogue with God.

One final observation: The bells were placed beside pomegranate-shaped objects. A midrash teaches that since the pomegranate is so full of seeds, it symbolizes the capacity of even the greatest sinner to sprout forth goodness. Hence, when entering the sanctuary, the bells could be heard ringing out as they clanged next to the pomegranates, teaching us that even the most wicked person could wake up and reconnect.

This concept can help us to understand whose voice was heard in the bells. The term *v'nishma kolo* is initially found in the Torah when Adam and Eve hear the voice of God in the Garden of Eden (Genesis 3:8). All "firsts" in the Torah teach us the real meaning of the term. From this perspective, it could be argued that the voice present in these verses refers to God—it was God's voice that was heard through the bells.

Some think that a synagogue is intended only for the most pure. But this is not the case. A synagogue is a spiritual hospital where all of us, with our imperfect souls, come to be healed. The bells clanging next to the pomegranates is a soft call telling each of us that no matter how far we've strayed, we have the capacity to hear His voice, the inner voice of God, and return.

When we understand the reality of our imperfections, and our ability to return only with the help of our inner godliness, we become more humble. And no individual was more humble than Aaron's (the first High Priest) brother and mentor, Moses.

No individual is mentioned more often in the Torah than Moses. In fact, in the Books of Exodus, Leviticus, and Numbers, which deal with his life, Moses is mentioned in every portion, except one—this portion of *Tetzaveh*.

Some suggest that Moses's name is omitted in this portion because it is usually read during the week marking Moses's death. Still others insist that this portion occurs after the incident of the Golden Calf when Moses tells God: "Now, if You will forgive their sin, [well and good]; but if not, erase me from the record which You have written!" (Exodus 32:32). Having made this statement, the name of Moses never appears in *Tetzaveh*.

There is, yet, another suggestion. After all, it's not as if Moses does not play a role in this week's portion. He does. The Torah tells us that Moses (who, according to the medieval commentator Ibn Ezra was the first priest) brings his brother Aaron "near" to become High Priest (Exodus 28:1). Moreover, Moses speaks to the wise-hearted men to make Aaron's priestly garments (Exodus 28:3). Additionally Moses prepares the sacrificial service to be offered on the day that Aaron would assume his post (Exodus 29:1). Finally, Moses washes Aaron and his sons and actually dresses them in their priestly garments (Exodus 29:4–9).

But in every instance, without exception, there is no mention of Moses's name. He is only mentioned through the use of a pronoun. Why? Why does the Torah text not record Moses's name in this portion?

Perhaps this underscores that Moses is prepared to share leadership, to shine the spotlight on his brother—and when doing so, rather than feeling jealous or cheated, he feels joyous.

Hence, Moses's name is not mentioned because even as he steps forward to facilitate every step of Aaron becoming the High Priest, he does so graciously and remains absolutely self-effacing. Moses, the leader of leaders, is true to the Torah's description of him: "Now Moses was a very humble man, more so than any other man on earth" (Numbers 12:3).

Moses teaches us the power of stepping back, making space for others—joyously and with humility. In the process, he transmits this teaching to his brother, Aaron, who can now enter the sanctuary, reflecting the message of the humble bells.

In a world where men are increasingly judged through their public success and by economic and professional yardsticks, these messages are especially true. Humbly tapping into our inner godliness connects us to the elements in life that we often take for granted. It is the small divine acts that we do when the doors are closed and the cameras are off that are the true measure of our humanity and, in turn, our manhood.

כי תשא
Ki Tisa

On Not "Facing" God

RABBI DANIEL GORDIS, PhD

"Oh, let me behold Your Presence!" (Exodus 33:18)

Like many of us, Moses is not entirely comfortable with uncertainty. We learn this from the very beginning of Moses's relationship with God. Moses "discovers" the presence of God in the bush that is burning but is not consumed, and soon thereafter, he is called upon by God to head to Egypt and to undertake the liberation of the Israelites from bondage. Moses does not refuse, but neither does he leap at the opportunity. He says of himself that he is "slow of speech and slow of tongue" (Exodus 4:10) and asks, "What if they do not believe me and do not listen to me?" (Exodus 4:1).

Yet Moses's main objection is actually the one that he raises first:

> Moses said to God, "When I come to the Israelites and say to them 'The God of your fathers has sent me to you,' and they ask me, 'What is His name?' what shall I say to them?" And God said to Moses, "Ehyeh-Asher-Ehyeh." He continued,

RABBI DANIEL GORDIS, PhD, is senior vice president of the Shalem Center in Jerusalem. Before moving to Israel in 1998, he was the founding dean of the Ziegler School of Rabbinic Studies at the University of Judaism in Los Angeles, California. His work has appeared in the *New York Times*, the *New York Times Magazine*, and *The New Republic Online*, among others. He is author of several books, including *God Was Not in the Fire: The Search for a Spiritual Judaism* and *If a Place Can Make You Cry: Dispatches from an Anxious State*.

132

"Thus shall you say to the Israelites, 'Ehyeh sent me to you.'"
And God said further to Moses, "Thus shall you speak to the
Israelites: 'The Lord, the God of your fathers, the God of
Abraham, the God of Isaac, and the God of Jacob, has sent me
to you: This shall be My name forever, this My appellation for
all eternity.'" (Exodus 3:13–15)

Now, Moses does not know how his life will unfold. He can have no
intuition that he will lead the Israelites, soon to become the Jewish
people, for eighty years, until he dies at the age of 120, never having
entered the Promised Land. But he does know that the task is daunting, perhaps risky. He intuits that he will meet resistance both from
Pharaoh and from the Israelites, and he is right. Thus, with no small
degree of justification, he asks God, "Who are You?" I want to know
something about You, Moses says, before we embark on this long
and complex relationship. Before I set out on this path, tell me
something about You.

But God's response, which reaches its apex in *Parashat Ki Tisa*, is
peculiar. God does give Moses a "name" of sorts, but it's a strange
name. It is Ehyeh, or "I will be." What does that mean? That God
will be what each of us allows Him to be in our lives? That God, too,
is changing (a notion that medieval Jewish philosophy rejected out
of hand)? Could it be something else (and there are many other
interpretations)? We cannot know.

Yet despite this peculiar response, Moses sets out on his way.
Through thick and thin, he gives this task his all. But then, in
Parashat Ki Tisa, comes one of Moses's greatest trials. He has been
gone, atop Mount Sinai, for a long time, and the people, restless
without their leader and worrying that they have been abandoned,
create for themselves an alternative "god," the Golden Calf.

God is enraged and intends, He says, to destroy the Jewish
people. He will save Moses, but He wants nothing to do with the
people: "Now, let Me be, that My anger may blaze forth against them
and that I may destroy them, and make of you a great nation"
(Exodus 32:10). But Moses will not relent. He has not come this far

with this people to let them be destroyed, even if God will make of him—Moses—something greater. In his anger, Moses, the ultimate leader, intercedes on behalf of the people, imploring God not to destroy them. God relents. Moses punishes them, and then God sends a plague to wipe out many of those responsible. And it seems that despite the drama, the episode has passed.

But it has not. Now, Moses, having stood on the very precipice, needs more than he's gotten before. The Ehyeh answer that God had given him earlier will no longer suffice. As we would say, he asks "nicely":

> Moses said to the Lord, "See, You say to me, 'Lead this people forward,' but You have not made known to me whom You will send with me. Further, You have said, 'I have singled you out by name, and you have, indeed, gained My favor.' Now, if I have truly gained Your favor, pray let me know Your ways, that I may know You and continue in Your favor." (Exodus 33:12–13)

It seems to be a thoroughly legitimate request. After all he has been through, Moses seems justified in wanting to know more about this God—this commanding Presence who has a plan, but who is still so hidden. Who of us would, or *could*, spend a lifetime devoted to a being—a lover, a spouse, a parent, a child, a friend—about whom we knew virtually nothing? Why, Moses asks himself and God, should a god be any different? "Tell me about You," he says. It's a perfectly natural phase of building a relationship. He has earned an answer.

At first, it seems that God will tell Moses what he wants to know: "And the Lord said to Moses, 'I will also do this thing that you have asked; for you have truly gained My favor and I have singled you out by name'" (Exodus 33:17). But Moses presses his case, and implores God, "Oh, let me behold Your Presence!" (Exodus 33:18). And with that, Moses has pushed too far.

God answers:

> "I will make all My goodness pass before you, and I will pro-claim before you the name Lord, and the grace that I grant

and the compassion that I show. But," He said, "you cannot see My face, for man may not see Me and live." And the Lord said, "See, there is a place near Me. Station yourself on the rock and, as My Presence passes by, I will put you in a cleft of the rock and shield you with My hand until I have passed by. Then I will take My hand away and you will see My back; but My face must not be seen." (Exodus 33:19–23)

Moses can see what God *does* in the world—God's grace and compassion—but Moses cannot see God's "face," for "man may not see Me and live." He can see God's outline, but not God's face.

Does that mean that Moses would die were he to see God's face? Perhaps. But more likely, it means that were Moses to behold God's true nature, he would no longer be human. It is the nature of the human condition for us not to know everything we "need" to know, for us to learn to be in relationships even with those we cannot fully understand.

This is true, and difficult, in both the human and the divine realms. We *imagine* that we know the people we love—the people we pursue, the people we marry, the children we create and raise—but we don't. We do not know them because the godly in them, like the godly in God, cannot be known. That is the nature of the human condition. There are secrets in their souls that we can never unearth, just as we know that they, too, cannot completely know us.

Perhaps, on a certain level, we don't want to know everything about them; the mystery is part of the sanctity. Accepting not-knowing and the limits on our ability to know is part of the challenge of growing as a human being. Could that be why we close our eyes (in *Crimes and Misdemeanors*, Woody Allen called eyes "windows into the soul") in our most intimate kisses? Could it be that the intensity of that intimacy is too much, so we *have* to move away—by not looking into our lover's eyes?

If we cannot know the people who shape the contours of the most significant and intimate portions of our lives, then we certainly cannot know God. The midrash tells us that to be human is to be suspended in uncomfortable equidistance between angels and animals. Animals do not wonder about God and thus are not frustrated by their inability to comprehend, to make sense of the universe. Angels, presumably, know whatever they wish. We, however, share with the angels the desire to know; and with animals, we share a limitation. Like them, we will never comprehend the universe in which we will live out our days.

In this week's *parashah*, God and the Torah seem to suggest that the challenge of being human is to learn to see the sacred in our not knowing and to discover in the vulnerability that comes with uncertainty the space in which we can uncover our potential greatness.

Our world does not celebrate uncertainty. Indeed, our world seems to fight against uncertainty, with the passion—but foolishness—of Don Quixote charging at the windmill. We equip ourselves with ever more (and smaller) gadgets, providing us with ever more (and more rapid) information; but we can never banish uncertainty. We ought not even try.

Yet, we find it difficult to desist. Though we know it is foolish, we do seek to banish uncertainty from our lives. For ours is too often a culture in which we—especially as men—feel that we are expected to know, to have solutions, to be prepared. Not to know, to be mired in uncertainty somehow strikes us as a failure, as a disappointment of those who, we imagine, have the right to expect more of us.

But uncertainty is not a failure, and those who love us as the men we are must come to understand that not knowing is the root of our humanity. It is the source of the profound within us, the piece of our nature that opens us to the Divine, the core of the "us" that they love. That is their challenge; and our challenge is to allow ourselves to believe that they can, and will, come to understand that.

Yes, *Parashat Ki Tisa* is correct. It is, indeed, in the moments of not knowing that we are the most human. It is next to the bed of a spouse who has received a terrifying diagnosis, holding his or her hand, facing the uncertain future together, that our capacity to rise to great human heights presents itself. It is in not fleeing the hospital room, which "reeks" with uncertainty, that we face our limitations, and our greatest capacity for love—a gift of not being able to know. It is when our teenage and adult children begin to discover how little they know about the world, and how little we know—that the truly human and sacred response is not "to look it up," but to face the unknowable together, to understand that the truly religious life is the quest for sanctity in the face of uncertainty. It is in our willingness to make lifelong commitments to other people—even though we know that they may abandon us, they may betray us, they will undoubtedly hurt us, and they may die and leave us horribly alone—that we give possibility to the most wondrous dimensions of our lives. Love is as powerful as it is because it stares uncertainty in the face and defies it, because it is about commitment even in the face of vulnerability.

In the end, that is what God was telling Moses: "Yes, you want to know, but you cannot." You cannot know because were I to allow you to know all that you seek to understand, you would no longer be human. And with that, the potential for the glory that is inherent in every human being—what some mean by human beings created in the image of the Divine—would be destroyed.

And that, too, is what Jewish life is about. Yes, it is belonging to a people. It is celebrating, and mourning, a history. It is a way of life—with customs, and holidays, and, in its traditional formulation, a not insignificant set of restrictions about diet, dress, time, sex, money, and much more. It is about nationalism, and language, and beyond.

But at the end of the day, Jewish life is the way in which we bond, hopefully as families, with close friends, as a community and as a nation, and face uncertainty together. We celebrate and mourn. We draw inspiration, and passion, from the past, and devotion to ideals from the texts we've been studying for centuries. We learn, and study, and argue, and debate—not because we believe that in the end we can locate truth, or dispel the inability to "know," but because it is in facing that very inability to know that we confront our vulnerabilities and, therefore, our need to find each other, to love each other, and to work to create lives of meaning.

It is in accepting our "epistemological humility" that we learn to strive. It is in not knowing that we discover the capacity to believe. It is in not knowing that we find not limitation, but grandeur, and the capacity to worship, to wonder, to make the very most of our often frustrating humanity.

ויקהל-פקודי
Vayakhel–Pekudei

In Search of Bezalel

RABBI CHARLES SIMON

And Moses said to the Israelites: See, the Lord has singled out by name Bezalel, son of Uri son of Hur, of the tribe of Judah. He has endowed him with a divine spirit of skill, ability, and knowledge in every kind of craft and has inspired him to make designs for work in gold, silver, and copper, to cut stones for setting and to carve wood—to work in every kind of designer's craft—and to give directions. (Exodus 35:30)

Now Bezalel, son of Uri son of Hur, of the tribe of Judah, had made all that the Lord had commanded Moses; at his side was Oholiab son of Ahisamach, of the tribe of Dan, carver and designer, and embroiderer in blue, purple, and crimson yarns and in fine linen. (Exodus 38:22–23)

RABBI CHARLES SIMON is executive director of the Federation of Jewish Men's clubs, the male volunteer arm of Conservative/Masorti Judaism. He has produced films, created products, founded synagogues in North America and Europe, and published widely. He teaches regularly at The Jewish Theological Seminary in New York and the American Jewish University in Los Angeles. He is author of *Building a Successful Volunteer Culture: Finding Meaning in Service in the Jewish Community* (Jewish Lights).

Bezalel is one of the least understood characters in our tradition. The Rabbinic commentators briefly comment on the process of his being selected, his lineage, and his age. According to the Talmud, Bezalel was thirteen years old when he was given the tasks of constructing the furniture, the tabernacle, and the Ark of the Covenant (*Sanhedrin* 69b). Some commentators also attempted to explain his name. Bezalel means "in the shadow of God," "because he constructed the dwelling place of God, and as a result all of the children of Israel lived in God's shadow" (*Berachot* 55a).

It's a wonderful thought that all of us should consider ourselves as if we were living in the shadow of God, but does the Torah teach us about Bezalel the person? Who was Bezalel? What was his life like? Did he marry? Was his life a meaningful one? Did he experience the loss of a loved one? Was he always viewed as "the architect" and never the person?

The Torah teaches us nothing. But what of the legends and midrashim that have been written for thousands of years? No matter where one searches for texts relating to Bezalel, Bezalel the person is absent. Our tradition never recorded who he *was*, only what he *did*. No matter how hard we search, his essence escapes us. We can never know him, and so perhaps like so many others with whom we come in contact, much of his value is lost to us. The Torah presents us with the persona, but not the person, and to a great extent, I fear that many of us have learned that lesson too well.

Imagine for a moment: what if Bezalel had been a "geek"? Artists tend to see things from different perspectives. Perhaps he wasn't like the rest of us. Maybe he stood out as a talent, or just stood apart. We assume he was heterosexual; perhaps he wasn't. Perhaps after having achieved fame, he became accepted, or perhaps it went to his head and he became arrogant and egotistical. "Look at me," his attitude projected. "I am what I did."

This is both wrong and sad. The characters in Torah aren't supposed to reinforce our shallow views of one another; they are intended to challenge us to see beyond them. Don't tell me what he did! Tell me who he was! If he were your son, what kind of concerns would you have? Imagine yourself saying, "Well, thank God he has a job, but what about a relationship? I'm ready to be a grandfather!"

The Torah should challenge us to look beyond a man's accomplishments in his field and to see his life in the larger perspective as a member or potential member of a community—as a person who experiences joy and sorrow, love and loneliness. Bezalel might have been able to build a house and even do his own plumbing and electrical work, but did he know people who could reach across the divide, who refused to be awed by his success and could invite him to a Shabbat dinner or a card game or a fishing trip?

Both our secular and religious cultures have taught us how to view people. In our current age, we are constantly challenged to reimagine our relationship to women. We read that we need to open ourselves up to our feminine side, to stop compartmentalizing, and to concentrate on our feelings. But neither secular nor religious cultures have taught or challenged us how to understand and develop our relationships with other men. Look at how limited our understanding of Bezalel has become!

Was Bezalel successful? It is an interesting question, because at different times in our lives each of us asks ourselves the same question: "Am I a success?" Have you asked yourself what that means? Does it mean to be a success in business or a success in relationships? If I feel successful, does it provide me with the courage to understand the Bezalels in this world a little bit better? Does it provide me with the courage to reach into myself and to reach out and establish connections with those who are a bit different?

Vayikra/
Leviticus

וַיִּקְרָא
Vayikra

Sacrifice Play

RABBI JOSEPH B. MESZLER

When any of you presents an offering of cattle to the Lord ... (Leviticus 1:2)

We all make sacrifices, but how do we feel about them?

The beginning of the Book of Leviticus focuses on the theme of sacrifice. Starting with the Hebrew word *Vayikra*, "God called" (Leviticus 1:1), we start the third book of the Torah with God calling to Moses to tell the ancient Israelites how to bring offerings of grain or livestock for worship in an acceptable fashion.

The ancient Israelites brought sacrifices for all sorts of reasons. There were different offerings, depending on the mood of the occasion. On Pesach, they remembered (as we do now) the sacrifice of the lamb to mark the doors of the Israelites' homes in Egypt so the Angel of Death would pass over. On Shavuot, they recalled the sacrifice of the first fruits of the land. On Sukkot, they commemorated the harvest. Most of these sacrifices were not simply burning up an animal entirely to God as a gift to the Divine. Instead, they were family meals

---

RABBI JOSEPH B. MESZLER is spiritual leader of Temple Sinai of Sharon, Massachusetts. He is author of *A Man's Responsibility: A Jewish Guide to Being a Son, a Partner in Marriage, a Father, and a Community Leader* and *Witnesses to the One: The Spiritual History of the Sh'ma* (both Jewish Lights). He helped found three different Jewish men's study groups in Reform Jewish settings. He is married to Rabbi Julie Zupan and is the father of two children.

for holidays. The inedible parts were "turned into smoke" on the altar, carrying "a pleasing odor" up to God (Leviticus 1:9). A portion was given to the priests who officiated, for their labor. The majority was brought back to the family's tent, where they would enjoy a large feast. The man who brought the sacrifice to the altar was really supplying food for his family to enjoy.

Men know all about sacrificing in order to feed their families. Much of our identity is caught up in providing for others, and we work hard in order to do so. However, unlike the joy that the Israelites must have felt carrying their sacrifice in great celebration, the daily toil of today's Jewish man is often filled with feelings of anxiety, exhaustion, and isolation. Many men have talked about how they feel that they have done the best they can being a provider, yet their inability to bring in a living wage or, even with good compensation, a lack of feeling appreciated can leave some men demoralized.

One man put it this way: He felt he had done his job in raising his family, sending his children to school, and providing for them. He was even able to send each of his children to college and have them come out debt-free. In addition, he had also given to his synagogue, donating a large sum of money. In exchange, he expected others to be full of warm gratitude, to want to take care of him, and to affectionately appreciate his sacrifice. He made a secret pact in his mind that what he gave financially should be rewarded with love and concern. Instead, he received polite acknowledgment, but not warmth. He looked at the money that he gave and felt that life was unfair, filled with only more burdens to carry. He felt resentment. He could not see that many of his gifts were given with high emotional demands, as if those around him owed him something and should be in his debt. I cannot imagine that anyone's monetary sacrifice, considerable as it may be, if done without love and joy can bring "a pleasing odor" to the Eternal. Many of the poor among us are still able to give emotionally and create connections that enliven, while there are plenty of wealthy, unhappy people whose significant financial contributions are not rewarded with love or affection.

How many men come home from work and simply want to be left alone? Working hard all day, sacrificing pieces of ourselves, we pull into the driveway, and we have nothing left to give. Instead of getting a chance to relax, we are instead hit with a crying child, a broken faucet, or a ringing phone demanding our attention. The time between 5:00 and 7:00 p.m. when everyone is tired, hungry, and needy demands the most from us, yet we have already given that away.

Worse, sometimes we come home from work, and we feel incompetent. At work, we knew what we were about. We knew how to get the job done. We were respected. We had a coat, a tie, a badge, a uniform, a stethoscope, a tool, or something else about us that proclaimed our worth. These things mean nothing once we cross the threshold of our homes. We are reduced to being tired human beings, yet the demands seem even greater.

Memories of our fathers might also paint a similar picture. Did he come home, pour himself a drink, and read the newspaper? Was the message clear that he was not to be disturbed? Some men had fathers who were full of joy; others did not. Many had fathers who surrounded themselves with silence, and we were forced to interpret that silence in order to discover our place in relation to him. Did we feel like he carried us, his family, like a burden, a sacrifice to the altar?

Many men believe that a great deal of their identity derives from their work. When we are asked about ourselves, many of us will answer with what we do as the response to who we are. It is not that we simply work as doctors, lawyers, or mechanics. We are doctors, lawyers, and mechanics. Our career is at the core of our identity, usually more so than for women.[1]

This emphasis on the sacrifices we make for work, however, brings problems. First of all, when we err or fail at work, we can take it very personally. As one man once related to me, it is not simply that he "screwed up" at work; it was that he was a "screw up."

A second major problem is that we neglect other parts of our lives. Judaism understands that being a partner in a marriage, a father, a son, and a member of a community are all equal, if not more important parts to being a Jewish man than our profession.

Manhood contains many mitzvot (sacred obligations). When we neglect these other deep parts of our lives, we might feel that our overinvestment in our work has exacted a deep price from us.

If people feel like they are a burden to us, if they feel that they are simply part of the sacrificial system that we have created, they cannot love us for who we really are.

How can we offer our sacrifices in a way that does not feel like a burden but rather enlivens? How can we feel the joy that our ancestors felt as they offered their sacrifices?

Perhaps the secret is found in the first word of Leviticus, our textbook about sacrifice. As previously noted, the Hebrew word that starts the book is *Vayikra*, "God called." In the Torah scroll, there is a scribal tradition to write the last letter of this word, the letter *aleph*, smaller than the rest. For an unknown reason, scribes writing Torah scrolls decided to write this letter in miniature, and it is preserved this way to this day.[2]

Perhaps the writing of the small *aleph* was simply a mechanical way of not confusing it with the next word, which also happens to begin with an *aleph*.[3] The Hasidic rabbis of eastern Europe, however, thought that this was no simple typographical function. Instead, they found great moral meaning in the small *aleph* in our relation to others. To them, the small *aleph* meant humility.[4]

Aleph is the first letter of the *aleph-bet*. It is also the first letter in the word *anochi*, meaning "I." The Hasidic masters taught that having a miniature *aleph* meant we ought to think of ourselves first and foremost as small when we offer our sacrifices. When fulfilling a mitzvah for others, such as providing for our families or giving donations to our community, we might become inflated with our own self-importance. This feeling of importance cannot hold, however, because in truth we are simply doing our part and fulfilling the commandment that God has set before us. Rather, we should feel humility from the start. We should realize that God has put us in a larger pattern of the universe, and our small self was meant to give to others with joy.

Each of us might even feel "called" to a certain profession, but that does not mean that we should inflate ourselves so that it overwhelms our identity. To do so risks arrogance and the neglect of family and community. Instead, a humble, small "I" accepts that God has cast us in a role in a drama that involves more than ourselves.

A traditional role of being a male is to provide for others. Even today in the twenty-first century, we men still feel it is primarily our duty to provide sustenance for our families. To define ourselves solely as providers, however, falsely inflates our roles as masters of the material world and makes us neglect our roles as loving and caring companions.

Even when we have succeeded in paying our bills, providing our children's education, or giving charitable donations, Judaism teaches that not for a moment should we consider this solely the work of our hands. Everything we give we have once received, and we are fortunate if we receive enough to be able to give. We are the stewards of wealth, not the owners. We may think of ourselves as a "breadwinner," but that alone does not entitle us to receive honor. We should think of ourselves as having a small *aleph* when it comes to managing what good come our way, for "the earth is the Eternal's and all that it holds" (Psalm 24:1).

It is the giving and demonstration of love that is rewarded with love. Loveless sacrifice, done with a sense of burden, brings nothing but hardship. It is focused solely on the self, often in a pitying kind of way.

Sacrifices done out of a sense of humility, knowing that it is a privilege to be able to give to others, knowing that our loved ones are in themselves gifts from God and that our homes to which we return at the end of the day are miniature sanctuaries—these are all gifts that fill us with life. A healthy perspective on who we truly are in the larger scheme of things makes us feel grateful to be alive and enables us to count our blessings.

Another phrase in this portion of Leviticus illustrates this idea. The person who brings forth a sacrifice in the Torah is a called a *nefesh*, literally meaning a "soul" in Rabbinic Hebrew (Leviticus 2:1)—in Rabbinic Hebrew, literally, a "soul." When we give our sacrifices, we should give from the heart, or even more deeply, from the soul. We should do so as a labor of love. We may not always succeed, but the ideal compels us. We reach out from our soul to connect with the souls of others.

Coming home in the evening may never be easy. It may always entail feelings of loss of competence and power. No longer the big shot at work, we are reduced to merely being a part of the family, vying for attention.

But what a privilege to be a part of a family, to be connected to a community, or simply to be a piece of the whole! These connections bind us and hold us together, and through all of them, behind every sacred relation, there is a tie to the Holy One of Blessing, the Soul of the Universe. We have the honor of giving to that larger unity that begins with those people around us.

Sacrifices that are performed out of joy will bring joy. Sacrifice from our souls connects us to the souls of others.

צַו

Tzav

The Family Business

RABBI BRADLEY SHAVIT ARTSON

And this is the ritual of the meal offering: Aaron's sons shall present it before the Lord, in front of the altar.... What is left of it shall be eaten by Aaron and his sons.

(Leviticus 6:7, 6:9)

In quantum theory, one of the most alluring (and misused) concepts is that of togetherness in separation—that two particles, once linked, continue to "track" each other even when no longer together, even when beyond the reach of the speed of light! These two particles will move in tandem, seeming to "know" each other's as yet unfinished "choices." This "non-locality" means that the two particles are entangled in each other's futures, no matter how separate they may be spatially.

Togetherness in separation is very much alive in the relationships of many fathers and sons. Prior to the birth of the son, a male finds himself the dream and hopes of the would-be father. As the two grow to know each other, each projects expectations, requirements, love, and identity onto the other. Given the complexity of all

RABBI BRADLEY SHAVIT ARTSON is dean of the Ziegler School of Rabbinic Studies and vice president of American Jewish University in Los Angeles, California. He is author of many books, including *Gift of Soul, Gift of Wisdom: A Spiritual Resource for Mentoring and Leadership* and *Everyday Torah: Weekly Reflections and Inspirations*.

human relationships, it is no surprise that this most intimate of relationships is also among the most complex. The father defines manhood for the son. The son embodies the projection of the father into the future. One is the base of identity; the other offers immortality. In the potent mix of dependence and shared identity, real men battle out their distinct individuality, their shared manliness, and their abilities to relate to each other, other men, humanity, and the world.

Tzav opens a window onto this world of men as we listen in on the instructions offered to male priests, the *kohanim*, at the establishment of the sacrificial system in the *mishkan* (the portable desert sanctuary) and later in the Holy Temple in Jerusalem. The lineage is a setup—a priesthood that begins with the house of Levi through Aaron, the first *kohen gadol* (High Priest), and continues through his sons. His male descendants inherit their *kahunah* (priesthood) from their fathers. It's a living laboratory of dads and their boys, of sons and their old men—all of them working in the family business, all of them seeking to make their mark.

As our story begins, Aaron is ready for his close-up. Everything up until now has brought him to this moment, when he can take over the sacrifices that establish a connection between God and Israel, when his meticulous attention to detail can ensure blessing for the entire Jewish people. And at this big scene, does he get the solo he deserves? No. Time and time again, his big scene has interlopers:

> And this is the ritual of the meal offering: Aaron's sons shall present it before the Lord, in front of the altar.... What is left of it shall be eaten by Aaron and his sons. (Leviticus 6:7, 6:9)

> The Lord spoke to Moses, saying: This is the offering that Aaron and his sons shall offer to the Lord on the occasion of his anointment. (Leviticus 6:12)

> The Lord spoke to Moses, saying: Speak to Aaron and his sons thus: This is the ritual of the sin offering. (Leviticus 6: 17)

And on, and on, and on. Instead of getting the spotlight all to himself, Aaron must share it with his sons and grandsons. Instead of a superstar, he comes across sounding like a law firm or a furniture store: Aaron & Sons.

Not only the key moments, but even the list of privileges associated with the priesthood are shared with the sons and grandsons:

> Those shall be the perquisites of Aaron and the perquisites of his sons from the Lord's gifts, once they have been inducted to serve the Lord as priests; these the Lord commanded to be given them, once they had been anointed, as a due from the Israelites for all time throughout the ages. (Leviticus 7:35–36)

For seven days in a row, "Aaron & Sons" are inducted into the priesthood—donning special robes and tunics, anointed with special oil, eating sacral meals, and making inaugural sacrifices. Seven days of Aaron & Sons, with an eternity of service stretching ahead of them!

What must have Aaron thought, as his sons moved to share the spotlight, even at this first glowing moment? How do fathers across time welcome their sons into their lives, giving them a future, even as they realize that these younger men will succeed them? That these vibrant youths will radiate energy and strength when their own energy and strength begin to recede? The Talmud notes poignantly, "The power of a son is preferable to the power of a father" (*Chullin* 49b; *Yevamot* 69b). What ambivalent emotions must that knowledge entail?

And what of Aaron's sons? How do they take their father's greater stature, expertise, and fame? As they scramble to make a name for themselves, must they always be the "sons of Aaron?" Here too, the Talmud reminds us, "Concerning one's father's affairs, even an adult is like a minor" (*Ketubot* 18a; *Gittin* 50a). How that must have chafed!

The key to navigating this complex and promising stream is to embrace the multifaceted nature of the father-son connection. Rather than falsely settling on one end of the spectrum, while seeking to make the opposite end invisible, the Torah tradition offers a model of embracing the rich incompatibility of the different aspects of father-son connections.

The Talmud notes, for instance, "The Merciful One gave the father credibility in all things" (*Kiddushin* 63b). Children naturally look to their fathers to represent wisdom, maturity, generosity, and strength. And parents are programmed as well, to rejoice in the achievements of their children: "A person is jealous of everyone except for a child and a disciple" (Talmud, *Sanhedrin* 105b). There is reciprocity in our giving each other the benefit of the doubt, in celebrating each other's greatness, in using that greatness as a stimulus to our own greater achievements.

Built into the structure of the father-son connection, like the directionality of time, is a forward motion, as love cascades unequally between the generations, from father to son, and then on again. In the sage words of Rav Huna, "A father's love is for his children; the children's love is for their children" (Talmud, *Sotah* 49a). That is not to say that sons don't love (even revere) their fathers, but that the intensity of emotion flows down across the generations, always favoring the newest and the youngest. The flow of male love embraces children. The periodic strains between fathers and sons can be reconciled in their shared love of the next generation.

That same transition across generations invites a renewed (and more sympathetic) assessment of fathers. As sons struggle to balance professional achievement, supporting their families, being there for colleagues and for spouse and children, sons gain a new understanding of the constraints under which their fathers struggled, new sympathy for the balancing act of being a man, a husband, and a father. Abraham Mendelssohn, son of the great philosopher Moses Mendelssohn and father of the great composer Felix Mendelssohn, quipped, "Formerly I was my father's son, now I am my son's father." As life moves forward, we experience, *seriatim*, being a grandfather's grandson, a father's son, a son's father, and a grandsons's grandfather. This cycle of love invites us to revisit the ways our own grandfathers lavished love despite their own advancing years and financial concerns, the ways our fathers carved opportunities to share insight and caring, despite ongoing business and social pressures, and forewarns us that we won't be more perfect in these tasks than were the men who came before us.

Armed with that awareness, perhaps it becomes possible for us to see what a privilege our time together is. We can use our hard-won empathy to look to our father as the most recent flow of love and devotion of all the men whose love welled up to launch us into life and whose disciplines and cautions (and support and enthusiasm) made our own characters possible. As a midrash reminds us, "It is an honor for children and fathers to be with one another" (*Shemot Rabbah* 34:5).

Beyond honor, it is a terrifying joy to see one's father in one's own gestures, thoughts, and expressions and then to see oneself in one's sons. Such continuity is a blessing of the deepest kind. Commenting on the biblical verse, "Blessed shall you be when you go out" (Deuteronomy 28:6), the Rabbis comment that this comes true when "your children will be like you" (Talmud, *Baba Metzia* 107a).

When we can stand together, generations of caring men, strong in our love and resolute in our commitments, then we truly are a source of blessings to our progeny, our spouses, and our communities. Such blessing requires real strength—not the coercive overwhelming so often mistaken for power, but the life-changing ability to influence, to educate, and to inspire—that is the special heritage that Jewish men can offer their children.

We see that, too, in *Tzav*. After "Aaron & Sons" launch the family business, the Torah portion ends with a quiet reassurance: "And Aaron and his sons did all the things that the Lord had commanded through Moses" (Leviticus 8:36). Father and sons are united in service, devotion, and values.

A pretty potent blessing, isn't it?

שמיני
Shemini

How Could God...?

RABBI STEPHEN S. PEARCE, PhD

Now Aaron's sons Nadab and Abihu each took his fire
pan, put fire in it, and laid incense on it; and they
offered before the Lord alien fire, which He had not
enjoined upon them. And fire came forth from the Lord
and consumed them; thus they died at the instance of
the Lord. (Leviticus 10:1–2)

A child expects to lose a parent some day. The loss of a sibling or a
spouse also can be anticipated. But the loss of a child is beyond anything imaginable—a parent's worst nightmare, a wound that never
heals, an event so horrendous that it stuns a mourner into silence.

The sudden death of Aaron's sons, Nadab and Abihu, is briefly
reported in two Torah portions. *Shemini* records the unauthorized
action of these novice priests, who are immolated because they offer
"alien" fire (Leviticus 10:1). Chapters later, *Acharei Mot* offers an
equally cryptic explanation: "They drew too close to the presence of

RABBI STEPHEN S. PEARCE, PhD, is senior rabbi of Congregation
Emanu-El of San Francisco, California. He was ordained by Hebrew Union
College–Jewish Institute of Religion and earned his doctorate in counselor
psychology from St. John's University. Named one of the fifty most influential
rabbis by *Newsweek* magazine, he is author of *Flash of Insight: Metaphor and
Narrative in Therapy* and co-author with Bishop William E. Swing and Father
John P. Schlegel of *Building Wisdom's House: A Book of Values for Our Time.*

the Lord" (Leviticus 16:1). This tragedy seems especially incompatible with the privileged status of the priestly inner circle that witnessed a divine encounter: "Then Moses and Aaron, Nadab and Abihu, and seventy elders of Israel ascended; and they saw the God of Israel ... and they ate and drank" (Exodus 24:9–11). But this pedigree does not afford Nadab and Abihu immunity to punishment for infraction of cultic rules.

The haftarah (prophetic reading) for *Shemini* records another untimely fatality that magnifies the injustice of undeserved death. When the oxen pulling the Ark being transferred to Jerusalem stumble, Uzzah, an innocent bystander, dies immediately upon touching the Ark in an attempt to steady it. In response to this tragedy, David is described as distressed and afraid (2 Samuel 6:3–9).

The death of Aaron's sons demands the examination of theodicy—the impenetrable paradox of affirming a good omnipotent God who permits malevolence. Commentators, uncomfortable with the unjust nature of the death that befell children who had dedicated their lives to serving God, aligned their theology to avoid the issue of theodicy by validating the young priests' untimely deaths. In so doing, they enumerated a variety of sins that blamed the victims and justified God's "justice." Rationalizations for this heartbreak include arrogance, ambition, insolence, alcoholism, jealousy, idolatry, religious fanaticism, immodesty, single marital status, failure to wear requisite garments, deficient personal hygiene, and disrespect for their elders. None is particularly satisfying, because the punishment does not fit the crime.

Archibald MacLeish succinctly defines indefensible unjustified death—the dilemma of theodicy—in his play *J.B.*: "If God is God He is not good, if God is good He is not God...." Because this tension between belief in a good and all-powerful God and the existence of evil is often not acceptable to biblical authors and rabbinic commentators, the theme of theodicy finds recurrent expression in sacred writing. Unable to understand why God would destroy the innocent along with the evil inhabitants of Sodom and Gomorrah, Abraham asks, "Shall not the Judge of all the earth deal justly?"

(Genesis 18:25). God's fairness is questioned in the Book of Job, the classic story of a righteous man who suffers in spite of his uncompromising obedience to God. Job's plaintive challenge, "Why do You hide Your face, and treat me like an enemy?" (Job 13:24), is echoed elsewhere in the Bible. Jeremiah (12:1) asks, "Why does the way of the wicked prosper? Why are the workers of treachery at ease?" Ecclesiastes, Isaiah, and Psalms all pose similar challenges. None provides a satisfactory answer.

In spite of the Rabbis' attempt to sidestep the question of a God who does not prevent evil, the Talmud (*Kiddushin* 39b) wrestles with the problem of how to reconcile belief in God's unlimited power with the injustice of evil and suffering by providing a troubling illustration. A father sends a perfectly innocent child up a ladder to chase away a mother bird before taking the eggs from her nest. While fulfilling the multiple mitzvot of obeying a parent and not taking fledglings in the presence of their mother, the child falls to his death.

Interest in theodicy is not limited to Jewish literature. For example, Ivan Karamazov, in Dostoevsky's *Brothers Karamazov*, speaks of the Russian nobleman whose hunting hound's paw was injured by an eight-year-old boy who threw a stone at the animal. After taking the boy from his mother and imprisoning him overnight, the next morning he ordered the boy to be stripped naked. Shivering in the cold, numb with terror, daring not to cry, the boy stood silently as the nobleman commanded, "Make him run." As the boy ran in terror, the nobleman set his whole pack of hounds on the child. Quickly overtaking the terror-stricken child, they tore him to pieces in front of his mother. Karamazov asks the bitter question that is at the heart this matter: "What did this child or any child have to do with evil?" In the third century CE, Rabbi Yannai best framed the unsolvable problem of theodicy: "It is not in our power to explain either the prosperity of the wicked or the afflictions of the righteous" (*Mishnah Avot* 4:19).

Beyond the tension between God's omniscience and the existence of evil, responses to untimely death merit additional scrutiny.

The deaths of Nadab and Abihu are not the only occasion when the Torah records a father's grief over the loss of a child, even when the child does not die. For example, upon considering the loss (although not death) of Ishmael, the Torah reports, "The matter distressed Abraham greatly" (Genesis 21:11). After the abortive sacrifice of Isaac, the father and son descend from the mountain; the lack of any further record of interaction between the two implies estrangement. Upon learning of the supposed death of Joseph, Jacob refuses to be comforted, saying, "'No, I will go down mourning to my son in Sheol.' Thus his father bewailed him" (Genesis 37:35).

King David's profound grief upon the separate loss of two sons is palpable. David fasts, prays, and grieves while the child of his illicit union with Uriah's wife lies dying. Upon learning of the child's death, he ends his bereavement and resumes daily routines. Puzzled by this seemingly out-of-character behavior, his courtiers question him, "While the child was alive, you fasted and wept; but now that the child is dead, you rise and take food!" (2 Samuel 12:21). David's response reveals the depth of his grief:

> "While the child was still alive, I fasted and wept because I thought: 'Who knows? The Lord may have pity on me, and the child may live.' But now that he is dead, why should I fast? Can I bring him back again? I shall go to him, but he will never come back to me." (2 Samuel 12:22–23)

The text describes David's palpable grief upon learning of the death of another son, Absalom:

> The king was shaken. He went up to the upper chamber of the gateway and wept, moaning these words as he went, "My son Absalom! O my son, my son Absalom! If only I had died instead of you! O Absalom, my son, my son!" (2 Samuel 19:1)

When Job learned of the sudden death of all of his sons and daughters, he "tore his robe, cut off his hair, and threw himself on the ground ..." (Job 1:20). Eli, upon hearing of the death of his sons and the theft of the Ark by the Philistines, "fell backward off his seat beside the gate, broke his neck and died ..." (1 Sam 4:18). These emotional reactions are surprising when contrasted with modern societal values of strength and silence—the expected so-called stiff upper lip in the face of loss. Aaron's silence is in keeping with the notion that undemonstrative dignity and decorum are a resolute expression of male strength, a sign that distinguishes boys from men; but his lack of response may also be viewed as a stunned silence in the face of his very personal tragedy. The reaction to the death of Ezekiel's wife makes a case for being stoic in the face of death:

> O mortal, I am about to take away the delight of your eyes from you through pestilence; but you shall not lament or weep or let your tears flow. Moan softly; observe no mourning for the dead: Put on your turban and put your sandals on your feet; do not cover over your upper lip, and do not eat the bread of comforters. (Ezekiel 24:16–17)

Following this model, Moses's words of consolation to Aaron on the deaths of Nadab and Abihu, "This is what the Lord meant when He said: 'Through those near to Me I show Myself holy, and gain glory before all the people'" (Leviticus 10:3), seem ill timed, especially in light of Jewish tradition that later will provide specific guidelines for the silent encountering of a mourner. Although the meaning of Moses's message is difficult to apprehend, any comment he offered would have been unsatisfactory in the face of such an unspeakable loss. Indeed, Scripture usually does not make note of someone not speaking, as it does of Aaron's silence, a silence that seems even more powerful than words. Aaron's unspoken response reveals his inability to find words that describe his tragic loss and the depth of his grief.

The mitzvah of silence—not speaking to a mourner until spoken to—developed out of the deep understanding that at the moment of most intense grief, no comment can offer genuine consolation. Restraint often saves a consoler from offering trivial thoughts and clichés. Thinking before speaking, a difficult activity for many, prevents the embarrassment of inappropriate probing for details of a death, the offering of trite theological explanations, or even the changing of the subject when the mourner wishes to speak about the deceased. Mourners hear the echoes of Aaron's silence in their wish not to articulate the complex emotions felt at a time of death. Thus, the Jewish tradition of saying nothing to a mourner until spoken to can only be accomplished if a consoler is comfortable with a mourner's stunned silence. The prophet Amos (5:13) reinforces the notion that "the prudent man keeps silent, for it is an evil time." The Talmudic noteworthy Rav Papa (Talmud, *Berachot* 6b) advises, "The merit of a condolence call is in the silence observed." Similarly, Rabbi Yochanan (Talmud, *Mo'ed Katan* 28b) utilizes Job's losses to illustrate this convention:

> Comforters are not permitted to say a word until a mourner opens (a conversation), as it is said: "They sat with him on the ground.... None spoke a word to him for they saw how very great was his suffering.... Afterward, Job began to speak.... Then Eliphaz the Temanite said in reply ..." (Job 2:13–3:1, 4:1)

Far more soothing than empty words is the comforter's presence and warm embrace that might allow the mourner to share his heartache and pain if he so chooses. It is this custom that fosters drawing a mourner out of utter aloneness and a sense of abandonment. The comforter's silence allows a mourner to know that a friend or family member shares the heartache and pain, as Howard Thurman's eloquent words suggest:

> *I share with you the agony of your grief*
> *The anguish of your heart finds echo in my own ...*
> *I can but offer what my love does give ...*
> *The warmth of one who seeks to understand*
> *The silent storm-swept barrenness of so great a loss....*[1]

Had Moses followed the custom of silent presence and not offered an explanation that is impossible to put into words, his presence alone would have proved to be healing. Thus, Judaism requires the human action of being fully present but not offering words that shatter the silence. That simple action allows the consoler to embrace the mourner and infuse his tragedy with dignity and even hope.

There is no protection against tragedy, just as there is no satisfactory way of reconciling God's omnipotence with the presence of evil. However, the death of Nadab and Abihu teaches how to understand and respond to grief when silent comfort for those touched by heartache is what is required.

A Father's Silence

RABBI DANIEL G. ZEMEL

And Aaron was silent. (Leviticus 10:3)

What are we to make of this silence? Wasn't it just a few chapters earlier in the Book of Exodus, before yet another fiery appearance of God at the burning bush, that God advised Moses to enlist his brother Aaron to be the spokesperson before Pharaoh? At that moment, Aaron was the one with the gift of speech; now Aaron is the one who looks on in silent horror. His sons have died, killed by a deathly fire emanating from God for what we are told is their foul play in making an offering that "[God] had not enjoined upon them" (Leviticus 10:1).

What does Aaron's silence reveal? We can only speculate. Is this a "manly" silence? He bears his wound internally and stoically hears his brother's rebuke. Has Aaron now become the "strong silent type"? Or is this a wounded silence? His grief is so complete, his horror so consuming that no words come to the one who is able to stand before Pharaoh. Might this possibly be the silence of a parent who feels that he bears some of the guilt for his sons' mischief? Did

RABBI DANIEL G. ZEMEL has been the rabbi of Temple Micah in Washington, D.C., since 1983. He has been a Synagogue 2000 Fellow and served as president of the Central Conference of American Rabbis (CCAR) Mid-Atlantic Region and on the CCAR national board. He is married to Louise Sherman Zemel and they have three children— Shira Michal, Adam Solomon, and Ronit Elana.

he not bring them up the mountain with him so that they, too, could see God along with the elders and Moses? Did he have them accompany him at too young an age? Was it an experience that they were in no way ready for, and now, like addicts not appreciating the potency of what they have tasted, they set out on their own for more—this time dangerously unsupervised? Or perhaps is this a silence of fear and intimidation as one who cowers before a bully as the bully gets his way? God has acted. Moses has spoken, and Aaron shivers in fear.

I cannot help thinking that there is some of all of this in Aaron's silence. How can he not be thinking in his own way, "What hath God wrought?"

תזריע

Tazria

Take Care of Yourself!

RABBI JACK RIEMER

**When a person has on the skin of his body a swelling, a
rash, or a discoloration … it shall be reported to Aaron
the priest or to one of his sons, the priests.** (Leviticus 13:2)

I have a good friend who began developing some serious medical
symptoms a few years ago. He was frequently tired, and when he
played tennis with his wife, he began losing more often.

She noticed something was wrong, even though he didn't. And
so, she insisted that he go for a stress test. He scoffed at her and
insisted that he was fine, but she continued to nudge him. Finally
and reluctantly, just to humor her, he gave in to her pestering and
took the test. Six hours later he was in the hospital, being prepared
for a bypass operation. His wife saved his life by pestering him, until
he finally gave in.

As *parshiyot* go, *Tazria* and its oft-linked "partner," *Metzora*, win
no popularity contests—neither with rabbis nor with congregants.
Rabbis do not like to preach about them, and congregants do not
like to listen to them—and for good reason. Who wants to preach
about bodily sores and skin disease and how they were cured in the

---

RABBI JACK RIEMER is editor of six books on modern Jewish thought,
and is a prodigious preacher and collector of sermons. He is coeditor of *So
That Your Values Live On: Ethical Wills and How to Prepare Them* (Jewish
Lights). He lives in Boca Raton, Florida.

time of the Torah? And who wants to hear a talk about scales and scabs and skin discolorations?

And yet, health is a topic that we need to talk about and that we need to hear about, even though we don't want to. The reason is clear: men are more reluctant to talk about their illnesses than women are.

I learned this truth from Doug Barden, who is the executive director of Men of Reform Judaism (formerly the North American Federation of Temple Brotherhoods). He made an observation that I had not thought about before. He said that it is not only blotchy skin and scales that men do not like to talk about. We don't like to talk about *any* of our illnesses—whether they are things that show up on the outside, like the diseases in this week's portion, or whether they are growths or polyps or feelings of depression, which show up on the inside.

Why are men reluctant to obtain proper medical care when they sense that something may be going on inside? Why do they have to be pushed and pestered to go for a checkup, the way my friend was by his wife, who saved his life?

Doug Barden suggests that the reason men do not obtain proper health care is not a function of economics. It is not that we cannot afford to. It is a matter of a macho misperception of masculinity. Just as "real men don't eat quiche"—whatever that means—"real" men don't run to their doctors with every real or imaginary ache that they feel. Men don't go for physicals as often as we should, because we don't want to think of ourselves as sissies or weaklings or hypochondriacs. The result is that men have a significantly shorter life span than women do. For many men, ignorance is not bliss. Instead, for many men, ignorance is deadly.

I propose that congregations, annually, set aside the week in which we read *Tazria-Metzora* as the occasion for providing education in health awareness to their members, especially to the men. There should be a panel of medical experts who will teach congregants how to detect possible signs of trouble in our bodies. Just as many congregations annually sponsor a Sunday-morning program where participants can donate blood for those who need it, they should also sponsor Sunday-morning programs where people can have their blood pressure taken and bone marrow screened. We will teach our people that it is not a *shandeh* (Yiddish, "a shameful thing") to be sick, and it is not a sign of lack of macho to have your health checked. On the contrary, it is a sign of strength to be willing to find out what the state of your health actually is.

One of the mitzvot in the Torah is *ushmartem et nafshoteichem*, "you shall guard your health." Just as we are commanded to guard and take care of our souls, so we are commanded to guard and take care of our bodies—for if our bodies are weak, we cannot do many mitzvot. Therefore, synagogues have a religious obligation to do whatever they can to educate their congregants about the importance of caring for their health. Just as our religious institutions are obliged to teach Jews how to observe the mitzvot, so, too, they are obliged to teach Jews how to maintain their health so that they can carry out the mitzvot. If we are not well physically, we will not be able to serve God spiritually.

Nobody likes to talk about such things as skin disease and blotchy skin—and yet the Torah includes this topic and devotes two full portions to it. Precisely because we find these things difficult to discuss, synagogues should provide opportunities to discuss them and to learn more about them—for the sake of our lives. My friend, whose life was saved only because he had a wife who pushed him to get himself tested, should be a lesson to us all. There is no virtue in being stoic when we feel pain. There is no virtue in putting off finding out what is wrong with our bodies until it is too late. There is no sense in doing self-diagnosis, instead of going to a doctor, when we need to find out what is going on inside us.

Synagogues need to get involved in teaching and promoting the mitzvah of health care. For if our bodies are not well, then our souls cannot be well either.

מצרע
Metzora

A Plague on All Our Houses

RABBI MITCHELL CHEFITZ

When you enter the land of Canaan that I give you as a possession, and I inflict an eruptive plague upon a house in the land you possess, the owner of the house shall come and tell the priest, saying, "Something like a plague has appeared upon my house." (Leviticus 14:34–35)

Is it true that men don't stop to ask for directions? I don't know. But I do know that when I teach courses on Jewish spirituality, women outnumber men four to one. Is there a connection?

Metzora may speak to this. Leviticus 14:34–35 states, "When you enter the land of Canaan that I give you as a possession, and I inflict an eruptive plague upon a house in the land you possess, the owner of the house shall come and tell the priest, saying, 'Something like a plague has appeared upon my house.'"

Note that you are not asked to correct the problem. You are asked to go to the *kohen* and admit, out loud, that there seems to be a plague in your house and it's beyond your control. (That's similar to the first of the Twelve Steps for recovery from addictive disorders—to admit that one is powerless, which is the most difficult step to take.)

RABBI MITCHELL CHEFITZ is scholar-in-residence at Temple Israel of Greater Miami and a novelist and story writer. His book *The Curse of Blessings* has been translated into German, Korean, and Mandarin.

In our time, what would be "a plague in the house"? Is your house in disorder? Are your children misbehaving? Is your partner depressed—so much so it might be considered a plague?

And who is the *kohen*? In those days, the *kohen* was the priest who served in all capacities—from physician to social worker to spiritual counselor. Nowadays, we have specialized *kohanim*, each one an expert at taking appropriate measures to do battle with particular plagues.

The spiritual lesson, especially for men, is to admit, out loud—in the hearing of another—that we don't have control, that we don't know where we're going. Direction and assistance are always there, waiting for that moment of surrender.

אחרי מות
Acharei Mot

Our Bodies, Our Selves

RABBI STEVEN GREENBERG

Do not lie with a male as one lies with a woman; it is an abhorrence. (Leviticus 18:22)

In gay Jewish terms, *Acharei Mot* is the "scene of the crime." In this portion (and again, a few chapters later), we find two of the verses that are traditionally understood to excoriate gay male sex.

In 1969, those two verses were both to be found in my bar mitzvah portion as well. At age thirteen, I had no idea that this *parashah* would come to mean so much to me. By the time Leviticus 18:22 and 20:13 exerted their full caustic power on my life, I was a closeted Orthodox rabbi living in Riverdale, New York, and involved in my first gay relationship. The high-wire anxiety of this time led me to a showdown of sorts. I needed to make some sense of my life in light of these verses in order to continue in good faith—not only as an Orthodox rabbi, but as a committed Jew.

RABBI STEVEN GREENBERG is director of the CLAL Diversity Project and a senior teaching fellow at CLAL—National Jewish Center for Learning and Leadership. He is the first openly gay Orthodox rabbi and a founder of the Jerusalem Open House, the Holy City's GLBT community center. He is author of *Wrestling with God and Men: Homosexuality in the Jewish Tradition*, which won the Koret Jewish Book Award for Philosophy and Thought. Rabbi Greenberg is currently scholar-in-residence for Hazon, the Jewish environmental organization, and for Keshet, a national organization for GLBT inclusion.

I spent roughly the next ten years working on the emotional, intellectual, legal, and spiritual ramifications of these two verses. My efforts eventually became a book, *Wrestling with God and Men: Homosexuality in the Jewish Tradition* (University of Wisconsin Press, 2004). What I discovered, in exploring these verses, turned out to be relevant not only to gay sexuality, but to desire and fulfillment for any couple, straight or gay.

The verse in Leviticus 18:22 is usually translated: "Do not lie with a man as one lies with a woman; it is an abhorrence." The only difficult phrase is *mishkevei ishah* (usually translated as "as one lies with a woman") because the phrase appears nowhere else in the Bible. A similar phrase, "the lying of a male" (*mishkav zachar*), appears in Numbers 31:18, and it is understood to mean what women experience in intercourse, that is, penetration. Consequently, *mishkevei ishah* is what men experience in intercourse, that is, engulfment.

If so, then the verse prohibits a man from lying with a male in such a way that his penis is engulfed in the other man's body. And where is a man penetrable? Here the Rabbis make use of the fact that the word "lyings" is in the plural form. The lyings of a woman are plural because she may be penetrated vaginally or anally. A man, missing the vagina, is only penetrable anally. Consequently, for millennia the Jewish tradition understood that Leviticus 18:22 prohibited anal intercourse between men, and Leviticus 20:13 reiterated and punished the crime with death by stoning.

By far the most intriguing element of the puzzle is the fact that the Torah never addresses the issue of lesbian relations. The simplest explanation for this lacuna is that the Torah is utterly uninterested in "homosexuality" per se. The sameness of the sex (homo = same) that so dominates contemporary thought in regard to homosexuality is missing here. Instead, there is something about anal sex between men that is at the center of the biblical concern.

Why does the Torah consider anal sex between men to be so problematic?

Some writers have suggested that the prohibition of anal intercourse between men is about cultic purity. The Torah forbids *maasei mitzrayim*, acts associated with the land of Egypt, which are consequently taboo for Israelites. If so, then sex between men is a ritual prohibition, like eating pork or shrimp or cooking meat with milk. Some contemporary rabbinic authorities in both Orthodox and Conservative circles have claimed that intercourse between men is a ritual transgression similar to the prohibition of intercourse with a menstruating woman in Leviticus 18:19. While this approach has led to more permissive rulings, in my view it doesn't hold up to scrutiny.

The transgressions enumerated in Leviticus 18 were understood not only to be common among Egyptians, but also to be the epitome of wickedness. In his commentary on Leviticus, Jacob Milgrom powerfully demonstrates that immorality is cultic impurity. The punishment for both "ritual" and "moral" violations of the sacred order—whether contamination of the Temple by contact with the dead, or the oppression of the orphan and widow—is exile from the land. Leviticus 18 mentions various sexual violations as defiling—not merely because they improperly mix fluids, but because they are deemed to be immoral.

Moreover, the punishment for this sexual violation is the death penalty. Such a penalty is generally reserved for severe moral transgressions like incest and adultery. It doesn't easily fit a ritual transgression, roughly akin to mixing linen and wool or eating a ham sandwich.

So then, I return to the question, what sort of moral argument can be made for the prohibition of sex between men?

One of the best ways to understand the meaning of any law is to explore the stories that provide the law with narrative contexts. There are a number of Rabbinic readings that discover homosexual relations in the Book of Genesis. For example, in Genesis 9, Noah's son Ham does not merely *see* his father naked and drunk in his tent, but either castrates or anally rapes him. Rape of the father (or the father's wife, as happens later in Israel's monarchic history) is an act of Oedipal appropriation, short of patricide, that could propel a son into the father's role.

Of course, the most overt biblical narrative depicting male-male sexual relations is the story of the destruction of Sodom (Genesis 18).

It is surprising to note that neither the later prophets (who use Sodom as a symbol of evil) nor the Rabbis of the Talmud portray Sodom as a den of sexual iniquity. The city is singled out instead for cruelty—for its refusal to care for the poor, inhumanity to strangers, inhospitality, and violence. Sodom was no more about sexual license than are the humiliations of the prisoners of Abu Ghraib in our own time. The aim of the people of Sodom, according to the Rabbis, was humiliation as punishment or sport, gang rape rather than sexual intimacy.

Moreover, this understanding of the verse actually fits the chapter well. The chapter is dominated by rules against incest, the violation of which makes the family a dangerous place. Incest victims experience their torment as a form of violence and abuse that has been rendered utterly invisible to the outside world. Adultery violates stated commitments, and in premodern contexts, it typically led to violence. Intercourse with a menstruating woman has the appearance of violence, and the ritual of sacrificing children to the Canaanite deity, Molech, was nothing less than pure violence.

Understood in this light, the verse in Leviticus 18 might reasonably be prohibiting the use of penetrative sex as a tool of humiliation and domination, while leaving open the acceptance of a committed loving relationship between two men. And this may be why there is no direct biblical prohibition of lesbian relations in the Torah. Women are simply not capable of penetrative aggression. My proposed, albeit radical, interpretation of Leviticus 18:22 is then: "And a male you shall not sexually penetrate to humiliate; it is abhorrent."

However, this interpretation of the prohibition poses a problem. If the text is condemning power-driven, humiliating, or violent sex, then it should surely only punish the penetrating partner of such a dyad. The verse in Leviticus 18 works well with this reading, since it only prohibits the activity of the penetrating partner and says nothing about the penetrated partner.

But Leviticus 20:13 holds both parties liable. "If a man lies with a male as one lies with a woman, the two of them have done an abhorrent thing; they shall be put to death—their bloodguilt is upon them." If in prison, for example, the strong and aggressive men take advantage of the weaker of their fellows and enforce sustained relationships of individual or gang rape, how can the victim be blamed?

Remarkably, the Talmud itself asks this question. In *Sanhedrin* 54b, the Rabbis read Leviticus 18 as the "warning" and Leviticus 20 as the "punishment." Why are both parties punished (in Leviticus 20) but only the penetrative party warned (in Leviticus 18)? According to Rabbi Ishmael, the answer is found in the verse "... nor shall any Israelite man be a cult prostitute [*kadesh*]" (Deuteronomy 23:18).

What is a *kadesh*? Among the more common interpretations is that the male *kadesh* and the female *kedeshah* served as "sacred" prostitutes in pagan temple rituals. According to Rabbi Ishmael, the *kadesh* is the receptive male who has sex with other males as a part of a pagan rite.

Consequently, sexual relations that occur without violence or humiliation, that are not part of the dramaturgy of pagan rites but are marked by intimacy and love, care and commitment, ought to be permissible.

While these two contexts may seem a bit extreme or historically distant at first blush, we should not be too quick to dismiss them. There are manifestations of public or group sex in certain gay circles that are not so far from the pagan dramaturgy described by Rabbi Ishmael. The link between sex and power is even more common. Is there not an anarchic lure for men toward sexuality as an expression of power?

While the most common real-life victims of this sort of sexual power fantasy come alive are women, the themes of domination and submission surely have their destructive expressions, both straight and gay. Leviticus is taking a clear stand. If there is a choice to be made between heightened sexual experience and intimacy, between risk and reliability, between the thrills and dangers of the chase and the mutuality and safety of commitment, there is no question where the Jewish tradition will place its bets.

And yet, despite this cultural prevalence, one can find within the biblical, Rabbinic, and mystical traditions a celebration of seduction. The patterns of the marital laws that keep couples sexually separate for twelve days a month were seen as a way to revive desire by removing constant availability. As Esther Perel asks in her book *Mating in Captivity: Unlocking Erotic Intelligence* (Harper Paperbacks, 2007), which is about the challenge of sustaining sexual passion in marriage, "How can one desire what one has?" Without barriers of one sort of another, sexual expression can become tired and pedestrian.

Scholars in the tradition were to provide their wives with sexual intimacy at least once a week on Sabbath. On Friday night, it was the custom for men to read the teasingly erotic biblical text Song of Songs before coming home to their wives. The same mystical tradition that marked the Sabbath for sexual union between husbands and wives is likewise filled with similar delights of the chase and the ultimate union between the feminine and masculine expressions of God. Remarkably, God, too, satisfies a renewable longing and fulfillment, by the parting of *tiferet* and *malchut* (two of the mystical *sefirot*, aspects of the divine personality) during the week, and their ecstatic reunion on the holy Sabbath.

In the medieval sex guide *The Letter of Holiness*, Rabbi Moses ben Nachman (Ramban or Nachmanides) instructs that a husband ought to seduce his wife but never force her. How should a man navigate the line between seduction and force? Must "no" always mean "no" between married partners? According to the *halachah* (Jewish law), finding the line between playful and intrusive aggression is best determined by the receiver. If sex can easily slip into abuse or (more commonly) boredom, then the only way to navigate the dangerous and fickle waters is to achieve a high degree of awareness and communication between partners. The challenge is to find a way to keep sex intimate and relational while leaving room for mystery, risk, and play so that we create a reliably renewable excitement that fulfills the common human desire to be repeatedly overwhelmed—by love.

קְדשִׁים

Kedoshim

The Hardest Mitzvah?

RABBI REUVEN KIMELMAN

You shall not take vengeance or bear a grudge against your countrymen. Love your fellow as yourself: I am the Lord. (Leviticus 19:18)

Mishnah Avot (4:1) defines a mighty man as one who is mighty enough to overcome his urges. The Talmudic commentary *Avot d'Rabbi Natan* 23 adds that the really mighty man turns his enemy into his friend. How does one turn an enemy into a friend? The following verses from *Kedoshim* show the way:

> (A) You shall not hate your kinsfolk in your heart. (B) Reprove your kinsman (C) but incur no guilt [or "sin] because of him. (D) You shall not take vengeance or bear a grudge against your countrymen. (E) Love your fellow [often rendered "neighbor"] as yourself: (F) I am the Lord. (Leviticus 19:17–18)

RABBI REUVEN KIMELMAN is professor of classical Rabbinic literature at Brandeis University. He is author of the Hebrew work *The Mystical Meaning of "Lekhah Dodi" and "Kabbalat Shabbat,"* and three audio books, *The Moral Meaning of the Bible: The What, How, and Why of Biblical Ethics* (two volumes) and *The Hidden Poetry of The Jewish Prayerbook: The What, How, and Why of Jewish Liturgy*. His forthcoming book is *The Rhetoric of Jewish Prayer: A Historical and Literary Commentary on the Prayerbook* (Littman Library of Jewish Civilization).

What is the process of moving from regarding someone negatively to regarding someone positively? After all, these verses, which begin with hatred ("You shall not hate"), end on love ("Love your fellow"). To understand this shift, let us trace the steps from A to F.

(A) "You shall not hate your kinsfolk in your heart": Why are you on the verge of hating at all? Is it because of what happened in the previous verse (19:16), which prohibits trading in juicy tidbits about others and standing by (at the expense of) the blood of your neighbor? In the first case, you hate X because he badmouthed you; in the second case, you hate him because he "finked out" at your moment of need. Neither slander nor by-standing is a culpable crime. Slander is limited to words, however hurtful, and by-standing is passive. His behavior, however repugnant, consists in doing nothing, declining to get involved. Having no legal recourse, you are left hating him in your heart. Lest you think that only hateful actions, not feelings, are prohibited, the verse specifies "in your heart," that is, even in your heart.

(B) "… [rather] reprove your kinsman …": Work out your hatred through properly reprimanding him, otherwise the resentment is prone to fester and grow. Express your feelings lest they erupt under uncontrolled conditions. Both the reprimanded and the reprimander benefit from the reproof. By properly ventilating one's feelings to the right person, at the appropriate time and in a constructive way, the reprimander can free himself from his hatred, whereas the reprimanded can become aware of his wrong and how much he hurt.

(C) "… but incur no guilt/sin because of him": What sin is involved? There are five possibilities:

1. Continuing to hate, thereby transgressing A.
2. Desisting from rebuking—out of fear of confronting the wrongdoer or making it worse—thereby transgressing B.
3. Rebuking vindictively, thereby aggravating the situation, for when reprimands become disguised retaliations, they not only fail to fulfill the command of reproving for improving

but also compound the evil by creating another aggrieved party.

4. Rebuking ineffectively, thereby making one feel guilty for having tried but failed.

5. Remaining silent—refusing to get involved, thereby causing the victim to interpret your silence as agreement.

(D) "You shall not take vengeance or bear a grudge against your countrymen": Vengeance retaliates; grudges preserve enmity in the heart. Taking vengeance means refusing the use of your pen to one who had refused you the use of his pen. Holding a grudge means that you let the other use your pen, while muttering, "Sure, you can use my pen ..." Vengeance retaliates by deed, grudges by inflection that reflects the hatred festering in the heart.

(E) "Love your fellow/neighbor as yourself": The Talmud understands this to mandate treating one's neighbor as one would want to be treated, for "What is hateful to you do not do to your fellow." In context, it implies that just as you would not want someone to smear your reputation, do not smear his; or just as you would not want someone to stand aside in your hour of need, do not stand aside in his; or just as you would not want someone to hate you in their heart, do not do this to him. Act in a manner that helps others love you. As such, "as" means "as much as"—that is, love your neighbor as much as you love yourself. Its motto is: Perceive others as if they were you. The focus is upon acting lovingly with the hope that going through the motion cultivates the corresponding emotion. It is not enough to mean well; the recipient must perceive you as meaning well. You are not judged solely by your intention but also by his perception. Always ask: Do I come across as loving?

Hasidism understands "as yourself" to mandate loving your neighbor in the manner that you love yourself. Now, how do you love yourself? Self-love is not the result of ignoring one's faults but of focusing on one's virtues. Love magnifies virtue as hatred magnifies faults. Accordingly, we are commanded to utilize our remarkable capacity for magnifying our virtues and minimizing our faults and apply it to others. After all, why did God give us two eyes if not to see our faults with one and the other's virtues with the other? Alas, we suffer from inverted vision by highlighting our virtues and the other's faults. To avoid earthquakes in human relations, do not dwell on people's faults. Self-love as self-esteem involves the ability to let virtues overshadow faults. Low self-esteem, on the other hand, has the uncanny ability to focus on faults alone. Loving your neighbor as yourself mandates learning the art of self-esteem and applying it to others. Its motto is: Perceive others the way you perceive yourself.

According to the Talmud, "love your neighbor as yourself" applies especially to convicted murderers and spouses. With regard to murderers, eschew all slow and degrading punishments, for loving your neighbor as yourself means that you should "select for him a dignified form of death," as you would want for yourself. With regard to spouses, couples are to avoid situations that could bring about estrangement. Love is promoted by avoiding situations that lessen it while maximizing those that enhance it. Love of spouse means anticipating situations that can cause friction or lessening of love. The specific concern with a convicted murderer or a wife is because being farthest from and closest to us, their dignity is most susceptible to compromise. In the case of a murderer, it could be argued that one who has taken another's life forfeits the prerogatives of the image of God. As a divine grant, however, human dignity is inalienable. What society does not grant, it cannot rescind even from a murderer. In the case of a wife, a man may be tempted to take liberties with her dignity under the guise or pretext of love. Thus, make sure that you love her as you love yourself, dignity and all.

(F) "I am the Lord": Who needs to hear this conclusion, if not the rebuker who feels aggrieved? When nursing an injury, it is tempting to feel that the God of justice sides with the victim alone. Victimization can demand supererogatory moral prerogatives. But as "I am the Lord" also of the one you are about to hate, don't hate, for God does not side with the hater, whatever the justification.

For Rabbi Akiba, "Love your neighbor as yourself" is the most comprehensive principle of the Torah. For his student Ben Azzai, however, the verse dealing with humanity being created in the image of God (Genesis 5:1) is even greater. Wary of the subjective element in "as yourself," Ben Azzai was apprehensive of those of negative self-esteem who, reveling in self-humiliation, revel in the humiliation of others. Thus he anchors self-esteem in the objective reality of the divine image. How could one degrade the image of God? For Rabbi Akiba, this contingency is covered by "I am the Lord," namely, the Creator of both.

In sum: As the aggrieved party, you can respond in kind, provoking further recriminations, or you can admonish the perpetrator in a nonretaliatory manner. A considerate rebuke allows the other to reread the situation, adjust his image of you, and reassess his relationship to you. For example, if you respond to a derogatory comment by saying, "I'm really surprised you said that. I've always thought so well of you. There must be some misunderstanding," you throw him off balance. This allows for the emergence of alternative feelings such as remorse or his entertaining the possibility that your slight was inadvertent. By not playing by his rules, you throw him morally off guard, creating a situation of moral judo, granting you the leverage to defuse the situation. By responding in kind, you reinforce his negative image of you. He might even exult in your lowering yourself to his level, thinking, "I knew he meant to insult me; I just beat him to the punch." Being insulted in return validates his feelings. Rationalizing that you really meant to insult him all along, he deigns you worthy of further insults. However illogical, such psychological self-justifications create situations where retaliation begets greater retaliation. Nobody hurls his or her greatest punch first. Waiting in the rear is an ever greater insult just looking for a pretext to be unleashed.

Indeed, among decent people the guilt of having wronged may linger longer than the hurt of having been wronged. All the more will one appreciate the unanticipated kind words and try ever harder the next time around to compensate, even *overcompensate*, by acting especially nice. This is the paradox of conflict. The initial onslaught creates a situation with all the potential for escalating into enmity or sprouting into amity. The choice is ours.

For the Torah, the dynamic of subverting hatred by acts of kindness is subsumed under the rubric of aspiring for holiness: *Kedoshim tiheyu*, "You *can* be holy" (Leviticus 19:1).

Holy Aware

PETER HIMMELMAN

The Lord spoke to Moses, saying: "Speak to the whole Israelite community and say to them: You shall be holy, for I, the Lord your God, am holy." (Leviticus 19:1)

There are words that we use too often—words that have become cheapened and trivialized, words that are syllabic shells with nothing left inside them.

Take the word "holy," for example. It's a religious word, certainly. It refers to some ritual practice or prayer service. I once had a rabbi friend take me for a look inside the beautiful sanctuary of his synagogue. The place was monstrous—with a domed ceiling and stained-glass portraits of figures from the Bible, each looking more serene and contemplative then the next. "Doesn't this place feel holy?" he asked. Not wanting to offend, I said something innocuous like, "It sure is an amazing space." I really wanted to say, "What's amazing is thinking about what you paid for this place." But holy? No, I didn't feel it.

I asked around a bit and talked to other religious figures. "Holiness," they all said, "means 'separateness,' a state of being separate from the mundane." Unfortunately for me, I wasn't exactly clear on what "mundane" meant, either. "Ordinary"? "Mediocre"?

PETER HIMMELMAN is a Grammy- and Emmy-nominated songwriter and performer. He lives with his wife and four children in Los Angeles, California.

"Commonplace"? By that standard, a Triple Crown–winning race-horse or a platinum-selling rock band should be a thing of holiness. It didn't seem right, though, to judge something's worth by comparisons. And then, what of the honeybee or a glass of apple juice? What if no one's cheering for a particular thing? What if no one's delineating its specialness? Is it then relegated to the mundane?

I've long been interested by the length of time people are fascinated by a thing or an event. For example: how long is one moved by the birth of one's first child? Certainly, for me, the first half hour as a new father was pure giddiness. I'd been transported into a state of mind that was radically different from where I was before. All the things that filled my mind—shoe sizes, the shape of an eggplant, various brands of ketchup, and profound questions, like, "Should I choose leather interior, or do I opt for basic cloth seats?"—all left my mind when my son emerged, and I found myself awed like I had never been. It was clear that G-d was running the show. But then, after I'd made the calls to my mother and my siblings, and when I'd gone out to the car to pick up some extra socks for my wife, a little of that transcendent feeling left me. Of course, I was still incredibly happy, but there had been a palpable sense of "it" slipping away. How long, really, is a person moved by anything?

If the birth of a child can't keep us at a constant pitch of inspiration, why not search for a bigger miracle? How about a person rising up from the dead? Cynic that I am, I figure a guy coming up out of the ground would give the world eight to ten days of wonder, maximum. By two weeks, though, the news media would be onto another story.

Holy and mundane seem to be subjective terms. When *Kedoshim* commands us (no less than three times), "Be holy for I, Ha-shem, your G-d, am holy" (my translation—PH), we are being given a priceless hint into the way we could experience life. Perhaps holy could be understood as "remembrance" and mundane as "forgetfulness." What we can remember is that G-d is making the world at every moment and imbuing every experience with the potential for awe. What we almost always forget is our sense of wonder.

For a man, ever concerned with his career and with providing for his family, there's a lifetime of hard work ahead. After all, if it's difficult to "remember" the birth of a firstborn, then you know it's going to be hard as hell to hang on to holiness in a traffic jam on a Wednesday at rush hour, in the rain—with cloth seats no less.

אמר
Emor

Baldness, Beards, Body-Bashing, and Bereavement: Guarding the (Masculine) Image of God

Rabbi Simkha Y. Weintraub, LCSW

They shall not smooth any part of their heads, or cut the side-growth of their beards, or make gashes in their flesh. (Leviticus 21:5)

When we reach *Parashat Emor*, we are well into the "Holiness Code," chapters 17–26 of Leviticus, a section of the Torah with an unusual repetition of words based on the root *k-d-sh*, "set apart, sacred." The portion opens with two chapters, 21 and 22, which differ significantly from the rest of this Holiness Code in addressing primarily the *kohanim*, the priests, and not the people of Israel as a whole.

Among the salient interests of *Emor* are the laws of purity (*taharah*), which, in some detail, prohibit the *kohanim* from having contact with the dead and spell out marital restrictions—whom a *kohen* may, and may not, marry. After opening with a description of

---

RABBI SIMKHA Y. WEINTRAUB, LCSW, serves as rabbinic director of the Jewish Board of Family and Children's Services in New York City, guiding its New York Jewish Healing Center and National Center for Jewish Healing. He is editor of *Healing of Soul, Healing of Body* (Jewish Lights) and *Guide Me Along the Way: A Jewish Spiritual Companion for Surgery*, among other writings and publications.

the defilement that contact or closeness with corpses causes (Leviticus 21:1–4), the Torah text puts forward a very dramatic regulation: "They shall not smooth any part of their heads, or cut the side-growth of their beards, or make gashes in their flesh" (Leviticus 21:5). The Hebrew verb *k-r-ch*, "to make one's head bald," derives from the noun *korchah*, "baldness, bald spot" and the adjective *kereach*, "bald." It connotes the removal of all hair from the pate or even from a section of it, either by shaving with a razor or by pulling out the hair at its roots.[1]

The student of the weekly Torah portion is struck by this verse at the beginning of *Emor*, because a very similar prohibition appeared just last week in *Kedoshim*: "You shall not round off the side-growth on your head, or destroy the side-growth of your beard. You shall not make gashes in your flesh for the dead, or incise any marks on yourselves; I am the Lord" (Leviticus 19:27–28). These commandments are embedded in the wide-ranging and eclectic body of laws in Leviticus 19—sandwiched, in fact, between the prohibition of consuming blood and engaging in divination or soothsaying, and the law forbidding the degradation of one's daughter by making her a harlot.

Third and finally, a similar prohibition will appear in Deuteronomy 14:1: "You are the children of the Lord your God. You shall not gash yourselves or shave the front of your heads because of the dead." This verse, which opens a chapter that goes on to discuss holiness in diet and tithes, prohibits all Israelites from this activity, whereas our verse, in the middle of the Holiness Code, is specifically directed to the priests. Apparently, like gashing, shaving the hair and pulling it out were common rites of mourning in ancient Canaan (and, as anthropologists and others have shown, across the globe), and Israelite religion sought actively to prevent these practices and folkways.

Why? What is the issue here? Perhaps it would be good to first consider the motivations that may lead grieving individuals to injure themselves. Why would—why *does*—anyone harm himself in response to death, to loss?

There are many possibilities, of course. Here are seven—clearly interrelated and, in people's lived experience, often "interflowing."

While some may seem to apply equally to both genders, there are powerful lessons here for the way that men deal with grief.

1. Rage directed at self. Death and loss often trigger anger in survivors. In various studies, self-injury, interestingly, was more common among women, whereas anger directed outward was more common among men.[2]

2. Cutting through the numbness. Another reaction to loss—which, in many situations, can be helpful and adaptive—is a "feeling freeze," a state of emotional numbness. Some self-injurers have harmed themselves in order to feel something, to physically manifest their pain and intentionally draw tears.

3. Coping and "resolving" guilt. A very common response to the death of a near one is to feel guilt, sometimes generated by specific inadequacies or failures, but other times out of a general, diffuse need simply to blame someone. Self-injury may then serve the function of punishing oneself for the death.[3]

4. To rival or undo intolerable psychic pain. In his novel *Dead Souls*, written in 1842, Nikolai Gogol described the hero dashing his head against the wall and tearing his hair out, "enjoying the pain by which he strove to deaden the unquenchable torture of his heart." Gogol's understanding was that this great physical pain was in the service of blotting out mental anguish, which may be, indeed, harder to manage, contain, or tolerate.

5. Reclaiming a position of efficacy. In response to mortality and the overwhelming sense of not being in control, individuals may turn to self-injury to re-assert their own agency and power: "This act is my decision, and it reflects my will; it is my hand causing the harm to my body, and it will be mine that causes it to end."

6. To draw attention to one's agony and pain. In the dramatic encounter that appears in 1 Kings 18, 450 cult prophets of the Canaanite god Baal call upon their deity to answer their prayers, and their strategy includes cutting themselves with

knives and lances, apparently to gain Baal's notice (1 Kings 18:28). For some, the self-injury is designed to leave a visible mark that attests to the dramatic shifts in the bearer's life-journey, even serving as a testament to survival after trauma, to endurance, to resilience.

7. Joining—the act of identification, the desire to be with some-one. For some, the self-injury reflects a profound, if disturbing, desire to join the one who has departed—a powerful form of identification and even love. Even if not a fully suicidal gesture, it can represent an attempt to connect and relate to the deceased.[4]

To be sure, we can surmise why our tradition found these behaviors so objectionable. Since the body, mind, and spirit of the human being are, all together, created *b'tzelem Elohim*, in the image of God, we are not allowed to intentionally harm, mar, or destroy ourselves. The *kohanim*, as exemplars of the *mamlechet kohanim v'goy kadosh*, "a kingdom of *kohanim* and a holy nation" (Exodus 19:6), would be especially enjoined to avoid these destructive practices.

But the repeated connection of cutting or gashing alongside "shaving smooth the head" or "rounding off the corners and side-growth" poses the questions: What do these behaviors have in common, and what is the ultimate, shared purpose of these restrictions? And what aspects of these bans specifically relate to men, to masculinity?[5]

Rabbi Meir Soloveichik, in *Commentary*'s "Why Beards?" underscores how the Jewish penchant for beards is not just a cultural marker, but a serious religious imperative.[6] The ban against destroying the edges of the beard was regarded by the Rabbis as one of the 364 Torah prohibitions, and transgressing it was deemed as serious a sin as the consumption of pork.

Let's trace the evolution of Jewish attitudes toward beards and shaving.

Rabbi Soloveichik, drawing on Leon R. Kass's *The Beginning of Wisdom: Reading Genesis*, contrasts the biblical approach with that of ancient Egypt, which was marked by an obsession with achieving corporeal immortality. Kass describes how "the rejection of (bodily) change and the denial of death" characterized ancient Egypt.[7] In Genesis 41, Joseph is taken out of prison and brought before Pharaoh to interpret the Egyptian king's perplexing dreams. Before he is brought to Pharaoh, Joseph is shaved clean (Genesis 41:14); it seems that in order to appear in high or royal Egyptian society, one had to be barefaced. Soloveichik explains that in order to emphasize the cultural differences with Egypt, which challenged mortality and denied human aging and deterioration, the Torah repudiates "the false blessing of eternal youthfulness" and underscores "the fact of our eventual and inevitable mortality."[8]

Various biblical references to shaving the head and beard reflect that these were considered signs of both mourning and degradation. Thus, in Job 1:20: "Then Job arose, tore his robe, shaved his head [translation mine], and threw himself on the ground and worshiped." In 2 Samuel 10:4, the elders are humiliated by a forcible shaving of half of their beards—and because of this degradation, they are commanded to wait in Jericho until their beards grow in again. Ezekiel 5:1–5 shows how shaving was identified with spontaneous beard-plucking, which was a behavior that denoted massive sorrow.

In Talmudic times, the beard was regarded as "the adornment of a man's face" (Talmud, *Baba Metzia* 84a), and a man without a beard was compared to a eunuch (Talmud, *Yevamot* 80b and *Shabbat* 152a).[9] Young priests whose beards had not yet grown were not permitted to bless the people (Jerusalem Talmud, *Sukkah* 3:14 and 54a). According to the Talmud, the Assyrian king Sennacherib was punished by God for having his beard shaved off (*Sanhedrin* 95b–96a). The Rabbis in Roman times permitted only those who had frequent dealings with the Roman authorities to clip their beards (Talmud, *Baba Kamma* 83a).

When the great sage Rabban Gamaliel was temporarily relieved of his position, the Rabbis' ultimate choice of a replacement was Elazar ben Azaryah, who was known to be wise, affluent, and of prestigious lineage. But his wife quickly pointed out to him that he had no white hair—certainly not the respectable growth of facial hair necessary to be a Jewish religious leader. According to the Talmud (*Berachot* 27b–28a), a miracle was wrought, and, though he was only eighteen years old, he awoke the next day "and eighteen rows of hair (on his beard) turned white." This is why he is said to have stated, "Behold I am about seventy years old!" This quaint tale drives home the image of the beard as reflecting maturity, sagacity, and leadership strengths.[10]

A further dimension to the Jewish valuing of the beard emerges when one looks, centuries later, at the Catholic priesthood, in which the key element, Soloveichik mentions, is "the ideal not of youthfulness but of celibacy."[11] He quotes the historian Mark Zucker, who notes that it was one and the same pope, Gregory VII (1073–1085), who by decree "enforced not only celibacy among the clergy but shaving as well."[12] It seems that beards were connected with ordinary ("profane") human carnality, as shown by this quote from the medieval scholar Guilielmus Durandus (1230–1296):

> Cutting the hair of the beard ... denotes that we ought to cut away the vices and sins which are a superfluous growth in us. Hence we shave our beards that we may seem purified by innocence and humility, and that we may be like the angels who remain always in the bloom of youth.[13]

Judaism, it seems, had a very different understanding. It chose to "invest" in facial hair, and thereby located the sacred in the everyday—in the face of the mortal, with no expectation of cherubic hairlessness, angelic purity, or "other-worldly" sexlessness. The ideal was not the rejection or denial of the body, but its uplifting and consecration.

In the Middle Ages, Jews living in Muslim countries apparently grew long beards, while those in Christian Europe clipped them with scissors, which the classic legal code, the *Shulchan Aruch*, permitted (*Yoreh De'ah* 181:10).[14] It is interesting to note that rabbinic courts were known to punish adulterers by cutting off their beards.[15] The post of *hazzan* (cantor) was only granted to a man with a beard.[16] And, of course, the well-known *Hineni* prayer from the Middle Ages, which introduces the *Musaf* (the additional) service on the High Holy Days, has the humble *hazzan* supplicate, in deep fervor, earnestness, and piety:

> Receive my prayer [*tefilah*] as one offered by an old-timer, a veteran [*zaken v'ragil*], a respectful person [*ufirko na'eh*], with a fully grown beard [*uz'kano m'gudal*], whose voice is sweet [*v'kolo na'im*] and who gets along well with people [*um'urav b'daat im ha-briot*].

In his commentary to Leviticus 19:27, Don Isaac Abarbanel (1437–1508) states that objection to the removal of the beard was based on the fact that God gave it to man to distinguish him from woman, so that shaving it off was an offense against nature. In Kabbalah, mystical powers were ascribed to the beard and hair, and Rabbi Isaac Luria (1534–1572) is known to have refrained from touching his beard lest he cause hairs to fall out.[17] With the spread of Kabbalah to eastern Europe, leading rabbinic authorities began to prohibit even the trimming of the beard.[18] And with the rise of Hasidism, removal of the beard became regarded as a fundamental break with Jewish tradition, as if one were both defacing and denying the image of God.[19]

Living as we do in an age of Botox, with broad societal aspirations and nonstop commercial promises that one can be "forever young," the following midrash may bring us to a deep understanding of the Torah's valuing of physical manifestations of age:

> Rabbi Judah, son of Simon, said: Abraham requested [the appearance of] old age, pleading before God: "Sovereign of the universe! When a man and his son enter a town, none know whom to honor! But if You crown him [the father] with [the appearance of] old age, one will know whom to honor." Said the Holy Blessed One to him: "As you live, you have asked well, and it will commence with you." Thus from the beginning of the Torah until here, old age is not mentioned,

but when Abraham arose [the appearance of] old age was granted to him: "Abraham was now old, advanced in years ..." (Genesis 24:1). Until Abraham, the old and young looked alike.

> (Midrash, *Bereshit Rabbah* 65:9; see also Talmud, *Baba Metzia* 87a)

In other words, the physical evidence and image of age and aging are necessary for the moral order and ethical functioning of society. There is youth, and there is age—and we must be able to know who is before us.

Beyond the fundamental concern of honoring and caring for the divine image, then, the commandments prohibiting incising flesh or shaving smooth the head reflect—"embody"—a number of profound and interrelated concerns:

- Accepting aging, mortality, and the limits of this life
- Celebrating physicality and our bodily nature
- Expressing manhood and masculinity
- Manifesting maturity and leadership
- Encapsulating sanctity, piety, and humility
- Appreciating order in nature and society
- Representing divine love and direction

Many have experienced a profound Zionist moment when seeing, on the Israeli public transit system, a sign with the opening words of the following verse from last week's Torah portion, *Kedoshim*: "You shall rise up before the hoary head, and honor the face of the old man, and fear your God; I am Adonai [translation mine]" (Leviticus 19:32).

This, indeed, is a binding biblical obligation—to stand for elders, at any time and at any place. It is not just a symbolic gesture, and not only a social nicety. Rather, it is the act of locating the moment in the forward flow of time—a profound acceptance of the order of life and the privilege of years.

בהר־בחקתי

Behar–Bechukotai

Going to the Wild Places

RABBI MIKE COMINS

> When you enter the land that I assign to you, the land
> shall observe a sabbath of the Lord. Six years you may
> sow your field and six years you may prune your vine-
> yard and gather in the yield. But in the seventh year the
> land shall have a sabbath of complete rest....
>
> Leviticus 25:2–4

> Then shall the land make up for its sabbath years
> throughout the time that it is desolate and you are in the
> land of your enemies; then shall the land rest and make
> up for its sabbath years. Leviticus 26:34

In ancient Israel, every seventh year, the nation went wild.

During the *shemittah* (sabbatical) year, land reverts to divine stewardship so that it may rest and rejuvenate. The human "owner" must let the fields lie fallow (Leviticus 25:1–5) because the "real" owner is God (Leviticus 25:23). Every fifty years, during the *yovel* (jubilee) year, Hebrew slaves are freed; the land reverts to its original

---

RABBI MIKE COMINS is an Israeli desert guide, the founder of TorahTrek Spiritual Wilderness Adventures, and author of *A Wild Faith: Jewish Ways into Wilderness, Wilderness Ways into Judaism* (Jewish Lights).

tribal designation, preventing the growth of a landed aristocracy. The *yovel* year is also a *shemittah* year; for two years in a row, the fields return to their original, wild state.

From the viewpoint of slaves and the land, *yovel* and *shemittah* were a release from the domination of others. But consider what those institutions meant to the vast majority of ancient Israelites— free people who farmed for a living. The land—your particular piece of land—reverted to wilderness. You could only eat what grew on its own.[1] Just as the Israelites were forbidden to save the manna that fell in the wilderness (Exodus 16:16–18), hoarding was forbidden. You could not take extra for yourself; nor could you prevent anyone else, even livestock and wild beasts, from helping themselves to the produce of the land that you worked the previous six years (Leviticus 25:6–7).

That wild state, particularly in the form of wilderness proper, is a central character in the Hebrew Bible. Moses discovers God through a burning bush in the desert. He returns to civilization to liberate the people and takes them far from it to receive the great revelation at Sinai. The Israelites live forty years in wilderness before entering the Land of Israel. Various prophets are invested or receive their visions in the wild, including Elijah, who travels back to Sinai to hear the "still, small voice" (1 Kings 19:12).[2]

We structured our society based on the great teachings we received in the wild. Then, after our attempts to create a just society inevitably fell short, prophets and poets and kings returned to our origins, to the wilderness, to renew the relationship with God and to revitalize the vision of what our society ought to be.

And every sabbatical year, instead of going out to the wild, we brought the wild to us.

What makes wilderness so critical to biblical spirituality? As a rabbi who leads Jews on wilderness retreats, I find that the answer to this question is just as relevant today as it was to our ancestors, particularly for men.

Wilderness is a place where a man can recover his origins and remember what it's like to be a boy: to throw rocks, explore around the pond, lift a stone to see what's underneath, plot with friends to conquer a peak, or make a fire. For children, it's a place to discover the world and how we fit into it. In the wilderness, a man can return to the uncomplicated days of childhood to renew his vision of what his life might be. More importantly, wilderness is a place where a boy becomes a man.

In order to mature, boys must undergo tests and overcome obstacles, including the challenge of Judaism's high moral standards. Sometimes we agonize over what the right action might be. But for the most part, we know the right thing to do. The harder question is, will we do it? Will we sacrifice to bring justice to a stranger? Will we stick by a friend when the going gets tough?

Testing one's moral fortitude is a central theme—perhaps *the* central theme—in the Hebrew Bible. Take Jacob, for example. As his Hebrew name implies (*Yaakov* means "he will circumvent/get around/skirt"), Jacob, a prototypical "mama's boy,"[3] gains his inheritance, and his wives, through deception and trickery. When he returns to Canaan, the brother he duped (the stereotypical masculine warrior, Esau) rides toward him at the head of an army. Fearing for his life, Jacob sends gifts to placate Esau and splits his camp in two to avoid wholesale slaughter at the hands of his brother. He prays (Genesis 32:10–13).

And when he senses that the danger is already upon him in the middle of the night, he moves his family across the Jabbok River (Genesis 32:23). Here the story takes an unexpected turn. As Esau is coming from the opposite direction, Jacob has actually placed his children between himself and his brother![4] Left alone on the riverbank, at a place farthest away from Esau, he prepares to do what he has always done when deception can no longer save him. He prepares to run.[5]

But then a mysterious *ish* (literally, "a man" [Genesis 32:25])[6] accosts him and wrenches his hip. Suddenly, Jacob can no longer run from danger. And the stranger continues to attack. He finds himself in the very situation that his deception was meant to prevent. He must fight with his bare hands—for his life!

But this unexpected, perilous wrestling match is a gift. The *ish* gives Jacob exactly what he needs: a physical fight. He must learn what he could never think, reason, or deduce—his own strength, his resolve, his courage. He can succumb to fear and die, or he can fight and live.

Alone in the wilderness, threatened by an adversary he did not anticipate, Jacob discovers his wild heart, his fighting self, his God-wrestling spirit. The text is clear. The *ish* blesses him because *vatuchal* (Genesis 32:29), usually translated "you have prevailed." But the Hebrew literally reads "and you were able." Jacob becomes Yisrael, "God-wrestler," or in a more creative reading, "He-Will-Circumvent" becomes *Yashar-El*, "the Straight One of God," but not because he gains an intellectual insight or another clever strategy. The sweaty, physical, dangerous fight does not produce knowledge. Rather, it discloses ability. Jacob's hidden capabilities—honesty, resilience, and courage—are revealed to him.

Jacob's newly discovered physical strength gives him moral strength. The night before, as he prepared to flee, he placed his family between himself and Esau. Now, after the wrestling match, Jacob limps past his family and faces Esau, putting himself between them and harm's way, with no weapon other than his new name. For the first time, acting without fear, he risks his life to do the right thing. Esau embraces him with a kiss.

For any of us, wilderness can be the *ish*. We are challenged to overcome fear, to live near danger without anxiety. Our bodies are tested by mountains and rivers and deserts, and with them, our hearts. Do we have the internal fortitude to persevere in the face of unexpected danger, to improvise when difficulties arise, to keep going when we are tired, to look out for our friends the same way we look out for ourselves?

Every seventh year, the ancient Israelite farmers saw their fields revert to wild territory, reminding them of the desert where Torah was given. Like the *ish*, the wilderness is an agent of revelation—a place where awe is the norm, where God's snow-drenched mountains, wild rivers, and red stone deserts enliven the spirit, and where a sudden storm just might slap you in the face, or wrench your hip.

Wilderness reveals to us our power, and our powerlessness as well.

In the wild, we discover our true position in the world. We must cultivate and depend on our strength and courage, for our lives depend on it. At the same time, we must recognize that we are fragile beings, in constant need of *chesed* (grace, loving-kindness) from God and people.[7]

A boy becomes a man.

Bemidbar/ Numbers

במדבר
Bemidbar

The Wilderness Speaks

On the first day of the second month, in the second year following the exodus from the land of Egypt, the Lord spoke to Moses in the wilderness of Sinai, in the Tent of Meeting.... (Numbers 1:1)

It's hot and sticky. The cooling breeze of nightfall won't arrive for hours. I'm stuck behind an eighteen-wheeler choking in endless urban traffic, while the radio news ticks off the day's toll of rape, murder, gang warfare, drugs, governmental incompetence and corruption, intractable social dilemmas, and unfathomable moral lunacy. Something about Israel flashes on the news; don't ask.

The kids in the back seat won't stop fighting. The one in the front seat says he's carsick. And I'm late. At times like these I cherish the Book of *Bemidbar*.

RABBI EDWARD FEINSTEIN is senior rabbi of Valley Beth Shalom in Encino, California. He serves on the faculty of the Ziegler Rabbinical School of the American Jewish University, the Wexner Heritage Foundation, and the Shalom Hartman Institute in Jerusalem. He is the author of *Tough Questions Jews Ask: A Young Adult's Guide to Building a Jewish Life* and editor of *Jews and Judaism in the Twenty-first Century: Human Responsibility, the Presence of God and the Future of the Covenant* (both Jewish Lights), finalists for the National Jewish Book Award. His latest book, *Capturing the Moon*, retells the best of classic and modern Jewish folktales. He lives in the San Fernando Valley with his wife, Nina, and three teenage kids.

Bemidbar means "in the wilderness," for the book commences in the wilderness of Sinai. But more than a physical location, *Bemidbar* depicts a social wilderness, a human wasteland. This is a place where everything falls apart. It portrays a people wandering—without a shared vision, shared values, or shared words. Leaders attempt to lead, but no one listens. The people of this wilderness, driven by fear and jealousy, moved only by hunger, thirst, and lust, have no patience for God's transcendent vision. This is a book of noise, frustration, and pain.

Bemidbar may be the world's strongest counterrevolutionary tract. It is a rebuke to all those who believe in the one cataclysmic event that will forever free human beings from their chains. It is a response to those who foresee that out of the apocalypse of political or economic revolution will emerge the New Man, or the New American, or the New Jew. Here, *Bemidbar* offers, is the people Israel miraculously freed from Egyptian slavery. Here is the people Israel who stood in the very presence of God at Mount Sinai—the quaking mountain aflame and covered in smoke. Here is the people Israel who heard Truth from the mouth of God, the people instructed by Moses himself. And still, they are unchanged, unrepentant, chained to their fears. The dream is beyond them. God offers them freedom, and they clamor for meat. "How long will this people spurn Me, and how long will they have no faith in Me despite all the signs that I have performed in their midst?" (Numbers 14:11).

It falls heaviest on Moses. In the course of *Bemidbar*, everyone in his life will betray him. Miriam and Aaron—his family members—betray him, murmuring against him. His tribe rebels against him, under the leadership of his cousin Korach. His people betray him, accepting the dispiriting report of the ten spies over the vision of the two. And finally, even God betrays him. Told to speak to the rock, he hits it instead. And for this, he will not see the journey's end. But of course he hit the rock! Nowhere in *Bemidbar* do words function. Nowhere do words nourish, inspire, or heal.

Every man knows Moses's burden. Every man has found himself in that excruciating moment when words don't work—when we try and say the right thing, to heal and help, but each word brings more hurt. Every man has tasted the bitterness of betrayal—when no one stands with us, when those who should know better stand against us. Every man has felt the deep disappointment of the dream turned sour. It could have been so good! It should have turned out so differently! Where did I go wrong? Every man has tortured himself with the torment Moses feels in *Bemidbar*. And that's the ultimate lesson. Listen to the Torah's wisdom: the agony, the self-doubt, the frustration are part of the journey through the wilderness. Any man who has ever held dreams, ever championed an ideal, ever reached for greatness—any man who has ever worn Moses's shoes or carried his staff—knows the anguish of *Bemidbar*. But know this, too: You're not alone. You're not the first. You're not singled out. And most of all, you're not finished. The torturous route through the wilderness does come to an end. There was hope for Moses. There is hope for us.

At the end of the Book of *Bemidbar*, we arrive in the Promised Land. But we arrive exhausted, depleted, defeated. If the Torah ended here, we would be a very different people. But the Torah goes on to a new book. *Bemidbar* gives way to *Devarim*, Deuteronomy. This is much more than just turning a page. It is the turning of the heart, the changing of the world. *Devarim* means "words." This is a book of shared words, shared values, and shared direction. Moses talks; people listen. Moses leads; people follow. Where once there was division, there is now shared vision. Where once there was dissension, there is now dialogue and consensus. The key word of *Devarim* is *Shema*, "Listen!" *Devarim* is a book of listening.

This is the Torah's message of hope. Nothing worth doing in life can be accomplished without crossing the *midbar*, the wilderness. But wilderness is not the last word. Beyond the *midbar*, there is a promised land of *devarim*. Consensus, common direction, shared values can be reached. Peace is not idle dream. It's out there—at the edge of the wilderness, at the end of the journey.

נשא
Naso

His Own Unique Gift

RABBI ELLIOT KLEINMAN

His offering: one silver bowl weighing 130 shekels and
one silver basin of 70 shekels by the sanctuary weight,
both filled with choice flour with oil mixed in, for a
meal offering; one gold ladle of 10 shekels, filled with
incense; one bull of the herd, one ram, and one lamb in
its first year, for a burnt offering; one goat for a sin
offering; and for his sacrifice of well-being: two oxen,
five rams, five he- goats, and five yearling lambs.

(Numbers 7:13–17)

The program for a men's spirituality retreat arrived on my desk a few
months ago. It described the opportunities available for men to
come together, learn from one another, and reconnect with their
Judaism. The retreat offered such "traditional" Jewish ritual moments
as drum circles, sweat lodges, "sacred screaming," and yoga. At the

RABBI ELLIOT KLEINMAN is chief program officer for the Union for
Reform Judaism (URJ). He coordinates the work of the departments of
Outreach and Synagogue Community, Jewish Family Concerns, Worship,
Music and Religious Living, and Social Action, and is responsible for the
URJ Biennial Conventions, North America's largest Jewish gathering. He
was regional director for the Northeast Lakes Council/Detroit Federation
of the URJ and served as a rabbi at Temple Sholom of Chicago, Illinois. He
is also Shira and Avi's father.

bottom of the third page there was a brief mention that "traditional daily prayers would be available for those who desired."

The last few years have brought a plethora of spiritual alternatives. The whole notion of modern Jewish spirituality is something of an open question. Congregations are filled with attempts to combine tradition with relevance in order to brew some kind of spiritual elixir that would be capable of transforming an ever more alienated membership into a sacred community. Alternative minyanim and study groups arise, as if from nowhere, offering the spiritual vibrancy that so many claim is absent from the synagogue. Many of these new efforts are to be applauded. But I still find myself at a loss, for there seems to be little available, specifically, for men.

That's why that brochure interested me. I consider myself relatively open-minded, but I admit to being mystified. Where was the Jewish connection? What did this have to do with me and my own search for Jewish spiritual authenticity? Although I long ago discarded the brochure, the questions remained.

I began to find answers in the Torah. While sitting in a synagogue service listening to the usual sermon on the priestly blessing (Numbers 6), I found myself becoming bored and my mind wandering. Opening the Torah commentary, I began reading the *parashah* for myself. *Naso* is replete with great sermonic material. There is the census and the assignment of duties to the priestly class, the priestly blessing, the adulterous woman, and the laws pertaining to the Nazirites. There was so much there, yet so little spoke to the questions I continued to harbor.

The Torah portion raises a particular challenge. At the beginning of the portion, God commands Moses to conduct a census. However, Moses is instructed to count men *only*. It was important to know how many men were available to perform the rituals of the ancient desert tabernacle, for such sacred roles were reserved for men.

And yet, as I travel for my work with the Union of Reform Judaism, and I meet with leaders of Reform congregations from throughout North America. I notice that more often than not, these leaders are women. The engagement of women in synagogue leadership has been a hallmark of contemporary Jewish life.

But, I believe that it also raises questions for men: What is my role, as a man, in the contemporary synagogue? What is unique about our (men's) engagement in Jewish life? How can I find an authentic expression of spirituality? It is these questions that seem to have led us to "sacred screaming" and sweat lodges. In the pages of the ancient text, we apparently "counted." Do we still count?

Perhaps our role is not to find or create some new spiritual modes. Perhaps there is something about the "old ways" that warrants reexamination, even and especially in "new times."

The final section of the portion (Numbers 7) is a litany of gifts brought for the dedication of the ancient desert sanctuary. It is a lengthy recounting (seventy-six verses!) of the dedicatory offerings. The gifts brought by the princes of each tribe are recounted in detail, and each is identical.

> His offering: one silver bowl weighing 130 shekels and one silver basin of 70 shekels by the sanctuary weight, both filled with choice flour with oil mixed in, for a meal offering; one gold ladle of 10 shekels, filled with incense; one bull of the herd, one ram, and one lamb in its first year, for a burnt offering; one goat for a sin offering; and for his sacrifice of well-being: two oxen, five rams, five he- goats, and five yearling lambs. (Numbers 7:13–17)

As the ever-shortening sound bites of television news attest, modern readers have little patience for this kind of duplication. If every word of the Torah has meaning, why should it devote so many verses to the same thing—the same identical offering, brought by each of the tribal heads—over and over again?

Rabbi Samson Raphael Hirsch, the founder of modern Orthodoxy in Germany, observes that the repetition demonstrates that, at that moment of celebration, all of Israel, regardless of tribe or communal role, was equal. Equality? The Torah presents us with seventy-six verses in order to demonstrate equality? There must be something more to this. It cannot be that almost an entire chapter of Torah is used to simply demonstrate equality among the princes.

A midrash offers an alternative explanation. Could it be that although the gifts appear the same, there was something different about each one? The midrash suggests that there was one critical difference in each prince's offering brought to the tabernacle. Each prince had a different motivation for bringing the gift. Each prince had endowed his gift with a meaning that was unique to him and to his needs at the moment (*Bemidbar Rabbah* 13:14–14:18).

True, the outward form of practice was indistinguishable, one from the other. But, for each prince, the meaning was wholly and completely unique. Commentators through the years have attempted to describe what the meaning of each gift was for each particular prince. There is one theme that appears throughout these explanations: within each gift, each prince brought something of his own history and aspirations.

This brings me back to the men's spirituality retreat brochure and the apparent search for a new form of men's spirituality. The Torah portion suggests that we may not need to search for a men's spirituality that was lost and in need of being redeemed or a spirituality that is new and in need of being created.

Rather, it may be that the traditional forms of service—Torah, *avodah* (worship), and *gemilut chasadim* (acts of kindness)—are all we need. To the casual observer, it may seem that traditional rituals, practices, and opportunities for participation only present us with a dull sameness, year after year. Yet, if we endow each moment, each ritual, each opportunity with our unique history and our unique hopes and dreams, then each Jewish act becomes a real gift.

We don't need sweat lodges or "sacred screaming." What we need is to put some sweat into bestowing the gifts we bring to our Jewish community with the most precious gift we have to offer—ourselves. The sacred is not to be found in the appearance of the act of spirituality but in the spirit we bring to the act.

בהעלתך
Behaalotecha

Can Moses Teach Us How Not to Burn Out?

RABBI ELIE KAPLAN SPITZ

"I cannot carry all this people by myself, for it is too much for me. If you would deal thus with me, kill me rather, I beg You, and let me see no more of my wretchedness!" (Numbers 11:14–15)

Despair, the sense that life is hopeless, strikes men at different points in their lives. When we are worn out physically, emotionally, intellectually, and spiritually, we may say: "I can't go on." Yet, from these moments of darkness, we may later extract wisdom and compassion. When we are down, we may choose hope and thereby reclaim our verve, our sense that life is good. We may begin to draw ourselves out of a rut with the awareness that others before us, great people, have felt hopeless and have gone on to do great things.

RABBI ELIE KAPLAN SPITZ has served for over two decades as the rabbi of Congregation Bnai Israel, Tustin, California, and serves on the Conservative Movement's Law Committee. He is author of *Does the Soul Survive? A Jewish Journey to Belief in Afterlife, Past Lives, and Living with Purpose* and *Healing from Despair: Choosing Wholeness in a Broken World* (both Jewish Lights), and has written many *responsa* (Jewish legal decisions) and articles on Jewish spirituality. He and his wife, Linda, are the parents of Joey, Jon, and Anna.

Consider Moses. A model of service to God and the teacher of his people, he, too, encounters despair. Listen to his plea to God: "I cannot carry all this people by myself, for it is too much for me. If you would deal thus with me, kill me rather, I beg You, and let me see no more of my wretchedness!" (Numbers 11:14–15). What prompts Moses to express a yearning to end his life? How does God help him overcome his hopelessness? In examining this story, we learn about avoiding and overcoming despair.

Moses begins his leadership with vigor and a willingness to work hard. After leading the people from Egypt, Moses undertakes the responsibility of judging the cases that the Israelites bring him. Jethro, his father-in-law and an experienced leader, observes Moses judging the people, by himself, from morning to night. The older man cautions Moses, "The thing you are doing is not right; you will surely wear yourself out, and these people as well. For the task is too heavy for you; you cannot do it alone" (Exodus 18:17–18). Jethro offers a remedy: appoint a judicial hierarchy, leaving only the most difficult cases for Moses to judge in consultation with God. Moses displays the willingness to listen and learn—and from his father-in-law, no less. He implements the suggestion of delegation and avoids the kind of burnout that comes from sheer exhaustion. Yet, Moses will later reach a moment in his life when he will feel crushed.

During the course of the next two years of marching through the harsh desert, the newly freed slaves repeatedly lack hope and gratitude. When they express their frustration over lack of water and food, Moses will intercede on their behalf and God will find a solution. Finally, Moses reaches the limits of his patience, his strength, and his willingness to tolerate the Israelites' burdens. The crisis unfolds as follows:

> The riffraff in their midst felt a gluttonous craving; and then the Israelites wept and said, "If only we had meat to eat! We remember the fish that we used to eat free in Egypt, the cucumbers, the melons, the leeks, the onions, and the garlic.

Now our gullets are shriveled. There is nothing at all! Nothing but this manna to look to!" (Numbers 11:4–6)

"Nothing but this manna to look to!" the Israelites wail. Consider that God has graciously provided manna for the people to eat during their desert journey. It rests upon the dew each morning, except Shabbat, but with a double portion on Fridays to enable Shabbat rest (Exodus 16:11–27). Now, in response to the people's complaint, the Torah makes a point of describing how delicious the manna tastes, comparing it to coriander seed, a sought-after spice, and rich oil (Numbers 11:7–8). A comment in the Talmud will go even further by suggesting that the manna could taste exactly like whatever the person brought to mind (*Yoma* 75a; see also the midrash *Bemidbar Rabbah* 15:24). All the Israelites have to do to eat this extraordinary gift from heaven is gather the bounty nearby, with no need to till, plant, or weed.

The Israelites are wandering through the desert not only physically, but also spiritually—searching for their purpose, while waiting to enter the Promised Land. The biblical commentators wonder, what is really bothering the people in this particular moment of despair? They offer at least two possibilities with a common theme. First, the people resent the restrictions that come with being bound by a covenant with God. When the Israelites use the word "free," they do so not to refer to the cost of the food in Egypt, but to the lack of moral expectations (midrash, *Sifrei*; also, Rashi). The other analysis focuses on the people's boredom. All their needs are satisfied; there is little variety in the daily routine or what they eat, and they lack the possibility of achievement amidst radical equality (Rabbi Samson Raphael Hirsch, nineteenth-century Germany; Jonathan Eyebeschutz, eighteenth-century Germany). The link between these two explanations is that the people lack a sincere commitment—a calling—that would override the immediate demands and shortcoming of their daily lives; a purpose that would emerge from having an ongoing relationship with God or faith in reaching the Promised Land.

While the people obsess over trivial cravings, Moses unravels. The leader, who has dedicated his life to serving God and guiding the people to a new life, sees an ungrateful people looking backward, yearning with a distorted memory for Egypt. And more, he sees a people fragmented and unabashed in their shameful whining, each crying as a family in front of their tents (Numbers 11:10). The Torah records that Moses is distressed and God is angry, but it is Moses who speaks:

> "Why have You dealt ill with Your servant, and why have I not enjoyed Your favor, that You have laid the burden of all this people upon me? Did I conceive all this people, did I bear them, that You should say to me, 'Carry them in your bosom as a nurse carries an infant,' to the land that You have promised on oath to their fathers? Where am I to get meat to give to all this people, when they whine before me and say, 'Give us meat to eat!' I cannot carry all this people by myself, for it is too much for me. If you would deal thus with me, kill me rather, I beg You, and let me see no more of my wretchedness!"
> (Numbers 11:11–15)

Here, too, there is more to the story than meets the eye. Moses speaks to God of his inability to satisfy the people's physical demands. Yet, God's response shifts the focus from the people's complaint to Moses's need for support and meaning in this troubled time. God tells Moses to gather seventy elders and bring them to the sacred Tent of Meeting and "I will come down and speak with you there, and I will draw upon the spirit that is on you and put it upon them; they shall share the burden of the people with you, and you shall not bear it alone" (Numbers 11:17). Moses complies and "then the Lord came down in a cloud and spoke to him; He drew upon the spirit that was on him and put it upon the seventy elders. And when the spirit rested upon them, they spoke in ecstasy, but did not continue" (Numbers 11:25).

God will also provide quail for the people, but it is this act of sharing of the spirit that quells Moses's anguish and renews his strength to carry on. In what ways do the seventy leaders momentarily communing with the divine spirit respond to what is really bothering Moses?

First, Moses sees seventy elders step forward to serve on God's behalf. He can see that God matters to them, too, and that they are willing to help shoulder his load.

Second, he sees that the spirit that infuses the seventy elders, allowing them to experience the ecstasy of the Divine, is channeled through him. The early Rabbis will comment that Moses is like a candle, sharing without a loss of his own light (midrash, *Sifrei*; also, Rashi). God thereby demonstrates to Moses that he has a unique and necessary role.

Third, Moses can now feel that the voices of despair do not tell the whole story. There are others whom he admires who, with gratitude, share his commitment to God and the faith that the journey to the Promised Land will lead to a better future. The seventy elders do not need to persist in their role as possessors of the divine spirit. Moses reclaims his worldview, in which service to God is a core commitment and freedom is a blessing. He regains purpose by knowing that others care about him, that he has a unique role to serve, and that he and the people have much to look forward to.

There are several lessons to derive from this dramatic series of events for our own lives.

First, despair is part of life. Whether for a simple Israelite or for Moses, the leader, there are low points in life—moments marked by hopelessness, unhealthy cravings, and unreasonable expectations. Men may encounter despair when work is going poorly, when there has been the loss of a loved one, or when there has been betrayal in a relationship.

Second, when we find a purpose that allows us to serve or inspire others, we find the endurance to deal with the challenges of life and reframe the way we see the world. Our purpose need not be grandiose. It may be as basic as raising a family or providing care to one other person. We need to know that we matter to someone else.

Third, we may need to listen, to trust, and to take direction to reclaim our path. Men in particular often feel a pride that prevents us from taking advice or even sharing our burdens. To trust another in conversation and to listen may make a huge difference in reclaiming perspective and hope.

Fourth, protecting ourselves from burnout—the exhaustion of physical, emotional, intellectual, and spiritual responsibilities—requires that we seek out support and delegate. Even more, to face the demands of life without despair, we need to know that where we are going and what we are doing is grounded in worthwhile, meaningful commitments, which are validated by others.

The Hebrew word for "crisis," *mashber*, is the same as the word for "birthing stool," a set of stones used by a woman to steady herself in the act of giving birth (see Rashi on Exodus 1:16). The lesson of the word *mashber* is that crisis may actually give birth to new beginnings. When we encounter the feeling of "I can't go on this way," as Moses did, we can first gain comfort in knowing that even great people—our greatest—had such moments of anguish and overcame them. Moses's story prompts us to pause and consider what underlies our complaints. In doing so, we should consider examining the commitments that define us and give us strength and purpose. Unlike Moses, we need not be leaders of a vast people to serve as a conduit for God's light. The Jewish mystics teach that our good deeds also help gather and make more manifest the divine light in our midst.

In the biblical story, Moses reclaims his willingness to serve, but the frustrations of leadership will persist. What has changed is how Moses sees himself, the people, and his purpose. As with the Israelites and Moses in our story, we may find that out of crisis we emerge to a new beginning, emerging with renewed hope and the strength to deal with life's unfolding challenges.

שלח לך
Shelach-Lecha

Our Personal Minority Report

RABBI ELLIOT N. DORFF, PhD

Caleb hushed the people before Moses and said, "Let us by all means go up, and we shall gain possession of it, for we shall surely overcome it." (Numbers 13:30)

This was my bar mitzvah portion in 1956, and I still remember what the rabbi said to me about it on the pulpit. So, for all you parents and rabbis who speak to young adults becoming bar or bat mitzvah, take note: your words just may be remembered!

My rabbi, Louis J. Swichkow, spoke about the twelve spies. Only two of them had the faith in God and the courage to say that the Israelites could conquer the land of Canaan, but they were right. Indeed, the entire Jewish people had to spend the next forty years in the wilderness because of the faithlessness of the majority's report. Because I had spent the previous summer at Camp Ramah and wanted to go back, and because at the time you had to be tak-

---

RABBI ELLIOT N. DORFF, PhD, is rector and distinguished professor of philosophy at the American Jewish University in Los Angeles, California, and chair of the Academy of Judaic, Christian, and Muslim Studies. He is widely published on the topics of Jewish thought, law, and ethics. His books include *The Way Into Tikkun Olam (Repairing the World)*, a finalist for the National Jewish Book Award, and *The Jewish Approach to Repairing the World: A Brief Introduction for Christians* (both Jewish Lights). He is married to Marlynn and has four children and seven grandchildren.

ing at least six hours per week of Jewish studies during the year to enroll in Ramah, I was going to continue with my Jewish studies after my bar mitzvah. Most bar mitzvah boys did not do that, and so Rabbi Swichkow used me to say to the congregation that real leaders are often in the minority, but they, like Caleb and Joshua, are often right.

I was more than a little embarrassed by his talk. It was bad enough that I was being singled out in public; no thirteen-year-old wants to be seen as different from the crowd, even for purposes of praise. Moreover, in my case, I knew that the praise was less than completely warranted. After all, I was not continuing with my Jewish studies out of a pure desire for more Jewish learning; I just wanted to go back to Ramah! That made me feel guilty as well; I was being held up as a leader for reasons that were not worthy of real leaders who sacrifice something for the good of others. In my case, my motives were instead completely, and embarrassingly, utilitarian.

I have often thought about what he said on that day. In part, I suppose, this is because even though I knew that the rabbi was not accurately describing me at the moment, I somehow felt challenged to measure up to the kind of leader he said I was. I do not know whether I have accomplished that particular feat, but it is not a bad thing to give teenagers—and adults, for that matter—goals to reach for. As I learned from Rabbi Jack Bloom, a psychologist, the very act of presenting a person with a view of himself that is positive—perhaps even somewhat more positive than the person actually is—sometimes gets the person to think of himself that way and to strive to manifest that positive characteristic. "You are a leader," "You are a compassionate person," "You like to learn about your heritage," "You make sure that others feel good about themselves," and so on—these are all important things to say to people, not only when they are deserved because of what they have already done, but also when you want to reinforce their own desire to aspire to a good goal. This is an important lesson for parents to learn in raising their children, for supervisors to use in encouraging their workers, and for any person to know in interpersonal relations generally.

Another lesson that I learned from Rabbi Swichkow's message to me that day is that human actions are often motivated by a variety of desires. In fact, we rarely do things for one reason alone; we may have one primary motive in our consciousness, but when we think about it, there are also other reasons why we do what we do. A potential convert to Judaism, for example, may begin a process for conversion primarily in order to marry a Jew, but that person should only ultimately convert if over the course of the conversion process he or she also becomes motivated to become Jewish for the sake of Judaism itself. When I was bar mitzvah, I was not continuing my Jewish studies because I had made a conscious decision that I wanted to learn more about Judaism, and I certainly did not do that to be a model and a leader among my peers. But there was, in truth, a part of me, motivated by a previous summer at Ramah, that wanted to return there to be further exposed to living a Jewish life as it had been presented there. The desire to probe my tradition further became a greater part of my conscious motivations as life went on, but already on my bar mitzvah day, it was there in nascent form.

Another story that happened at the same time pulled me in the opposite direction, but it was equally important in teaching me how to become a man. My grandfather built houses in Europe and then in the United States, and my father followed suit. My grandfather had learned to do this on the job, and my father learned the same skills, during his teenage years and early twenties, by serving as his father's apprentice. Then, my dad earned a college degree in civil engineering from the University of Wisconsin. With that credential, he was licensed to build not only houses, but also apartment and office buildings, both of which he did. He had his own company, and as his only son, I knew that the empty desk next to his was meant for me some day.

I loved mathematics and science—two subjects that I knew my father had studied in order to become an engineer. In fact, I almost majored in mathematics in college. I took several science courses and wrote my bachelor's thesis on the philosophy of science. I also loved the pride that my father exuded as he took me to the buildings that he was constructing. Even the smell of the wood was enticing.

But then, in seventh grade, I got a D in wood shop. That was clear evidence of the fact that I am, to use the politically correct terminology, "mechanically challenged." (My father said it more plainly; he said I had eleven thumbs!) Dad, though, sat me down and told me that men spend a large part of their lives at their work and that there are many men who hate their jobs, which is really sad because they are then spending much of their lives doing what they hate to do. My dad told me that he loved civil engineering, but he understood that I might not like it or be good at it. The important thing, he said, was to find something I loved doing and did well. It should be legal, but otherwise it could be anything I wanted.

I remember that conversation as if it were yesterday. It relieved me of the burden of feeling that I was expected to do what my father did for a living. It gave me the freedom to accept my limitations and to look for something that I wanted to do and could do well. It also reassured me that my father would feel proud of me, even if I did not do what he loved to do.

Precisely because that conversation was so important in my life, when each of my four children turned thirteen, I deliberately had the same discussion with each of them. Thankfully, each of them has found something that they love doing. None of them, by the way, is a rabbi, and only one of them is a professor—a professor of law.

And so, I return to the spies. Caleb and Joshua saw the same land that the other ten spies had seen, but they reported that the Israelites could conquer it, despite its challenges. Sometimes that kind of positive self-perception and that kind of faith in oneself and in God are all that are needed to accomplish more than we ever thought we could. So even if my rabbi's bar mitzvah talk engendered embarrassment and guilt in me, I now want to thank him for challenging me in the way he did that day.

At the same time, I want to thank my father for recognizing that what he loved to do may not be what I either wanted to do or was suited for; that expecting me to follow in his own footsteps and those of his father constituted a challenge that was neither appropriate nor healthy. From Rabbi Swichkow and my dad together, then, I learned that being a man required that one know when to stretch oneself and when to acknowledge one's desires and limits. Few lessons could have been as important for the process of becoming a man.

קרח
Korach

Can Egalitarianism Be Heretical?

Dennis Prager

Now Korach ... betook himself ... to rise up against
Moses, together with two hundred and fifty Israelites,
chieftains of the community, chosen in the assembly,
men of repute. They combined against Moses and Aaron
and said to them, "You have gone too far! For all the
community are holy, all of them, and the Lord is in their
midst. Why then do you raise yourselves above the
Lord's congregation?" (Numbers 16:1–3)

It is difficult to imagine a more relevant portion of the Torah than
that of Korach, the man who led a rebellion against Moses.

Far more than Moses (unfortunately), Korach represents the modern Western mentality and value system. Korach is the quintessential

---

DENNIS PRAGER is co-author of *The Nine Questions People Ask about Judaism* and *Why the Jews? The Reason for Antisemitism*, as well as author of *Think a Second Time* and *Happiness Is a Serious Problem*. He is the recipient of the American Jewish Press Association's Award for Excellence in Jewish Commentary. His widely heard nationally syndicated radio talk show is broadcast daily on over a hundred stations across America and around the world on the Internet. Dennis Prager is also a Fellow at the Hoover Institution at Stanford University and writes a weekly syndicated column. Called by Toastmasters "one of the five best speakers in America," he gives over a hundred speeches a year.

egalitarian, someone who believes not only that all men are created equal—a basic Torah position—but that they are equal no matter what they do. Whenever I read the story of Korach, I wonder how egalitarians understand the story. I suspect that most moderns, if asked what was morally wrong with Korach's argument, would have no coherent response. Indeed, deep down, they must have some sympathy for him.

His argument is the egalitarian argument that permeates modern culture. In his words (Number 16:3): "All of the community is holy, all of them. Who are you, Moses and Aaron, to set yourselves above us?"

The Korach argument is appealing: We are all equal in our holiness, in our goodness, and in just about every way; no one is better than anyone else—not even the man (and his brother) who led the Jews out of Egypt and talked directly with God. No achievement is necessary. No excellence need be pursued. If you breathe, you're holy.

This egalitarian thinking is what has led to the increasing abolition of the title "valedictorian" in senior high school classes. After all, the term signifies that one or two students have achieved more than all the rest. That's not equality.

This is the thinking that underlies giving all American children awards in sports. There are no better or worse players, or better or worse teams. All the kids—the ones who struck out every time they batted, the ones who didn't even play, and the ones who regularly got on base are all equal, all champions, deserving of an award.

This is the thinking that fills so many contemporary Western art galleries with manure—often literally, given all the scatological "art" that has been made in the recent past. No art is better or worse than any other art; all art is equal. It's all a matter of personal opinion. One person prefers Rembrandt, and another prefers the menstrual blood exhibit. All art is equal, all artists are equal, and all of us who look at art are equal.

Egalitarian thinking is especially applied to the moral realm. No one is better than anyone else; who are we to judge? And no act is really evil: "One man's terrorist is another man's freedom fighter." One need only recall the anger at President Ronald Reagan for calling the Soviet Union an "evil empire." Who was he to make to such a judgment? the Korachs of the time asked. "Who are you, Ronald Reagan, to set America above any another country?" So what if the Soviet Union was a totalitarian state, and America a free society?

The dispute within Judaism and Christianity regarding same-sex marriage is also largely about egalitarianism. Those in favor of redefining marriage to include same-sex couples would argue, "All loving unions are holy, all of them. Who are you, Torah-based Jews and Christians, to set man-woman unions as *kiddushin* [the Hebrew word for 'marriage,' meaning 'holy'] and not grant the status of *kiddushin* to same-sex unions?" (We are, of course, talking only about marriage here, not individuals; the gay individual is, needless to say, the human equal of the non-gay.)

Egalitarianism now even applies to animals. Increasing numbers of non-Torah-based Jews and non-Jews regard humans and animals as equally holy; they claim to see no difference between the holiness of a human being and that of an animal. Thus, the animal rights group PETA (People for the Ethical Treatment of Animals) has a campaign on behalf of vegetarianism called "Holocaust on Your Plate," in which the group morally equates the barbecuing of chickens with the burning of Jews during the Holocaust. Today's Korachs argue, "All living beings are holy, all of them. Who is anyone to set human beings above animals?"

The French Revolution elevated equality above all other values, along with fraternity and liberty (naively ignoring the fact that liberty and equality are in conflict). Since that time, in the West, and among the multitude of non-Westerners influenced by Western thought, there is almost no area of life in which equality has not been elevated above all other values.

The Torah, of course, believes that all people are created equal. One of its many world-changing doctrines was that all human beings are created in the image of God. But the Torah does not believe in egalitarianism. Some people are morally better, holier, than others. God deemed Noah a better person than everyone else in his generation. Jews say in the Shabbat *Kiddush* over wine, "You chose us and sanctified us from all the nations." The very notion of chosenness—though it never meant Jews are inherently better than anyone else or that only Jews are rewarded in the afterlife—is clearly not an egalitarian doctrine.

So Korach's argument that all of the Jewish community is equally holy found no support in the Torah. When Moses called upon God to adjudicate between him and Korach, God made His decision known rather clearly by having the earth swallow up Korach and his followers.

The draconian punishment God imposed on Korach can only be explained by the Torah's rejection of the egalitarian ideal. In the final analysis, egalitarianism is a form of idol worship because it ultimately leads to believing that man and God are equal, too. How can it not? At its core, egalitarianism is an attempt to overthrow authority—no one is above anyone else—and to overthrow standards, whether in baseball (all the kids get awards) or in morality. Egalitarianism ultimately comes from a desire not to be judged. And if there is no judgment, there is no Judge.

That is why God swallowed up Korach and his followers. Were God to swallow up today's Korachs, however, there wouldn't be many people left on earth. In fact, the Book of Numbers may have been the last time the egalitarians lost so decisively—until the American Revolution, whose values, not coincidentally, were largely based on the Torah. While, like the Torah, the Declaration of Independence affirms that "all men are created equal," its three paramount ideals, unlike the French Revolution's, are "life, liberty, and the pursuit of happiness." "Equality," in the way Korach and the French Revolution meant it, is not mentioned.

We are not, as Korach and modern egalitarians would have it, "all equally holy." Some people do indeed achieve greater holiness than other people. Holiness is earned through holy/moral/ethical behavior. Moses earned it. Mother Teresa earned it. Korach did not.

Why is the egalitarian ideal dominant in our time? In part, it is because of the feminization of society. Feminine values incline toward compassion (and therefore equality); masculine values incline toward standards (of excellence, holiness, and so on). A balanced world needs both feminine and masculine traits and values.

From the Torah's perspective, however, the masculine (representing standards) is specifically necessary for society to function properly. If compassion supersedes standards, society will fail. That is why, for example, the Torah warns, "Nor shall you show deference to a poor man in his dispute" (Exodus 23:3). If a rich man and a poor man appear in court, the Torah warns the judge not to decide the case using compassion. The judge's task is to seek justice (using standards), not equality (yearned for by compassion).

This does not mean the Torah is sexist. It depicts women and men as equals. Indeed, the creation story, which gives woman pride of place as the final act of creation, seems to suggest that she is further removed from the animal than man is and is, therefore, in some ways on a higher plane than man. But the Torah's governing societal values are masculine.

It is the feminine instinct toward compassion that pushes for equality of result—everyone who plays gets an award, "all the community are holy, all of them." It is the masculine instinct toward standards of excellence that insists that an award be given only to those who earn it, whether that award is a trophy or a higher level of holiness.

Chukat

My Father's "Vestments"

Rabbi Steven Z. Leder

Take Aaron and his son Eleazar and bring them up on Mount Hor. Strip Aaron of his vestments and put them on his son Eleazar. There Aaron shall be gathered unto the dead. (Numbers 20:25)

There is one tiny verse, often lost among the greater questions of *Chukat*. Toward the end of the portion when Aaron knows he is going to die, God commands that his priestly vestments be removed and placed upon his son, Eleazar: "Take Aaron and his son Eleazar and bring them up on Mount Hor. Strip Aaron of his vestments and put them on his son Eleazar. There Aaron shall be gathered unto the dead" (Numbers 20:25).

A father's life's work, his struggle and courage, now rests upon his son. As my own father's mind and body slowly slip away, I am beginning to understand this verse in new and profound ways.

RABBI STEVEN Z. LEDER is a rabbi at Wilshire Boulevard Temple in Los Angeles, California, and author of *The Extraordinary Nature of Ordinary Things* and *More Money Than God: Living a Rich Life without Losing Your Soul*.

Dear Dad,

Soon it will be Father's Day and we are thousands of miles apart, as we are far too often and far too long. So it seems a good time to write you and tell you—Dear God, what to tell you? How can a son possibly say what a father means to him—how can I say what you mean to me?

From the time I was a little boy, I always knew you were different. You threw a baseball like a girl. You didn't help with homework. You didn't cook burgers on Sunday afternoon. I never really understood why, until much later. Later I learned that there was no time for sports, or even school when you were growing up. You grew up poor—"burning wax paper to stay warm in the Minnesota winter" poor; "picking tin cans out of the dump" poor. Had you been born to the Dalit caste in India you would have been one of the children they call "ragpickers." You earned your living from the garbage of others. Later, I learned that when you were young and you would come home from school with a book, the laughter and ridicule were too much for a little boy to take. "Look at the professor!" they would say.

So you could never be the "Little League coaching, algebra tutoring" kind of dad. But we had other things, you and I. Fishing. How I loved to fish with you. Watching you row the boat across the lake, shirt off, tan, strong, eyes sparkling like the water. You were a giant. You were my dad. And we had long walks in the woods, smelling, tasting, and feeling the wonder of the great, green earth. "God is the best florist," you said.

I remember those Sundays when you and mom piled all five of us into the station wagon for an afternoon at the roller rink. Gliding across the floor, holding mom's hand, whirling, bending, effortless, transcendent, grace and speed, smiling and alive. It was the only time I ever saw you dance. You learned it all working there as a kid, sweeping up the floor after closing time.

Work. If there was one thing you were going to teach your children, it was work. When I was young I never really noticed that you came home with bloody hands and frostbitten toes, wounds from the war you waged for forty years at Leder Brother's Scrap Iron and

Metal. You filled the bathtub and laid in it each late night when you came home, just trying to get warm.

I never considered the fear and the responsibility you must have shouldered. Married at eighteen with five children to feed by the time you were thirty. Yes, work was your salvation. Or so I thought. Now, I know better. Now I know you were never working for yourself. To this day, in spite of your success, you have a hard time spending money. For God's sake, Dad, how many guys who've made it still reuse their dental floss because they can't stand wasting a perfectly good piece? No, you were never working for yourself. You were working for me. For Marilyn, Sherry, Joanne, and Greg, too. And you were teaching us to work for ourselves. I started cleaning toilets and scrubbing floors on my knees at the scrap yard when I was five. "You have to start at the bottom," you'd bark. It was harsh. It was true.

Once, when I was supposed to pull the weeds around all the shrubs in the backyard, you made me do it again because I hadn't been thorough. Then, hours later you came and pulled me off the street where I was playing with my friends, to make me do the job a third time, until it was right. When I got caught shoplifting at Target, you had three truckloads of dirt dumped on our driveway, handed me a wheelbarrow and shovel, and said, "Spread it over the yard, front and back." It took the entire summer. It was a punishment, a humbling reminder, and it worked. I turned around that summer. Hard work was your salvation, and somehow, it had become mine. It still is and always will be.

Resorting mostly now to old Yiddishisms from your past—your sharp edges rounded by time and brain atrophy—when I nearly crumble from the expectations placed upon a rabbi who can only do so much, you smile and simply say, "Az m'schtupdis gatis [If you push it, it goes]." Can I ever thank you enough for teaching me about the folly of shortcuts and the salvation of a job well done; for teaching me to haul a load when it's dumped on me and shut up about it?

We never talked much about women, but somehow I grew up respecting women because you always demanded that I respect my *sisters and my mother. We never talked much about Judaism, but you brought me to shul with you to say Kaddish for your father. One December when I was six or seven, you walked the beach with me in Miami for hours, teaching me the blessing for the Chanukah candles so that I could take my turn along with my sisters. You sent me off to Israel when I was sixteen, and when we said good-bye at the airport, it was the first time I ever saw you cry.*

We never talked much about education, ideas, or the world, but from the time I was a little boy, you said, "There's always money for books." Later, you sent me to Oxford to study Shakespeare, to study in Israel, to tour Europe and Russia. You supported me through college and five years of graduate school. The boy who was teased by his ignorant, immigrant parents for wanting to read became the father whose mantra was, "There's always money for books. There's always money for books."

We never talked much about tzedakah, but somehow you were always helping someone who had much less. We never talked much about family, but somehow you raised five children who live today without a shred of sibling rivalry because we had a father who knew how to forgive. Somehow you managed to rework your worldview, a world of truck drivers and fag jokes, to embrace a son, my brother, who is gay.

We never talked much about marriage, but at our wedding you looked at Betsy and me, raised your glass with a wide smile, and simply said, "May you always be each other's best friend." After all these years of performing weddings myself, of counseling sessions with hundreds of couples, of volumes read on love and marriage, leave it to you to get to the heart of it all in one sentence—a good marriage is really a good friendship.

We never talked much about being a mensch, but I never saw you favor rich over poor, beautiful over ordinary, Jew over non-Jew, man over woman, white over black. Phoniness never impressed you. You always loved simple things: a perfect avocado or ripe tangerine—preferably free from the neighbor's tree; your old flannel shirt; Butter Brickle ice cream on a hot Saturday night; Hank Williams; the warm sun and a hot bath—you were always just trying to get warm. And no matter what sort of cold or trouble came our family's way, you reminded us that it was a lot better than a "geshveer off der hintin [a boil on your ass]!" And no matter how proud we were of any accomplishment, we had to keep our head about us because "ah kotz ken iss kaliyamachen [even a cat could f-ck it up]."

In this week's Torah portion when Aaron is about to die, he takes off his priestly vestments and puts them on his son Eleazar. It's our tradition's way of saying that we must carry on the work of our fathers—that eventually they must live through us. This Father's Day, I am beginning to understand that.

Lately, I've noticed something about us, Dad. We never used to, but now we end every phone call by saying, "I love you." I think it's because somehow we sense that ever so slowly, we're getting closer to Aaron and Eleazar—nearer to the end than we are to the beginning.

It's hard for a rabbi to have any pretty illusions about life, which is all the more reason why I am writing this letter. I have seen so many people lose their fathers this year, and there's a certain ache in them that I know will never leave. There are so many for whom Kaddish is no longer a mere collection of words. None of us gets to hold on to our fathers forever. How well I know it.

So my letter to you will also be my message to anyone with a dad who reads this week's Torah portion. It's a little reminder to thank God for Aaron and Eleazar; for Lenny and Steve; for all the fathers who teach their children about God's green earth, hard work, women and friendship, and money for books. It's a reminder to push forward every day, because trouble is fleeting and so is success. Most of all, as I am sure the Torah would put it to each and every son, it's a reminder to be a mensch while trying to stay warm in a sometimes cold world.

Happy Father's Day, Dad. I love you.

Steve

בלק

Balak

The Ass Sees What Man Cannot

RABBI WALTER HOMOLKA, PhD, DHL

Then the Lord uncovered Balaam's eyes, and he saw the angel of the Lord standing in the way, his drawn sword in his hand; thereupon he bowed right down to the ground. The angel of the Lord said to him, "Why have you beaten your ass these three times? It is I who came out as an adversary, for the errand is obnoxious to me. And when the ass saw me, she shied away because of me those three times. If she had not shied away from me, you are the one I should have killed, while sparing her."
(Numbers 22:31–33)

Balaam, the son of Beor, is a prophet living on the Euphrates River. According to the biblical narrative, Balaam's prophecy turns out to be in favor of Israel, despite his original adverse intentions. Balak, the king of the Moabites, promises Balaam great honor and gifts if he

---

RABBI WALTER HOMOLKA holds a PhD from King's College, London, and a D.H.L. from Hebrew Union College–Jewish Institute of Religion. He is an adjunct full professor of Jewish studies at the University of Potsdam (Germany). The chairman of the Leo Baeck Foundation, he serves as rector of the university's Abraham Geiger College for the training of rabbis and cantors. Rabbi Homolka is also an executive board member of the World Union for Progressive Judaism. He is coauthor of *How to Do Good and Avoid Evil: A Global Ethic from the Sources of Judaism* (SkyLight Paths).

will come to Moab with his emissaries to curse Israel. Balaam first replies: I cannot do that; I can only say what God tells me. Still, Balak desperately wants Balaam to come to Moab.

The figure of Balaam is ambiguous. His involvement in battle, his role as a royal counselor, and foremost of all, his occupation with the holy seem to represent typically male spheres. In the Jewish and the Christian traditions, he is described as a sinner: someone who loved money more than the truth; proud, cunning, duplicitous, cruel, and sanctimonious, someone who ended in hell. These judgments are based less on this week's passage, but rather on later passages in Numbers, Deuteronomy, and Joshua. In the Qur'an and in the later Islamic tradition, Balaam is not mentioned by name but is described as a miscreant and equated with a dog.

There are, however, other voices regarding Balaam. The Rabbis understood that he was, above all, a prophet. In the midrash *Sifrei Devarim* 357, he is even compared to Moses. God gave human beings such as Balaam and Job the gift of prophecy so that they, in turn, could lead others to God and so that other peoples could not say that God is accessible only to Israel (Midrash, *Tanna d'bei Eliyahu* 28). One thing is certain: Balaam has a special ability. He sees more than other human beings do. He experiences visions. And his words possess great power. What a man! Many believe that those blessed by Balaam remain blessed and those cursed by him remain cursed.

Balaam knows very well that he should not curse the people of Israel, a people blessed by God. Nonetheless, Balaam—tempted and in pursuit of advantage—finally agrees to travel to King Balak, and with this, his precipitous path begins. He takes quite a risk, and he could easily fail. An angel of God attempts to halt him, but Balaam does not even see this danger. Will he do what God commands?

With Balaam our text seems to draw a picture of a typical man: strong, bold, visionary, courageous, strategic, stopping at nothing, a leader. And it depicts the darker sides as well: unreliable, cruel, acquisitive, haughty, selfish, stubborn, obstinate, someone who plunges into things. It is good that his she-ass balks before Balaam walks straight into the angel's sword! The ass, which sees the danger, saves Balaam.

Is it not odd that of all creatures an ass should be the corrective counterpart of Balaam, the prophet? The ass is one of the oldest domestic animals and is mentioned often in the Bible as a mount and a draft and pack animal (Exodus 4:20; Genesis 42:26; Deuteronomy 22:10). Despite its usefulness, even to the present day it is often perceived with disdain.

In contrast to this, in Berlin in 1797, the Jewish philosopher Saul Ascher published a "Eulogy for the Ass" (*Lobschrift auf den Esel*). His friend, the German poet and Jewish satirist Heinrich Heine, also compares the respect that asses merited in earlier periods to the reputation they now have. "Modern asses are great asses," Heine writes. "The ancient asses, which were so highly cultured, would turn in their graves if they heard how their descendants were being discussed. Once upon a time, 'ass' was an honorable title. It was equivalent to the titles Counselor, Baron, Doctor Philosophiae. Jacob compares his son Issachar, Homer his hero Ajax, and nowadays we compare Lord ... to an ass" (*The Book Le Grand*, chapter 13). In his writings, Heine refers to Balaam and his ass several times.

Even today in the Orient, the ass is considered a notably intelligent animal that is not only patient, but also understanding. Asses were the traditional mounts of nobility (Judges 12:14) and later of kings (Zechariah 9:9), the favorite animal of prophets and of those who come in peace. In addition, an ass always leads the large caravans of camels. It sets the route and it sets the pace of the caravan.

And so, in the Torah portion under discussion here, the she-ass even begins to speak and says to Balaam, "Do I deserve this?" Its words are affectionate and show understanding of the wild threats of its rider. So, asses could speak wisely in the old days, and nobody found anything wrong with it. How exciting that asses should speak at all! With his usual sarcasm, Heinrich Heine writes, "Nor have I ever seen an ass, at least any four-footed one, that spoke as a man, though I have often met men who, whenever they opened their mouths, spoke as asses" (*Religion and Philosophy in Germany*, part 1).

So asses are depicted as wise and respectable, highly cultured, patient and affectionate, understanding, intuitive, as symbols of peace, and also leaders, if of a different style. To me, the ass seems to represent a contrasting, complementing character to Balaam.

Is it not a hint that this fine animal should be female? Perhaps we should abstract from the plain surface of the story—the interaction of a prophet with his donkey—and look at what might be behind it.

In an essay on the form of the fable, written in 1759, the German dramatist, philosopher, and aesthetician Gotthold Ephraim Lessing, who was a friend of Moses Mendelssohn, writes, "The miraculous is the highest degree of the new." In any fable, such as the narrative of Balaam and his she-ass, a moral thesis is illustrated by animals that talk and act like human beings while retaining their animal traits. As in George Orwell's famous work *Animal Farm* (1945), the animal needs to be seen in human terms, expressing a moral teaching and insight to us that was formerly hidden.

Even if some Jewish interpreters have tried very hard to reconcile the wonder of the speaking ass and the world of natural laws, I am convinced that our text is not about God's intervention in nature at all. Instead, it uses figurative language to demonstrate that this great and proud man is incapable of seeing with his abilities and gifts what his female partner could perceive—and that the faculty of rational cognition is limited and fragile in contrast to the feminine intuition, which is exerted by the she-ass. This presupposes the she-ass's intuitive ability, goodness, and loyalty as well as its strength to be stubborn. Through feminine intuition, loyalty, and perseverance, Balaam finally acknowledges God's will. He should bless, not curse.

The main emphasis of this story, one that is full of irony and hidden humor, lies not in the ass speaking. Rather, that it is Balaam's feminine counterpart—endowed with a love of peace, moderation, and intuition—who can peer into the future and into another world, whereas the seer himself, in pursuit of immediate advantage and opportunity, remains blind.

פינחס
Pinchas

The Seduction of Zealotry

RABBI TONY BAYFIELD, DD

The Lord spoke to Moses, saying, "Pinchas, son of Eleazar son of Aaron the priest, has turned back My anger from the Israelites by displaying among them his zeal for Me, so that I did not wipe out the Israelite people in My zeal. Say, therefore, 'I grant him My pact of friendship. It shall be for him and his descendants after him a pact of priesthood for all time, because he was zealous for his God, thus making expiation for the Israelites.'" (Numbers 25:10–13 [my translation—TB])

I stand up in honor of the Torah, and with my eyes and my posture, I follow it around the synagogue out of respect. But not as a sacred totem, or as a manifesto carefully crafted for ease of maximum buy-in. I know that this is a document touched by God because of its elusive character, its deceptive complexity, and the depth of challenge

---

RABBI TONY BAYFIELD, DD (Lambeth), earned a masters degree in law from Cambridge University before training for the rabbinate at Leo Baeck College in London. A former congregational rabbi, he now serves as head of the Movement for Reform Judaism in Britain. Rabbi Bayfield teaches personal theology at Leo Baeck College and is a specialist in modern Jewish thought. He is a widower with three children, one of whom received rabbinic ordination from Leo Baeck College.

that it throws down. Like God, it will not be possessed or summoned to yield simple truths. It does not provide an incontrovertible program with which to capture the souls of others. Rather, it bothers, provokes, disturbs. Sometimes even "touched by God" will not do. There are dark passages and characters in the Torah, passages displaying zealotry and applauding violence—by men.

Pinchas.

We are near both the end of the Book of Numbers and the borders of the Promised Land—in fact, at a place called Shittim (meaning "acacia trees"). The "sons of Israel" have become involved with local women, and they have embraced them in immoral and idolatrous practices. A plague is raging. Just as Moses is about to deal with the situation, Pinchas, grandson of Aaron and son of Aaron's son Eleazar, grabs hold of a spear, rushes into a private chamber, finds an Israelite man called Zimri having sex with a Midianite woman called Cozbi, and dispatches them both through the stomach. The plague is checked, the defection is halted, and God rewards Pinchas with the pact of hereditary priesthood.

By and large, the traditional Jewish sources accept and approve of Pinchas's act of zealotry. The end amply justifies the means. How could that not be so, since the text of the Torah itself explicitly endorses Pinchas's act? Yet hereditary priesthood is high reward, indeed, for the work of an impulsive, murderous moment—an act that is characteristically male.

During my student days at the Leo Baeck College in London, I remember being introduced to a particular midrashic sequence from a collection known as *Midrash Tanchuma*, in which both the ancient authors and my teacher Professor Raphael Loewe reveled in the details: where, precisely, the spear entered and exited, and the exact position that Zimri and Cozbi had adopted at the moment they were caught *in flagrante delicto* (in the middle of the sexual act). This midrash turns Pinchas into something of a strong man and has him running around the camp with the unfortunate couple impaled on his spear like an exotic kabab.

Pinchas turns up in later midrashic tradition in various positive places: at the head of the Israelites in their campaign against Midian, intent on completing the good work he himself had begun by slaying Cozbi (*Bemidbar Rabbah* 22:4); avenging his maternal grandfather Joseph, who had been sold into slavery by the Midianites (*Sifrei Bemidbar* 157; Talmud, *Sotah* 43a); miraculously slaying Balaam (Talmud, *Sanhedrin* 106b); as one of the two spies sent by Joshua to Jericho (*Targum Yerushalmi* on Numbers 21:22), where he managed to make himself invisible like an angel (presumably he could be trusted to enter Jericho without having recourse to the services of its best-known inhabitant, the harlot Rahab).

The Mishnah goes so far as to codify the incident: "If a man ... cohabits with a gentile woman, he may be struck down by zealots" (*Sanhedrin* 9:6). A midrash portrays Pinchas recalling this *halachah* (law) as legal justification for his own behavior (*Sifrei Bemidbar* 131)—even without Moses's permission, presumably because Moses was paralyzed by his own marriage to a Midianite woman (Exodus 2:16–21; Talmud, *Sanhedrin* 82a; *Bemidbar Rabbah* 20:24).

But the way the story is dealt with in contemporary Jewish biblical commentary is terribly fascinating. I quote at some length from W. Gunther Plaut, the renowned Canadian rabbi and scholar, whose master work, *The Torah: A Modern Commentary*, was first published in 1981.

Plaut raises the moral question of how a priceless reward could be given for an act of killing:

> By postbiblical and especially contemporary standards the deed and its rewards appear to have an unwarranted relationship. But the story is biblical and must be appreciated in its own context. To begin with, [Pinchas] is rewarded not so much for slaying the transgressors as for saving his people from God's destructive wrath. But, even if we assume that the text concentrates on the former merit, we must remember that the Moabite fertility cult was to the Israelites the incarnation of evil and the mortal enemy of their religion.[1]

Plaut then goes on to quote the biblical scholar George E. Mendenhall, who identifies the plague with bubonic plague, and he suggests that Zimri was following a pagan precedent for dealing with the affliction (it is remarkable what one used to be able to get in public health benefits!). Plaut, however, concludes:

> [Pinchas] did not act out of superior medical knowledge. He saw in Zimri's act an open breach of the covenant, a flagrant return to the practices that the compact at Sinai had foresworn.... This was the first incident in which God's power over life and death (in a juridical sense) passed to the people. [Pinchas]'s impulsive deed was not merely a kind of battle-field execution but reflected his apprehension that the demands of God needed human realization and required a memorable and dramatic example against permissiveness in the religious realm.[2]

Some voices from the classical period sound much more disturbed by Pinchas than Plaut appears to be. A passage in Talmud, *Sanhedrin* 82a struggles with the legal problems. Why was there no warning before Pinchas's violent act? Why was there no evidence presented? Why was there no trial? The answer that emerges is that the act was licit only because the couple was caught *in flagrante delicto*. If they had *finished* fornicating, then Pinchas's zealotry would have been murder. If Zimri had turned on Pinchas and killed him first, he would not have been liable to the death penalty, since Pinchas was a pursuer seeking to take his life. Even here the Rabbinic anxiety is more convincing than the conclusions at which they arrive to allay it. In the nineteenth century, Rabbi Samson Raphael Hirsch, the founder of modern Orthodoxy, offers the same lame explanation: "Pinchas acted meritoriously only because he punished the transgression *in flagrante delicto* in the act. Had he done it afterwards, it would have been murder."[3]

That same passage from *Sanhedrin* also reports Rabbi Hisda as explicitly stating that anyone consulting "us" (meaning, the Sages) about how to act in a similar situation would not be instructed to emulate Pinchas's example. It is interesting to note that a connection is made between Pinchas's slaying of Zimri and Cozbi, and Moses's slaying of the Egyptian overseer (Exodus 2:12). Because the Exodus text offers little comment and refrains from explicit praise of Moses, the Rabbis felt more able to voice doubts in this present context. Some even connect Moses's act of killing with the punishment of not being allowed to enter the Promised Land. But they are still a minority.

Let's go back to the passage from Rabbi Plaut: "This was the first incident in which God's power over life and death (in a juridical sense) passed to the people." I have severe doubts about religious traditions and religious authorities abrogating God's power over life and death, and those words "in a juridical sense" only increase my discomfort. For there is no juridical context for Pinchas's act. He acted alone; as the text implies, it was without the approval of Moses or the religious, political, and legal authorities of his time. There was no warning, no evidence adduced, and no trial. As Plaut says, Pinchas's act "reflected his apprehension that the demands of God needed human realization and required a memorable and dramatic example against permissiveness in the religious realm." In this, Plaut is in accord with an early twentieth-century Orthodox commentator, Baruch Epstein, author of *Torah Temimah*. According to Epstein, there is justification if such a deed is "animated by a genuine, unadulterated [sic] spirit of zeal to advance the glory of God."[4]

For me, that is the clearest remit for and definition of zealotry and fanaticism that I know. It is the ultimate reversal of a wonderful Hasidic adage, "Take care of your own soul and another person's body, not of another person's soul and your own body." It encapsulates that terrifying absolute certainty that you know what God requires and that others do not. It declares with total conviction that human beings can stand in God's place and hold sway over life and death, that we can execute, not in self-defense, not in the defense of the lives of others, but to advance our own religious agenda and protect our own religious point of view. It seems to me to be a peculiarly male failing.

I do not have to spell out contemporary examples of those who appear to have seen in Pinchas and in similar scriptural authorities not simply justification but inspiration for becoming God and doing God's supposed murderous will. In fact, I can explain part of my discomfort with Plaut's view by just how much the world has (apparently) changed over the last almost three decades since his Torah commentary was first published—how much more aware we are of the resurgence of fundamentalist zealotry, religious fanaticism, and violent patriarchy.

Jews recall Brooklyn-born physician Baruch Goldstein, who, just before Purim in 1994 and apparently with the story of Esther in mind, murdered twenty-nine Muslims in the Ibrahimi Mosque over the Cave of Machpelah in Hebron. We recall Yigal Amir, who believed that he was saving Israel by assassinating Prime Minister Yitzhak Rabin. Christians, too, have their fundamentalist zealots who are prepared to threaten violence, bomb, and commit murder at abortion clinics. Islam has been hideously defaced by kidnappers and suicide bombers, for whom every conceivable act of inhumanity—and some that were even inconceivable before they were perpetrated—is justified by their religio-political goals and "suitable" texts from the Qur'an.

For me, zealotry and fanaticism are deeply disturbing facets of religion. Pinchas is a terrifying role model, a dark character who seduces his fellow men from dark passages in our holy Torah.

So there we have it—a text against which I rebel from the very heart of my being. It is not that I cannot wrestle with it; it is not that I mind being challenged by it; and it is certainly not that I cannot find some things of merit, interest, and religious quality within the narrative. But I rebel because it can be read and heard as having authority, as being worthy of reverence, as being God's word—which it is not. It can be taken up and used in ways that are absolutely antithetical to religion, to humanity, and to the name of God. Too much of the commentary on this text, both ancient and modern, is self-justifying rather than self-critical, supporting blind obedience and justifying zealotry and fanaticism.

I stand up in honor of the Torah, and with my eyes and my posture, I follow it around the synagogue out of the respect that is due it. For this is a document touched by God. Like God, it does not offer a simple menu of impressive sound bites, homely truths, and responsibility-absolving instructions. Rather, it challenges us even to the extent of asking us to struggle with texts that we ourselves can misunderstand, misuse, or leave as hostages to fortune. It demands that we accept the fact that there are dark passages that are not God's but ours, still ours—we men—even in Torah.

מטות
Mattot

Jewish Warriors and Boundary Crossings

The Lord spoke to Moses, saying, "Avenge the Israelite people on the Midianites; then you shall be gathered to your kin." Moses spoke to the people, saying, "Let men be picked out from among you for a campaign, and let them fall upon Midian to wreak the Lord's vengeance on Midian." (Numbers 31:1–3)

Part I: A gathering of tribesmen of the tribe of Judah, somewhere outside the Land of Israel

Listen my brothers! Some of you know me; I am Yehudah ben Avraham ben Ben Zion ben Yehudah. I am your fellow tribesman of Judah, and I have the honor of being your new commanding officer. Many of you knew my older brother, Michael ben Avraham, who led you so valiantly in our war against the Ammonites last year, but, sadly, my brother died from wounds that he suffered in that campaign.

DOUG BARDEN is executive director of the Men of Reform Judaism (MRJ) and is author of *Wrestling with Jacob and Esau: Fighting the Flight of Men* and *Making Time for Sacred Fellowship: MRJ's BenAbbaZeyde Programs—A Men's Workbook and Facilitator's Guide.*

I have gathered you here this morning because I have just come from a meeting with the commanding officers of our fellow tribes. We met personally with our great leader, Moses.

This is what I have come to tell you—or, rather, this is what I have come to ask of you.

It has been nearly forty years since we left Egypt. Look around. Other than our war leader Joshua, the scout Caleb, and, of course, Moses, who remains from those years of slavery? No one! Our grandfathers, our grandmothers, our fathers, our mothers, maybe even your older brothers and sisters, all who endured and then fled from a world of bondage and slavery—they are all gone. Old age, plague, natural disasters, and war have taken their toll on our elders. We are all that is left. We are the new generation, hardened and tested by our years wandering in the desert. We are the men who must now take responsibility to ensure that our people finally reach the end of our wandering, the end of our common journey. We owe it to those who came before us—and to those who will come after us—to complete the mission.

My brothers, fellow Jewish warriors: Moses has heard from our Lord that we are commanded to gather a force of twelve thousand men—one thousand from each of our tribes—and to strike down our Midianite foes. I am sure I do not have to remind you of the ongoing treachery of our Midianites. No—rather than the Midianite men meeting us in the field of battle with swords and spears, they have used their women as lethal weapons to defeat us in a different kind of battlefield. You know the consequences. As our brethren have been weakened by coupling with these whores, our Lord's wrath has been felt, and the dreaded plague is upon us. Thousands have died, weakening our numbers, weakening our resolve. We must destroy the Midianites before they destroy us.

Join with me, and may Pinchas be your role model! I am sure you have heard the story. Pinchas, now High Priest Pinchas, son of Eleazar, grandson of Aaron the priest, was with Moses and others the day that Zimri, the son of a chieftain of the tribe of Simeon, brazenly paraded his Midianite whore Cozbi before them. What was Zimri thinking? Did he honestly think that the superstition that whoring with her, a wanton prostitute, was true and would cure the plague? Pinchas acted in the name of God, and drove a spear through the sexual organs of both Zimri and Cozbi, striking them dead on the spot (Numbers 25:6–9).

The plague has ended. Moreover, Pinchas has been rewarded by Moses, as God commanded, and received his *brit shalom*, the covenant of peace with God. If you have any doubts that Pinchas has acted as our Lord would want, know this: Pinchas, not Joshua, will now lead us in battle against the Midianites.

We are so close. We are nearing the end of our journey in the wilderness, and we are nearly at the gates of the Promised Land. We are about to cross into the Land promised to our forefathers and foremothers. But our enemies are doing more than preventing us from crossing a geographic boundary of valleys, rivers, and streams. The plague that befell us was not because our Lord was angered so much by our sleeping with Midianite women. No, much worse. It was because we were so ready to adopt their gods, especially their powerful god of fertility, Baal Peor.

This is not just a battle over olive fields, over cattle, donkeys, or sheep, or over women. Rather, we are engaged in a holy war. The way of our Lord is pitted against the idolatry of the Midianites. Before we can cross into the Promised Land, we must be prepared to defend a different kind of boundary. This is not a boundary of valleys, rivers, and streams, but of moral codes, of laws that say what is right and what is wrong. It is a spiritual boundary that says there is only one God and that the greatest transgression of all—the worse boundary crossing of them all—is idolatry. No shelter can be given to idolatrous behavior. It must be thwarted. It must end. We must protect our spiritual boundaries at all costs! Failure is not an option. If we fail to act, we abandon our promise, our covenant with our God. We cannot do that. We must not do that. We must protect our loved ones. This is what Jewish men, Jewish warriors, do! We are God's warriors!

I ask you to act decisively. Join me now in this campaign. As your leader, I vow to you that I will fight right there beside you to strike down every Midianite. I do not make or say this vow lightly. May my words be spoken from my heart, and may you, my community of brothers, and our Lord hold me accountable. For the sake of our wives, our sisters, our parents now gone, and especially for our children and our children's children, join me in this campaign to wipe out the Midianites once and for all!

Part II: The Israelite camp, several days later

My friends, my brothers, my comrades in arms: Congratulations! We have been victorious! By your hands and the hands of your fellow Israelite men, the Midianite men have been defeated, each and every one of them. Their fields and villages have been burned. We have wiped them off the field of battle. Yes—shouts of glory, back slapping, and hora dancing are in order! The booty is plentiful— gold and silver, and tens of thousands of cattle, donkeys, sheep, and, yes, women, have been taken and will be distributed to you shortly!

Can any one of you doubt that we acted in the name of the Lord? Not one of your brothers died in this battle. Not one! Surely this is a sign that God was on our side. Go now; the priests are waiting to assist you with the purification rituals. We cannot let the dead defile our community. Their blood, and their idolatry, must be ritually washed away.

My work is not yet complete. For, to be honest, when we, your commanders, returned from battle and reported our success to Eleazar and Moses, Moses's response was not the one we anticipated. His disappointment came fast and furious: "You have spared every female! Yet they are the very ones who, at the bidding of Balaam, induced the Israelites to trespass against the Lord in the matter of Peor, so that the Lord's community was struck by the plague" (Numbers 31:15–16).

Our orders are now clear: every Midianite male, no matter how young, is to be put to the sword; and every Midianite female who has had carnal knowledge is to be put to the sword (but, men, don't worry; there are still thousands of virgins left as booty for you to take as wives or concubines).

As your leader, I failed you. I failed my fellow leaders, I failed Moses, and most of all I failed our God. But, we will undo our failure and complete God's work.

Part III: The present day, at a gathering of men

On the one hand, we could start this section with just one word—one short question in Yiddish: "*Nu?*"—which we might best translate as: "So, what do you think? What are you going to do now? Are you prepared to be a Jewish warrior?"

But there is a longer version.

While the details of the preceding story come out of the Torah portion, I have obviously added my personal interpretation (including the invention of the character Yehudah ben Avraham as well as his older brother, Michael ben Avraham), in order to highlight what I feel is the real purpose of its inclusion in our Torah. Sometimes, there is no room for mercy; sometimes there is no other alternative but total annihilation of your enemy. This is especially true when our community of faith is threatened. You are free to either agree or disagree with that point, but our Torah scribes were trying to make precisely that point.

If we were to sum up the perceptions of many Rabbinic commentators on this *parashah*, the word would (once again) be a Yiddish expression: *Oy!* For those who have difficulty envisioning an avenging God, protecting His (yes, "His") turf; for those who like their God to be warm, merciful, and cuddly all the time; or for those who like to think Jews are at their best only when winning Nobel prizes, this *parashah* is nothing short of embarrassing.

On the other hand, I am someone who spends a great of time traveling around the country engaging Reform Jewish men, trying to help them find better ways to connect to their faith besides the traditional synagogue ushering and *sukkah* building. I have been trying to convince them that Torah study is an extraordinary well for contemporary adult Jewish men to draw from for their spiritual journey. Therefore, this *parashah* is on my "to do" list to share at workshops. Why? Because it raises so many important and difficult questions that contemporary Jewish men need to explore:

What does it mean to be a contemporary Jewish warrior? Rabbi Allan Tuffs makes an important distinction between a "warrior" and the modern soldier:

> The warrior should not be confused with the ideal of the modern solider although some modern soldiers are certainly warriors. While the soldier and the warrior share many of the same qualities, they differ in at least one significant way. The ideal solider is cut off from most of his feelings. He is encouraged to numb himself to all emotions except anger. The warrior, on the other hand, is a man who is in touch with the full spectrum of his feelings. He feels passionately about the causes he supports. Although fierceness is part of his emotional composition, the warrior can show tenderness and experience vulnerability.[1]

In part I of the story, our speaker and his audience are all prepared to be warriors. But, when the commanding officer goes off to kill women and little children, do we find ourselves still rooting for this Jewish warrior?

Do we, as fathers, even want our sons to grow up and become warriors? How can nice Jewish boys also be warriors? But this isn't just a story about warriors; it is a story about *Jewish* warriors. That is the most critical, and simultaneously, disturbing aspect of this *parashah*. The killing of the Midianite children and women may be disturbing to modern sensibilities. We often try to interpret and explain it, apologetically, by trying to place it within its historical context. For me, however, it is simply another example of the Bible's consistent attitude toward idolatry, in which no quarter can be given. If you worship anything other than our God, the consequences will be swift and terrible. No mercy. Expect harsh heavenly judgment.

Have we reached a point with our modern, liberal sensibilities that we can no longer imagine that "defending our faith" could ever require such extreme measures as resorting to total destruction of our enemy, young and old, male and female alike? Are we afraid that by admitting this possibility, we become too similar to those who preach jihad against us today? Does that place us too close to those whose ideology defined us as less than human and had no pangs of conscience when they sent our elders and small infants to the death camps?

As someone who considers himself a contemporary Reform Jew, and therefore, a "liberal," I can't help but pose the questions: When does it become ethnically incorrect to think of ourselves as "members of a tribe," with hard, solid boundaries dividing "us" from "them"? When does it become religiously archaic to think of a fierce, demanding, and potentially wrathful God who is supremely "Other"? When, in liberal Reform circles, does it become politically incorrect to wonder aloud whether our interfaith marriage rate is somehow the result of our own failure to "man" the boundaries? Perhaps the "nice Jewish boy" model hasn't served our community as well as we thought it would. Perhaps it is time for us to revisit our buried Jewish warrior spirit.

When we do so, let us also admit that it is time to open the gender gates. It is time for "Jewish warriors" to not only be *male* warriors. After all, is the warrior spirit—the basic instinct to defend what you love—only a masculine trait? Is the impetus to fight for what you believe is right and just only a masculine trait? Are traits such as bravery, duty, self-sacrifice, and discipline only reserved for men? If our community still admires and encourages those traits, then they must belong not only to our sons, but also to our daughters. I welcome opening a meaningful dialogue with my contemporary sisters and brothers to elicit what I am sure will be their varied responses.

Mattot is telling us that maintaining our covenant means ensuring our survival as a faithful religious community. That survival requires that we be ready to establish and defend our boundaries. Those who defend our boundaries and our community are Jewish warriors.

And sometimes, words are not sufficient.

מסעי
Masei

Resting Places on the Journey

RABBI ARTHUR GREEN

**These are the journeys of the children of Israel who
went forth from Egypt in their multitudes, by the hand
of Moses and Aaron. Moses wrote their goings forth to
journey by the mouth of God; these are their journeys
as they went forth.**
(Numbers 33:1–2 [my translation, here and in the rest of the
commentary—AG])

If there is a new Kabbalah, or Jewish secret doctrine, to be revealed
for our age, I have long suspected that its biblical basis will be this
seemingly obscure portion, which contains a list of the various stopping places in the course of Israel's forty-year journey through the
wilderness. The Torah reading tradition, at least as practiced in the
Ashkenazic synagogue, recognizes a mysterious quality in these
place names, chanting them in a special lilting tune that is used only
here and at the Song of the Sea.

RABBI ARTHUR GREEN is Irving Brudnick Professor of Jewish Philosophy
and Religion and rector of the Rabbinical School at Hebrew College in Boston,
Massachusetts. He is author or editor of many books, including *Tormented
Master: The Life and Spiritual Quest of Rabbi Nahman of Bratslav*; *Seek My Face:
A Jewish Mystical Theology*; and *Ehyeh: A Kabbalah for Tomorrow* (all Jewish
Lights). His newest book is *Radical Judaism: Hasidism for a New Era*.

Imagine Moses writing them down as he completes the Torah, just before giving his great final speeches. He knows that he is not to enter the Promised Land, that he will have no part in the "glory of battle" that lies ahead. Instead, he chooses to leave his people with a list of all those places in which they had camped along the way, back when they were still just wanderers. But this record of travels, seemingly meaningless and perhaps confused meanderings around the desert wasteland, is not written down just as a memento for future generations. There is something sacred in the list of place names—a secret yet to be revealed.

> They journeyed from Elim and camped at Yam-Suf. They journeyed from Yam-Suf and camped at Midbar Sin. They journeyed from Midbar Sin and camped at Dofkah. They journeyed from Dofkah and camped at Alush. They journeyed from Alush and camped at Rephidim, where there was no water for the people to drink. They journeyed from Rephidim and camped at Midbar Sinai. They journeyed from Midbar Sinai and camped at the Graves of Desire.... (Numbers 33: 10–16)

Journeys, wanderings. The reason we will write our own Kabbalah around them is because we, too, are wanderers. In the private religion of our own inner lives, we all have such sacred lists, all the important stopping places in our journeys. Our generation wanders as none before it, perhaps not since the days of our hunter-gatherer ancestors. After many centuries of relatively stable human settlement, created by agriculture and the deep bond it forged between men and soil, the twentieth century, with its great upheavals of population, broke that bond and set us loose. Born in places where our families had only the shallowest roots, we felt free to wander, to cover territory across the country and around the world, before settling down. The decision to stop wandering was a hard one; many of us never quite come to peace with it. When we do settle, it is often in yet newer places. Each generation, so it begins to seem, seeks out a new place to call home and make its nest.

> They journeyed from the Graves of Desire and camped in Hatzerot. They journeyed from Hatzerot and camped in Rithmah. They journey from Rithmah and camped in Rimon Paretz. (Numbers 33:17–19)

Lay out your own family's journey this way, as much detail as you know of it. "They journeyed from Berditchev and camped in Hamburg. They sailed from Hamburg and landed in Ellis Island. They journeyed from Ellis Island and camped on Rivington Street. They journeyed from Rivington Street and camped in the Bronx, on the Grand Concourse. They journeyed from the Grand Concourse and settled in Teaneck." Now your own travels, key stations along your road of life. "I journeyed from Teaneck and camped in West Philadelphia. I journeyed from West Philadelphia and backpacked in Europe. I journeyed from Europe and camped in Ann Arbor." Go ahead, do your own. Write it down, just like Moses did. Once you have your list, try chanting it aloud.

There is something of the nesting instinct that belongs to our feminine side; the man-soul within us always struggles with the desire to keep wandering, to see life as an endless journey rather than as the history of a growing home. Even when settled and loving our families, there is something in us that still hankers for the open road. That's how Jack Kerouac became the hero of an entire male generation, his readers mostly guys who had long given up such travels but still wanted to hear and dream about them.

We even have a word for it, an English term derived from the old German—wanderlust. What is it in us men that still desires, against all reason, to cut loose from ties and hit the road? How many good relationships have we ended, how many hearts lie broken, because we just couldn't "stay put"? Perhaps it is that old tribal wanderer, the one who has not quite left behind the "hunter-gatherer" stage of human history, who remains alive somewhere deep within us.

The ancient memory is embedded in our lives as Jews. Look at two of our oldest rituals and ask where they really come from. On the spring full moon, we used to sacrifice a lamb and then, for a week, eat only nomads' bread. We still eat that thin, crunchy stuff, bread like that which people made before we settled down, before we had ovens. The dough was carried on our backs, so we're told, baked only by the sun. At the fall full moon, we leave our houses and live in wanderers' huts for a week, covered with palm fronds or pine branches or whatever our climate provides. Only later did these rites come to be associated with one specific journey, that which took us out of Egypt. But their origins go back to the most ancient of human memories. What are they, if not nostalgia for the freedoms of that ancient age, passed by so many centuries ago, but not quite fully left behind?

Some of the old desert place names seem to have meaning, and might be translated that way: "They journeyed from Rissah and camped in Community. They journeyed from Community and camped at Mount Beauty. They journeyed from Mount Beauty and camped at Trembling. They journeyed from Trembling and camped at Choirs. They journeyed from Choirs and camped at the Bottom (or maybe at "Asshole"; anyway, it was a terrible place)." But we're not quite sure of those meanings. Perhaps we need another set of tools, not yet discovered, to really decipher them.

Here we are, still wandering through our wilderness, not knowing if we'll ever get to our Promised Land. Meanwhile we struggle with the meaning of all this travel, seeking to find out how each way station will reveal some holy secret. All we can do for now is write them all down. What they mean is something we'll figure out later, when we have time.

Devarim/ Deuteronomy

דברים

Devarim

Words Like Bees

RABBI STEPHEN B. ROBERTS

These are the words. (Deuteronomy 1:1)

Words have always had a central place in Judaism. As Jews, we have always understood that words have real power.

Words create. Words destroy. Words are holy.

The Torah begins with words being the tools of creation. Genesis 1:3 states, "God said, 'Let there be light'; and there was light." Torah educates, again and again, about the power of words. This portion teaches and reminds us about the destructive force that can be found in words.

Moses starts recounting to the Israelites the journey of the last forty years. He reminds them that a generation earlier—the generation of their parents—God had led them to the Promised Land of Israel and was ready for their parents to enter. "See, the Lord your God has placed the land at your disposal. Go up, take possession, as

---

RABBI STEPHEN B. ROBERTS, BCJC, is associate executive vice president and director of the Jack D. Weiler Chaplaincy Program of the New York Board of Rabbis (NYBR). The NYBR runs a major program, Dayenu: Enough Silence (www.Dayenu.org), which is focused on training clergy, both Jewish and non-Jewish, to help combat and eliminate domestic and family violence. Rabbi Roberts is past president of the National Association of Jewish Chaplains and coedited *Disaster Spiritual Care: Practical Clergy Responses to Community, Regional and National Tragedy* (SkyLight Paths).

the Lord, the God of your fathers, promised you. Fear not and be not dismayed" (Deuteronomy 1:21).

Moses then continues by reminding those assembled that it was words that stung so deeply and painfully that they ultimately led to the destruction of that entire generation. The spies who had gone to scout the Land of Israel came back and "gave us this report: 'It is a good land that the Lord our God is giving to us" (Deuteronomy 1:25).

However, the story then continues by explicitly documenting the destructive action of words: "But the men who had gone up said, '... All the people that we saw in it are men of great size; we saw the Nephilim there—the Anakites are part of the Nephilim—and we looked like grasshoppers to ourselves, and so we must have looked to them'" (Numbers 13:33).

Words can destroy hope, faith, self-confidence, a sense of self-worth and value, and so much more. The destructive impact of words is highlighted by Moses when he recounts that the people who heard the words of the spies indicated, "Our kinsmen have taken the heart out of us, saying, 'We saw there a people stronger and taller than we, large cities with walls sky-high, and even Anakites'" (Deuteronomy 1:28).

The Hebrew for "words," *devarim*, is written in the Torah scroll with no vowels, and it can be read and vocalized more than one way. It can be read and vocalized as *devarim*, "words." It can also be read and vocalized as *devorim*, "bees." Words can be sweet and sustain like the honey of a bee. And words can hurt and even lead to death, like the sting of a bee.

The most clearly documented use of *devarim* as *devorim*—to sting, to injure, to hurt—is domestic abuse. Domestic and family violence is a men's issue! Over 90 percent of victims of domestic violence are women. One in four women will experience domestic violence in her lifetime. Domestic and family violence is a men's issue because men are doing the violence. These men are most likely someone you know—your brother, father, best friend, doctor, lawyer, the camp counselor you looked up to, the coach who changed your life, the rabbi who influences you today.

Almost every case of domestic abuse and violence starts with words. And in the largest number of cases, words are the only sign we—the larger community of men—will see of the cycle of violence and abuse that is going on, because domestic and family abuse is most often done in private. Words are the exception.

Public words create environments for private thoughts and actions. A warning sign or red flag for known domestic violence is making sexist and offensive jokes about one's spouse. It is shocking, and yet it happens on a regular basis and most of us have participated.

A group of men gather, play a sport, start to drink, talk and joke around. In this process, one person tells an off-color joke. Everyone laughs. Another soon follows, and then someone follows with a sexist joke. Again, everyone laughs. It is in these words and actions, more specifically the action of inaction, that we create an environment of collusion that ultimately leads men to believe that domestic abuse and violence are their right.

Men's communities, particularly in American Jewish communities, have fought long and hard over the last generation to stop the use of the "n" word and all that it represents. We have understood that words create conditions that define what is appropriate thought and behavior. Words condition us. Almost no one laughs any longer if someone tells a joke with the "n" word. We know and understand that racism is a systemic societal problem that must be combated at all levels. Through the clear action of the last generation, starting with indicating that jokes with the "n" word in them are inappropriate and offensive, we have radically changed society. We have stopped *l'dor va-dor* (from generation to generation), a generational transmission of values of hate and racism.

It is time to do the same thing with sexism. Through something as simple as laughing at sexist jokes, we perpetuate a patriarchal system in which men and boys, consciously or unconsciously, learn that they are above women. It is a system where men want privilege and power. In this system, there are appropriate and inappropriate behaviors. It is a system in which it is OK when a man tells a sexist joke about his own wife or daughter. And the take-away message of telling this type of joke is clear: what is OK in public is OK in private. And it is exactly because of the messages we learn in jokes that we have tried to stop the use of the "n" word in them.

Words create environments that are holy or unholy. It is time we started to create holy environments wherever we go. This Torah portion makes it clear that leadership is both shared and communal. No one person can lead alone or make changes alone. Nor does God expect us to. Moses, our greatest leader, was not able to lead alone. He said publicly, "I cannot bear the burden of you [Israel] by myself" (Deuteronomy 1:9). Moses knew that communal responsibility and action must be widespread and at an almost universal communal level. Thus he took "tribal leaders, wise and experienced men, and appointed them heads over you: chiefs of thousands, chiefs of hundreds, chiefs of fifties, and chiefs of tens" (Deuteronomy 1:15).

It is time that we follow Moses's example. Domestic and family violence can only be eliminated at a universal and communal level. And men must be at the forefront of the change and become leaders. We must be "our brothers' keepers."

The first step to creating change is to understand the issue. Domestic and family abuse is multilayered. Much of it is in a private realm that is never seen by outsiders. It is a process that starts with words and often moves beyond words. The men involved in this often think it is acceptable for them to act the way they do. They have learned in school, at camp, in synagogue, at scouts, from their coaches and teachers, and from their relatives including fathers, uncles, and brothers that it is OK to belittle and demean girls and women.

The process of abuse almost always starts with words. And like *devorim* (bees), these *devarim* (words) sting—first, emotionally and spiritually. The words involved in making sexist/offensive jokes in public are coupled with name-calling, mind games, obsessive jealousy, and even silent treatment in private. The stinging from the *devarim* (words) increases as time goes on and if not stopped, the hurt increases. Like with the Israelites, the words begin to diminish the heart out of those abused and under duress. Harassing phone calls at work and threatening words are directed at a woman, her children, even the family pets. The progression goes further, as the victims begin to be isolated from others. Then the cycle can escalate and move beyond just *devarim*. *Devarim* changes to *devorim*—now, with a physical "stinging." Clothes are cut up, photo albums are destroyed, slapping with an open hand takes place, weapons are displayed and used as threats, punching occurs, and a person is thrown across the room. As the cycle grows in intensity and violence, there may be rape, stalking, followed by use of sharp objects to inflict physical damage, threats of murder, increased stalking, and murder.

We learn from Rabbi Elazar ben Azaryah in *Mishnah Avot* 3:21, "Where there is no proper conduct, there is no Torah." Domestic abuse and violence are not proper. Period. Thus, it is time to bring Torah back into the lives of men and men's communities by stopping domestic abuse and violence. The time to stop the cycle is at the very beginning. To do this we, as men, must change the environment among and between men about what is acceptable behavior.

There are specific actions we can take:

- If you are at services on Shabbat and a man tells a sexist joke, stop him. You can say something along the lines of, "We are here to celebrate Shabbat and God's creation. We are not here to belittle God's work."
- If you hear a generic sexist joke, ask yourself, would this be funny if it was about my mother, my sister, my daughter, or my wife? Ask the same question publicly.
- If you hear a man tell a sexist joke about a loved one of his own, ask him, "What makes this 'joke' funny?" "Rabbi Elazar of Modin taught: He who puts his fellow to shame in public ... even though he has Torah and good deeds to his credit—has no share in the world to come" (*Mishnah Avot* 3:15).
- Take such jokes as real warning signs. Seek out professional help on ways to safely address a possible perpetrator of domestic and family abuse and violence. Also, reach out to a professional about how to safely approach the women in his life

about what is domestic abuse and domestic violence, how it functions, and options she may have if she sees it.

- Think about how this scourge gets transmitted over the generations. Work to change the systemic pattern in the following ways: Speak with your sons about words, sexism, and domestic violence. Use the example of the "n" word and racism. Show how a large societal change took place starting with the action of changing words. Involve and encourage them to help change the world regarding this issue. Work with other fathers to approach a congregation's rabbi or educator and suggest the inclusion of training for healthy dating as part of the school curriculum. Work with the public and private school systems to institute these classes. Camps, youth groups, Boy Scouts, and Hillel should all be part of the focus of change.

This Torah portion begins with the words "These are the words that Moses addressed to all Israel" (Deuteronomy 1:1). We too must address our words and our actions involving change to all Israel.

Like Moses, no one person can do the work alone. If each of us found a way to positively change ten other men, we could change the world for the better within one generation. It is a long and difficult task. Let us learn from Rabbi Tarfon in *Mishnah Avot*: "You are not required to complete the task, but neither are you free to desist from it" (2:12).

ואתחנן
Va'etchanan

Teach Your "Sons"?

WAYNE L. FIRESTONE

Take to heart these instructions with which I charge you this day. Impress them upon your children [l'vanecha]. Recite them when you stay at home and when you are away, when you lie down and when you get up.
(Deuteronomy 6:6–7)

During the past year, the halls of our home rang with the sweet sounds of a young woman practicing her Torah portion. Our oldest daughter, Lital, became a bat mitzvah—the culmination of a process that has engaged our entire family, including Lital's two younger sisters, in preparing her to enter Jewish adulthood.

As I reflect on this special moment in Lital's life and in the life of our family, I am reminded of the unique emphasis the Jewish

---

WAYNE L. FIRESTONE is CEO and president of Hillel: The Foundation for Jewish Campus Life. He has held leadership positions in Jewish communal affairs, dating to his days as a Soviet Jewry activist at University of Miami Hillel and the Georgetown University Law Center. He lived and studied in Israel for almost nine years, serving as director of the Israel Regional Office of the Anti-Defamation League; lecturing at Technion, the Israel Institute of Technology; and founding Siliconwadinet Ltd. He was twice named by the *Forward* as one of the "Forward 50" influencers who are making a difference in the way American Jews view the world and themselves. He lives in Rockville, Maryland, with his wife, Stephanie, and three daughters.

tradition places on youth and on the role they play in enriching the Jewish people and the world. I am also reminded of the emphasis placed on active, experiential education as a means of developing and actualizing that role over several years of emerging adulthood and self-actualization.

The text of *Va'etchanan* contains two of the most easily recognizable passages in the entire Torah: the quasi-repetition of the Ten Commandments (*Aseret Ha-dibrot*) and the first paragraph of the *Shema*. Much has been said and written about both, but I would like to focus my discussion on a small but tremendously meaningful segment of the latter.

Deuteronomy 6:6–7 reads: "Take to heart these instructions with which I charge you this day. Impress them upon your children [*l'vanecha*]. Recite them when you stay at home and when you are away, when you lie down and when you get up."

The word *vanecha* is inherently unclear in its gender. While the singular *ben*, "son," is distinctively male, the masculine plural (*banim*, "sons," or *vanecha*, "your sons") can also be used to refer to a mixed-gender group. Therefore, the word can mean "your children" generically or "your sons" specifically, and it is often difficult to discern which meaning fits a given context.

The word first appears in Genesis 6:18 in reference to Noah's children, all males. As though to further emphasize the masculinity of the term in that context, the text goes on to mention *neshei vanecha*, "the wives of *vanecha* [your sons]," thus clarifying the gender of *vanecha*. Similarly, another early appearance of the word, in Genesis 19:12, is accompanied by *uvenotecha*, "and your daughters," leaving little room for confusion.

And yet, the word's ambiguity is manifest. The 1611 King James Bible, for instance, translates *banim* as "sons" 2,893 times and as "children" 1,570 times. The common biblical reference to the Israelites as *benei Yisrael*—which first appears in Exodus 1:1— clearly means "the *children* of Israel," not "the *sons* of Israel."

I have always been particularly moved by the Talmudic exposition of Isaiah 54:13. The verse reads: "And all your children shall be disciples of the Lord, and great shall be the happiness of your children." In the Talmud (*Berachot* 64a), Rabbi Elazar says in the name of Rabbi Hanina: "Torah scholars increase peace in the world, as it is written: 'And all your children shall be disciples of the Lord, and great shall be the happiness of your children.' Read not *banayich* [your children], but rather *bonayich* [your builders]."

The implication here is quite beautiful. The interchangeability of "children" and "builders" is one that speaks to the very core of the Jewish tradition, a tradition that calls upon human beings to partner with God in the act of creation. It may well be that because I am the father of three daughters I am unwilling to accept the gender-specific rendering of *vanecha* in Deuteronomy 6. Yet, I believe the more inclusive reading of the charge—to teach our tradition to the next generation, both females and males—is a moral necessity. If in the Talmud Rabbi Elazar already saw the necessity to universalize the meaning of *banim*, we can hardly do less. We live in an age when Torah study is and should continue to be more accessible to more people than ever before.

Over the past several years, I have had the good fortune of working for Hillel: The Foundation for Jewish Campus Life, which combines these two perspectives—that of the *Shema* and that of the Talmud—by engaging our young people in experiential education under the assumption that they truly are the builders of our people and of the world. In *Pirkei Avot*, the Ethics of the Fathers, our organization's ancient namesake, Hillel the Elder, states, "A shy person cannot learn" (*Mishnah Avot* 2:6). Today, our organization encourages Jewish students to leave their comfort zones, to push their personal boundaries, and to take an active part in enriching the Jewish people and the world.

In record numbers, Jewish university students are actualizing this role in a very real way—taking hammers and power tools in their hands to help rebuild the Gulf Coast. This is not a comfortable experience. For many, it represents their first experience with manual labor; for others, it is their first encounter with widespread poverty and devastation. This is a departure from the normal and the mundane. It is growth through discomfort as students push themselves to the limit and labor to better the world around them.

Elsewhere, students are taking part in building themselves and their communities through active, experiential learning. They are discussing, debating, arguing, and agonizing over our ancient texts. They are inspiring their universities to develop innovative instruction techniques based on the dialogical *chevruta* (partnered study) method. By engaging the sources—and one another—in active conversation, the students are taking ownership of their Jewish identities and helping to build themselves and the future of our people.

My wife, Stephanie, and I were proud to witness Lital's own decision to adopt an active approach to her mitzvah project. She chose to work with wounded servicemen and servicewomen at Washington's Walter Reed Army Medical Center as her cause—not only raising funds to ease their convalescence, but also developing and participating in an entertainment program aimed at providing the soldiers with a moment of levity in the midst of their suffering. Though we worried how our daughter, surrounded by such immense pain, would handle such a challenging environment, we found ourselves filled with wonder upon witnessing the care and grace with which she engaged and comforted the wounded. By leaving behind the comforts of a suburban teenage existence, Lital found herself better able to relate to the soldiers, many of whom responded in kind, opening their hearts in a way that moved us all to tears.

And so, as we watch our three daughters develop into young Jewish women, we will continue to look to the *Shema* for inspiration. In order to teach our *banim*—as the *parashah* instructs—we must look to them as *bonim*, responsible for actively engaging their surroundings in *tikkun olam*, "perfecting the world." We must challenge them to challenge themselves, to embrace the uncomfortable, and to engage the world in active dialogue.

עֵקֶב
Ekev

Making a Living and Making a Life

RABBI DAVID B. ROSEN

Man does not live on bread alone. (Deuteronomy 8:3)

If ever there was a Torah reading that should be required reading for today's man, it is *Ekev*, for in this portion not one, but three, passages speak directly to issues affecting—and, some would say, afflicting—a great many men.

Few verses in Scripture are more familiar than Deuteronomy 8:3: "Man does not live on bread alone," a verse that would appear to be perfectly clear to even the most uninitiated Torah reader. Indeed, almost all our sages concur that it addresses the need for our lives to be in pursuit of meeting not only our physical requirements, but our spiritual ones as well.

The verse thereby cuts to the heart of a well-known dilemma in Jewish life—namely, the withdrawal of many men from the ongoing life of the American synagogue. The excuses given are typically the

---

RABBI DAVID B. ROSEN is senior rabbi of Congregation Beth Yeshurun, a Conservative synagogue in Houston, Texas. Previously, he served congregations in Providence, Rhode Island, and East Meadow, New York. He was invited by President George W. Bush to represent the Jewish community at the National Day of Prayer in 2005, which took place at the Washington National Cathedral in the aftermath of Hurricane Katrina. Rabbi Rosen is married and is the father of two children.

need to work longer hours in pursuit of professional goals or the lack of interest in religion in general (fueled, men often say, by unhappy memories of their childhood religious school experiences).

The passage from Deuteronomy 8:3 anticipates these claims by affirming the distinction between *working to live* and *living to work*. It argues that the man who becomes so engrossed in the pursuit of wealth, prestige, or material possessions is, in a way, not fully living. He is choosing a life in slavery over one of freedom, which is a denial of a core Jewish value.

Indeed, as significant a teaching as this verse is, the words commonly quoted are only a portion of a longer sentence—the whole of which teaches something of even greater significance and deeper meaning:

> [God] subjected you to the hardship of hunger and then gave you manna to eat ... in order to teach you that man does not live on bread alone, but that man may live on anything that the *Lord* decrees [emphasis added]. (Deuteronomy 8:3)

Rabbi Harold Kushner wisely sees in the complete quote the lesson "that people can survive on 'less than bread'—namely, the manna from heaven with which God sustains them."[1]

It is one thing to argue that working hard to earn a living is not enough, that there needs to be a spiritual dimension to make us fully human. But even more important, we need to recognize that the faith in God on which the Israelites had to rely each day as they collected just enough manna to last for the next twenty-four hours was ultimately as important as the physical act of eating itself. The Torah seems to be saying that what we want and what God feels we need may be two different things.

But Deuteronomy 8:3 serves, too, as a prelude to the second of the three passages that speak to us in this Torah portion.

As the Israelites' journey approaches its conclusion, Moses cautions the people that when they arrive in the land promised by God and live in fine houses with large herds and much silver and gold, they must "beware lest your heart grow haughty and you forget the Lord your God ... and you say to yourselves, 'My own power and the might of my own hand have won this wealth for me.' Remember that it is the Lord your God who gives you the power to get wealth" (Deuteronomy 8:11–18).

When you have worked hard and sacrificed so much for all your material wealth, never forget that it all ultimately is a gift from God, who created us and gave us the strength, the wisdom, the very skills to succeed as we have. And therefore we must acknowledge this through words of gratitude and appreciation, which, when spoken to God, are called "prayer."

Some years ago, a cherished colleague of mine invited me to a special service in celebration of his sixtieth birthday, which coincided with his thirty-fifth anniversary at his synagogue in New York. The leader of the congregation, reflecting on the rabbi's humble origins, introduced the rabbi as a "self-made" man.

My colleague rose and began by tactfully discounting that title. "I am the farthest thing from a self-made man," he said.

"I am what I am, first, because of the fateful decision made by parents so many decades ago, to leave Russia and come to America.

"I am what I am because of the encouragement of my own rabbi in New York, who saw in me a latent spark that, with some fanning, he felt could make me into a fine rabbi myself.

"I am what I am because the Seminary, knowing I was all but destitute, provided me with a generous scholarship, without which I would never have had the resources to study.

"I am what I am because a friend in the Seminary suggested in my senior year that I take a look at this small pulpit out in the sticks, a place where both the new congregation and I might grow together.

"And I am what I am, and I am here today," he concluded, "because I said 'yes' to that congregation, and thirty-five years later, we have grown and shared so very, very much.

"A self-made man? I am the farthest thing from it," he said.

It would be nice if more of us possessed my colleague's sweet humility.

How well Moses understood the need to caution against the all too prevalent tendency to regard our blessings as proof of our ability or our virtue!

"Beware lest your heart grow haughty and you forget the Lord your God ... and you say to yourselves, 'My own power and the might of my own hand have won this wealth for me.'"

Yes, how often we fail to show gratitude to those who have helped us in our journey through life. And most of all, how many of us have lost sight of our indebtedness to God. Too seldom do we credit Him even partially for our successes; too little do we think of Him except in times of pain and suffering. Then we are only too eager to cry out to Him for relief, for respite.

"Answer us, O Lord, when we cry out to You," we pray each day in the Jewish tradition. But another prayer is more in the spirit of gratitude. "*Modim anachnu lach,*" we pray. "We thank You and praise You, O Lord, morning, noon, and night for Your miracles that daily attend us and for Your wondrous kindnesses." This is a great prayer—a prayer that affirms that we are thankful to God, who created us, who nurtured us, who established a world of such beauty and poetry and love. It is a grateful heart that utters this prayer.

There is a beautiful tradition in which Jews, on a daily basis, strive to find one hundred opportunities to say a blessing of thanks to God. In assembling our own lists, what might we include? In a matter of minutes, we could easily come up with twenty-five, fifty, or even one hundred opportunities to thank God for the simple realities that allow existence itself.

And those sacred opportunities would not consist of gratitude for our big-screen televisions or our cutting-edge phones. No, we know only too well what really counts in life. We know—deep down, we really *do* know—how blessed we are for the right things.

Henry Ward Beecher put it this way:

> If one should give me a dish of sand, and tell me there were particles of iron in it, I might look for them with my clumsy fingers, and be unable to detect them; but let me take a magnet, and sweep through it, and it would draw to itself the most invisible particles. The unthankful heart, like my finger in the sand, discovers no mercies; but let the thankful heart

sweep through the day, and as the magnet finds the iron, so it will find some heavenly blessings.[2]

Or in the words of a small and succinct prayer: "Blessed is our God, in whose abode is joy, of whose bounty we have partaken, and through whose goodness we so enjoy life."

At the close of Judaism's central prayer, the *Amidah*, we daily recite these words: "For all you do for us and for all Your creatures, O Lord, we truly offer thanks."

Finally, we come to the third passage in our Torah portion that speaks to today's men: "When you have eaten and are satisfied [my translation—DBR], give thanks to the Lord your God for the good land which He has given you" (Deuteronomy 8:10).

To me, the key word is *savata*, "and when you are satisfied." Typically it is not enough just to eat; rather, we need to feel some sense of satisfaction, of fullness, when the meal is finished. The difficulty many of us have is that we don't know when to stop eating; we are, in truth, never fully "satisfied" and tend therefore to overeat. The result is a population of men (and women) who keep a weight-loss industry running on all cylinders.

When it comes to food, we have many guidelines to help us. When we reach for that second serving of potatoes, we may get a stare from our spouse. When we take for ourselves too big a piece of pie, someone may suggest we've had enough, and, embarrassed, we might feel the need to put the pie down.

But it is far more difficult to discern such "hints" when it comes to other failures of being satiated—like the number of hours we work, or the amount of money we believe we must earn, or the number of vacation days and evenings we are prepared to sacrifice to make life "better for our families."

When, exactly, do we know we've got "enough"? We have enormous appetites for work; do we ever feel full?

After a long meeting in my synagogue one night, a congregant was leaving and happened to notice that the light was on in my study. Sticking his head into my office, he asked, "You're really working late. What are you working on?"

"My desk," I explained. "It's piled with correspondence, papers, mail. I have to clean it up or I'll start tomorrow on the wrong foot."

"So let me ask you something," my congregant asked. "If you don't clean your desk tonight, will your sermon not be ready this Shabbat morning?"

"No," I replied.

"And will you not be able to visit sick congregants at the hospitals this week?"

"No."

"And will you not be able to teach your adult education class on Thursday morning?"

"Well—no."

"So really," he said, "if you stay late tonight, the only thing you won't be able to do is be home tonight with your family."

He was right. We sometimes have enormous appetites for work—to finish up a project or task, to make one more phone call, to answer that last wave of e-mails, to follow up on one more lead. But in the end, what is the price we pay for this inability to say "enough"? The only things we end up sacrificing are the things that, in the end, we know matter the most: time with family, time in prayer, time at peace with ourselves and those we love.

No, man does not live on bread alone. We constantly need to cultivate a sense of gratitude for all we possess because God created us in a world also of His creation. We must acknowledge, too, that for all we seek—and for all the time we are often prepared to invest in that search—some things (time with family, time to renew ourselves through prayer, and acts of loving-kindness) are even more vital. And we must never lose sight that, for all we have and are, our hearts should be filled with gratitude to those who helped us—and, most importantly, to God Almighty Himself.

ראה
Re'eh

Choosing *Is* a Blessing

RABBI DAVID J. GELFAND

See: This day I set before you blessings and curses.
(Deuteronomy 11:26 [my translation—DJG])

In William Styron's haunting novel *Sophie's Choice*, we encounter one of contemporary literature's most frightening moments. In the midst of the hell of Auschwitz, Sophie must make the most horrible choice a parent could possibly confront: which child will live, and which child will die? The core of her being exploding, she screams, louder and louder, "I can't choose! I can't choose!" Threatened with the real possibility that both children will be killed, she blurts out, "Take the baby! Take my little girl."

Even when we are confronted by the worst kinds of existential choices—even in the darkness of the Shoah—Jewish tradition demands that we strive to use our uniquely human gifts. *"Re'eh,"* this *parashah* tells us—see, discern, and make life-affirming choices, as best we can.

RABBI DAVID J. GELFAND is senior rabbi at Temple Israel of the City of New York, and previously served congregations in New York, Ohio, and New Jersey. He serves in a leadership capacity on many local, national, and international nonprofit boards. He helped found and currently serves as vice-president of the Interfaith Alliance as well as on the board of the World Union for Progressive Judaism. He and his wife, Kathy, have four grown children.

Today, men especially continue to be challenged to make choices that shape our present and set us on a course for the future. The strong cultural expectation that we will be caretakers adds pressure to our lives. Life is never simple, and as a friend of mine, a therapist, once taught me, "Where in the Good Book is it written that life is fair?"

Throughout Jewish history, we have argued about why bad things happen to good people, or in the words of the Talmud, *Tzaddik v'ra lo; rasha v'tov lo*, "Why do the righteous suffer while the wicked prosper?" It is no accident that *Re'eh* occurs at the beginning of the High Holy Day season. As we read *Re'eh* in the annual Torah cycle, and as we journey toward the Yamim Noraim, the Days of Awe, the shofar can be heard in traditional synagogues each morning. Like the shofar blasts of the Hebrew month of Elul, which leads into the Days of Awe, the opening words of this *parashah* call out with a clarion blast. They shake us and call out to us, stopping us in our endless rush, demanding that we recognize daily that "this day I set before you blessings and curses." This is a text about making choices and recognizing how our choices will affect the nature and the quality of our lives and of those around us. For as God called out in the Garden of Eden, *Ayekah*? "Where are you?" (Genesis 3:9).

We live at the beginning of the twenty-first century, amidst unbridled wealth but anxiety-provoking uncertainty, technological wonders yet computerized nightmares, scientific breakthroughs and yet medical limitations, contemporary blessings and modern curses. We realize that things are not always what they seem to be.

In *Stories from Far Away*, storyteller Joel ben Izzy confounds us as he helps us reflect on the challenge of choosing wisely. He tells the story of a man who acquired a beautiful horse. "How wonderful!" his fellow villagers exclaimed. "What a blessing has come to you!" He responded, "What seems like a blessing may, in fact, be a curse."

The villagers were puzzled by his reaction. Sometime later, the man awoke one morning and found that his beautiful horse had run away. The villagers rushed to his side to comfort him on the loss of his prize possession. Again, he puzzled them by saying, "What seems like a curse may be a blessing."

Sometime later, his horse returned, surrounded by a whole herd of beautiful stallions—each one worth a fortune. The villagers, struck by the man's extraordinary good fortune, enthusiastically congratulated him. He replied, "What seems like a blessing may, in fact, be a curse." Sometime later, the man's son, while riding one of the stallions, was thrown from his mount, and he broke his leg. The villagers rallied to offer support to the man. The man was sanguine, saying, "What seems like a curse may be a blessing." Sure enough—soon after this, all the young men of the village were conscripted into the army and forced to fight a terrible war far away from their village. All of them died in battle—except for this man's son, who could not fight because of his broken leg. What seems like a curse may, indeed, be a blessing.

In our macho male roles, we often assume that we can determine the future, just by the sheer force of personality. But our eyesight is not always clear, though our hindsight is sometimes 20/20. Our lives are often filled with challenging moments of endless choices. Some moments that are filled with light suddenly turn dark and agonizingly painful. Out of some traumas, a thousand blessings appear. We need to make intelligent choices. Our free will to choose and the responsibility in making those choices is one of God's greatest gifts to us. It is the part of us that makes us most godlike as we strive to give honor to the teaching that we are each created *b'tzelem Elohim*, "in the image of God"—and we are therefore endowed with the power, and intelligence, to choose.

"Intelligence" comes from two Latin words: *inter* and *legere*. *Inter* means "between," and *legere* means "to choose." "Intelligence" is the ability to choose between alternative courses of action, to make decent moral decisions. Each of us has free will. While in ancient days pagans felt forever doomed, our forefathers and our ancient texts have taught us that we have the ability to help choose our destiny. Hindus see man tied to a wheel of karma. Muslims are ruled by kismet (fate) and have no real choice other than to submit to Allah's will. We must find the strength and the courage to deny that we are puppets manipulated by the powers about us—by our bosses, our coworkers, our lovers, our families, and our friends.

The great sage the Vilna Gaon explained to his students that there is a reason "I set before you" is written in the present tense and not, as one might expect, in the past—"I *have* set before you." Every day of our lives, God continually gives us choices. Each day, each hour, each minute, each second, we are given choices for blessings and curses.

Perhaps the most articulate evidence to this is the testimony of the Holocaust survivor and contemporary thinker Dr. Victor Frankl. "We who have lived in concentration camps can remember the men who walked through the huts comforting others, giving away their last piece of bread," he wrote. "They may have been few in number but they offer sufficient proof that everything can be taken from man but one thing: the last of the human freedoms—to choose one's attitude in any given set of circumstances—to choose one's way."[1]

And yet, there are those who do not see and seek to avoid choices. In *Spoon River Anthology,* the poet Edgar Lee Masters writes of one who reflects that "I have not chosen nor rejected, whatever life has for me selected."

And then there are those who seek to make only emotional choices. Dennis Prager, author and radio personality, has written that when we make choices, we sometimes mistake fun for happiness. In our narcissism, we pursue immediate gratification, and we search for instant pleasure rather than long-term satisfaction that will ultimately bring us happiness. In his book *Happiness Is a Serious Problem: A Human Nature Repair Manual*, Prager teaches us that fun and happiness are really opposites: "To understand fun doesn't create happiness and can even conflict with it. We must understand the major difference between fun and happiness: fun is temporary; happiness is ongoing. Or to put it another way, fun is during, happiness is during and after."[2]

The real test is found in our ability to hear the call and to see how our choices will affect us, our loved ones, and beyond. The eternal question, *Ayekah*? "Where are you?" beckons to us. That first question in the Bible was not about geographical location. Cain failed his test when God asked, "Where is your brother?" (Genesis 4:9). Abraham was tested on Mount Moriah through the *Akedah*, the binding and almost-sacrifice of his beloved son Isaac. Leah was tested in her troubled marriage to Jacob. Joseph was tested when his brothers appeared in his "new business location" in Egypt, and he had to struggle about whether to exact vengeance. Moses was tested, time and again, in the wilderness. These were all ancient tests of words and faith. We are tested constantly with contemporary choices with the call to see—*Re'eh!* "For the Eternal your God is testing you to see whether you really love the Eternal your God with all your heart and soul ... and to whom you should hold fast [my translation—DJG]" (Deuteronomy 13:4–5).

No matter how much we may feel overwhelmed and no matter where our life's journey takes us, life's choices are neither all dramatic nor existential. But each of them, small and large, are the threads that create the tapestry of our journey. When this Torah portion arrives with its clarion call of "*Re'eh*," I always think about it in the context of the coming High Holy Days, and I urge my congregants to think about how we can choose wisely in the month of Elul and then peer into the distance, into the New Year, and reflect on the decisions we might choose to make.

Then, together, we recite the prayer that my own rabbi taught me to say with the dawn of each new day—a day that would, invariably, be filled with opportunity and choices: *Modeh ani lifanech....* Thank God for the gift of breath, of spirit, of life and for the light after the darkness of each night and for the privilege of seeing and of choosing. *Modeh ani lifanecha*, "let us give thanks," and let us *re'eh*, "see," and choose only blessings.

שפטים
Shoftim

Judging the Judges

RABBI DOV PERETZ ELKINS

You shall appoint magistrates and officials for your tribes ... and they shall govern the people with due justice. You shall not judge unfairly; you shall show no partiality; you shall not take bribes, for bribes blind the eyes of the discerning and upset the plea of the just. Justice, justice shall you pursue, that you may thrive and occupy the land that the Lord your God is giving you. You shall not set up a sacred post—any kind of pole beside the altar of the Lord your God.... (Deuteronomy 16:18, 16:21)

We are always criticizing our judges. They are too lenient with hardened criminals, or they are too tough with first-time offenders. No one is ever overjoyed with a judge's decision. How should a judge

---

RABBI DOV PERETZ ELKINS is rabbi emeritus of The Jewish Center of Princeton, New Jersey, and an internationally known speaker and workshop leader. Winner of the National Jewish Book Award, he is author and editor of many books, including *The Wisdom of Judaism: An Introduction to the Values of the Talmud; Jewish Stories from Heaven and Earth: Inspiring Tales to Nourish the Heart and Soul; Rosh Hashanah Readings: Inspiration, Information, Contemplation*; and *Yom Kippur Readings: Inspiration, Information, Contemplation* (all Jewish Lights). He and his wife, Maxine, live in Princeton, New Jersey, and have six children and nine grandchildren.

make his call? Today's Torah lesson offers some advice, through the creative comparison by the Rabbis of seeing a verse in its context.

> You shall appoint magistrates and officials for your tribes ... and they shall govern the people with due justice.... You shall not set up a sacred post—any kind of pole beside the altar of the Lord your God.... (Deuteronomy 16:18, 16:21)

What possible connection could there be between these two matters? Why does the Torah so abruptly change gears from three brief verses on the theme of justice, to discuss the subject of divine altars?

A Rabbinic commentator makes an astute observation. What is the common thread between a judge and an altar? Just as an altar is made of earth inside and brass outside, so, too, with a judge. He should be humble on the inside, like the dust of the earth, and yet be strong, proud, and dignified on the outside. He should be strong enough to resist the power of exploiters, manipulators, and oppressors and should protect the poor and the innocent. And he should be soft and humble enough to have mercy on a guilty defendant who evidences a sincere sense of contrition or who committed a crime with mitigating circumstances.

What may be said of a judge can be applied equally to all human beings. All of us occasionally need to call upon the quality of a stern, firm veneer. In the face of injustice around us, we must fiercely resist the temptation to go along, and certainly not sit by and be a spectator to the act of evil. On the other hand, when we have been wronged and our natural inclination to revenge grips us in its tough jaws, we must be prepared, provided forgiveness is requested and restitution made, to be forgiving and merciful.

What the tradition is asking of us is not easy. The decision to be strong or soft, proud or humble, unbending or flexible, is often a hard call. Not many people are given the ability to apply both sides of themselves at the right time and place.

Abraham Lincoln was one who did.

In an address to a joint session of Congress, on the 150th anniversary of Lincoln's birthday, Carl Sandburg said:

> Not often in the story of mankind does a man arrive on earth who is both steel and velvet, who is as hard as rock and soft as drifting fog, who holds in his heart and mind the paradox of terrible storm and peace unspeakable and perfect. Here and there across the centuries come reports of men alleged to have these contrasts. And the incomparable Abraham Lincoln ... is an approach if not a perfect realization of this character.

The Rabbinic commentator could not have described his intention more vividly. A judge—and at times we must all judge, ourselves and others—must be like an altar, humble as the dust within, and strong as brass on the outside; velvet covering her heart, and steel covering her body.

Our Israeli brothers and sisters are also reputed to possess this rare quality of a soft heart and a firm exterior. One who is born in Israel is called a sabra. The *sabra* is a plant that blooms in the Israeli desert—a kind of cactus, with a strong, prickly exterior, and yet one that is tender and soft and juicy inside. So, too, the native Israeli. He is strong and tough and hardened by life's tragedies and war's brutalities. Yet, his vigorous outward appearance has been tempered by the mercy and compassion of his Jewish roots. His sense of decency and his own dour historical experience have prevented him from becoming callous and impervious to mercy. The sabra's sharp and bristly points have been watered by the softening teachings of Torah. He is velvet wrapped in steel. Only a great people and a great nation can combine these two disparate polarities in one personality. The image that most epitomizes the Israeli soldier is the tough man with a steel helmet resting on his head, an Uzi flung in readiness over his shoulder, standing at the *Kotel* (the Western Wall) with tears falling down his cheeks in his prayers for *shalom* (peace).

That is the challenge that Torah presents us. Israel has abundantly demonstrated its capacity to build the strongest military force in the Middle East, and one of the most powerful anywhere in the world. Yet, it is also prepared to make serious compromises, exhibit the most extraordinary flexibility, go more than halfway in meeting its former enemies—Palestinians and other Arab neighbors—and show its soft, bending capacity to reckon with new world circumstances, new realities, and new attitudes on the part of some of its neighbors.

Fathers who want to raise healthy children have to show both paradoxical qualities—toughness and tenderness. One best-selling psychologist named his approach to child rearing "tough love." This is not an oxymoron. It is the blending of two qualities that must be mixed in a crucible of maturity and creativity to transmute a small selfish child into a selfless, compassionate teenager and adult. Fathers, and all who have a talented hand in bringing up children, have to discover within themselves the capacity to find the seat of their righteous indignation and appropriate anger, when necessary, and to unsheathe their most seasoned softness and quiet caring, when they must bring balm to a young one's pain, or show the light of a new truth to an intractable and self-satisfied learner.

In an op-ed article written just before the 1988 presidential election, when George H. W. Bush faced off with Massachusetts governor Michael Dukakis, former senator George McGovern wrote that many people were looking for a "tough" candidate in a president. McGovern argued that while toughness is certainly an admirable trait, the presidents in American history whom he respected the most—Washington, Jefferson, Lincoln, Wilson, and FDR—may have been tough, but they all had another side to them, the side that McGovern characterized as that of the "preacher." He meant the soft side, as symbolized by the pastor—the man who tenderly nurtures his flock.

McGovern described the late Martin Luther King Jr. as one who was "tough-minded and tender-hearted." He was, said McGovern, "one who had the capacity to make judgments with a tough mind and a compassionate heart guided by a sense of moral purpose." McGovern wrote that the strongest president is the one who has the courage to cut back the military budget when the country is adequately defended, and the soft-hearted president is the one who is demanding enough to insist on increases for school lunch programs for our hungry, deprived youth.

Two years later, Boston columnist Ellen Goodman described how Dianne Feinstein won the election for the United States Senate. "The former mayor of San Francisco," wrote Goodman, "fused the images of two genders into one description as omnipresent as the tagline to her ads: Dianne Feinstein: Tough and caring. The emphasis is on the word 'and.'"

Goodman explained how the pollsters predicted that certain words would challenge the mettle of female candidates—words like "strong," "decisive," and "leader." People would want to know if a woman candidate could measure up to the boys when it came to toughness. Feinstein won, she explained, because she came out in favor of capital punishment and was pro-choice. She was tough and caring—tough on criminals, caring of families. She quoted Feinstein, who said in a campaign speech, "Californians want to have someone who is strong, who is going to take care of them and take care of their families. They really don't care what kind of shell that individual comes in." Goodman applauded Senator Feinstein for using campaign tactics that embraced both "tough" and "caring," "one word from the old male vocabulary and one word from the old female dictionary. Add them together and then perhaps the title Governor, even President, may not have a gender anymore."

Perhaps we should add a phrase to Malachi's prophecy for Shabbat Ha-gadol (the Sabbath that immediately precedes Pesach) when he says that the messianic age will be a time when the hearts of the children will turn to their parents, and vice versa (Malachi 3:24). Perhaps also the messianic age will be a time when the fist of a man will be thrust forward by a powerful woman, and the compassion of a woman will be exercised by a caring man.

Do you recall the riddle of Samson in the Book of Judges? Samson had killed a lion with his bare hands. A short while later he turned to look at the lion and saw that a swarm of bees had settled in its body and deposited honey there. Samson then thought of the following riddle with which he challenged his friends: "Out of the strong came something sweet" (Judges 14:12–20).

It took the assembled group an entire week to unlock the riddle, and even then, they did it only with help. For it is not often that something sweet comes from someone strong. We tend in our very nature to be either strong or sweet, proud or humble, steel or velvet.

Our tradition tells us we can be both as men. This is our challenge, our mandate toward human perfection and ultimate wisdom. To be gentle, yet strong. "Hard as rock and soft as drifting fog."

Velvet wrapped in steel.

כי תצא
Ki Tetzei

(Young) Men of War

RABBI DANIEL LANDES

**When you go out to war against your enemies, and
the Lord your God delivers them into your power and
you take some of them captive....**

(Deuteronomy 21:10 [my translation—DL])

"Gabe," one of my students, from southern California, made *aliyah*
(emigrated to Israel) with his family at approximately the same time
that we did. Back "home," we had studied ethical texts ranging from
Maimonides to Moses Chayim Luzzatto (the eighteenth-century
Italian-Jewish thinker). Gabe had a good head, a wonderful heart,
and a deadeye shot on the basketball court. A year or so later, he
walked into the *beit ha-midrash* (study room) of the Pardes Institute
of Jewish Studies in Jerusalem in uniform. He'd been trained as a
specialist—a sniper. His job was to take out "the bad guys" from
impossibly long ranges. Those texts we learned together, he gently

---

RABBI DANIEL LANDES is director and *Rosh HaYeshivah* of the Pardes
Institute of Jewish Studies in Jerusalem, where he also teaches the senior
Talmud class and theology. He edited *Genocide: Critical Issues of the
Holocaust*, as well as *Confronting Omnicide: Jewish Reflections on Weapons of
Mass Destruction*. He was the Jewish law commentator for the *My People's
Prayer Book: Traditional Prayer, Modern Commentaries* series (Jewish
Lights), winner of the National Jewish Book Award. As a rabbi, he served
Bnai David-Judea Congregation of Los Angeles, California, and served as a
judge on the Los Angeles Rabbinic Court.

told me, did not seem to speak to the fact that the requirement for his new job was that he take human life. This commentary on the first verse of the Torah portion emerges from my encounter with Gabe and with those young men who serve—my own son and other students.

Ki—"when." Going out to war is an anticipated part of Israeli culture. In the *shevi'it* (junior year of high school), the boys (and girls as well, but it's different with girls, who deserve their own narrative) receive their *tzav giyus* (draft notice). It simply arrives in the mail. They are excited. They eagerly compare notes on what service they will try out for and the demands that each division entails. There are physicals, as well as emotional and mental testing. As a dad who has never gone through it, I have no particular wisdom to offer—just support. As a teacher (again, me) who did not choose to go into the army when I was a visiting American teenager learning in Israel, I have little to offer my "twenty-something" *talmidim* (students) who agonize over the decision to serve, except to give support—readily, eagerly, hungrily, but (usually) humbly. The ones who will serve will tell their own stories and supply their own commentaries—and theirs are the crucial ones. No, now I am speaking to fathers and to teachers.

Actually, each moment of "going out" is a jolt: the draft notice, the testing, the decision making by young men, and then the real decision by the army, the induction, the training, and finally the posting to dangerous places.

It shouldn't be a surprise. The process is laid out. When, years ago, we made a quick *aliyah*, life was a blur. We gradually got a hold on things, but there was one issue I could never figure out: why do Israeli parents let their boys run so wild? A half-year into our *aliyah*, our son Isaac had a birthday party. The boys were playing some rambunctious game in the park nearby, running and pushing while kicking a ball and a can. There were two workmen fixing the telephone line, and they stopped to watch. One asked, "*Abba*? [Are you the father?]" I nodded "yes." "*Ben kamah*? [How old is your son?]" "*Shemoneh* [eight years old]." The second workman noted, "*Od eser shanim* [ten more years]."

It took me a moment to realize that they were referring to the fact that he would eventually go into the army. That fact is always on Israeli minds. A few minutes later, my wife, Sheryl, came out and was disturbed by both the lateness of the hour (it had gotten dark) and the roughness of the game. "Let them play a little longer," I pleaded with her.

As it turned out, our son spent two years after high school learning in a fine yeshiva as part of *hesder* (the "arrangement" that combines yeshiva learning and training in the Israel Defense Forces [IDF]). That "won" him two more years in the park, allowing him to remain "young" just a little bit longer.

Tetzei—"you go out." The commandment to go out is in the singular. It is the nature of an army that it has one persona. An army can only be successful if it has the support of the nation.

But the closeness of the IDF to Israeli society has staggered my imagination. One sees the faces of the soldiers—young, vital, but usually so tired—as the faces of your own family. Being a small country, this is literally often the case, but it doesn't matter. They are our children, our brothers and our sisters. Yom HaZikaron—Memorial Day for Israel's fallen—has the intensity of both Tisha B'Av (the traditional fast day in remembrance of the destruction of the Temples in Jerusalem) and Yom HaShoah (Holocaust Memorial Day). Yom HaZikaron is not a memory or a reenactment; it is a fresh wound that is constantly torn. It is a day of pain and resolve, but also of fear.

This binds us, but it also separates us. Those sectors of Israeli society that don't participate in the IDF anger me. For the ultra-Orthodox *haredim*, their reasons for not fulfilling the mitzvah of defending their people all revolve around the notion of "holiness"—their need for their studies and to maintain separation from the more secular elements of Israeli society. But the net result is that this creates a climate in which their sons and their students feel their own blood to be more precious than that of their fellow Jews, which clearly violates the Talmud (*Sanhedrin* 74a), which teaches that no one's blood is redder—more precious—than any one else's. Unlike the "simple Jews," religious or secular, who identify so closely with the IDF that they fulfill "when you take the field" with their hearts and their bodies, the *haredim* remain distant, unsupportive, and disdainful.

Tetzei—"you go out." Our young boys go out of their childhood, and they become men. From a shallow teenager with an ungainly gait and sloppy behaviors, they become toughened men with hard and, yes, graceful, bodies who know how to exercise responsibility. The transformation is expected, but nevertheless, it is startling.

I turn to the children of my *haredi* cousins, friends, and acquaintances. Those children are fine people; some of them have attained great book learning at an early age. But, they remain "soft" kids. They have become infantilized. Their talk is strangely abstract and narrow, and their vision is hazy. Their moral compass is limited. They lack the fundamental challenges that a man can have: the defense of family and nation, real moral decision making in the face of life-and-death decision and responsibility for your group. I despair of the Torah and these lives that it somehow creates. This culture of stilted learning justifies their abandonment of their people, and that culture is only compounded over the generations.

Those who serve—and not only those who serve in combat—recognize the urgency of life. "Screwing up" is no longer a phrase or a metaphor. "Screwing up" can cost a life. The stakes are real, and not symbolic. The lives of those who serve—and their Judaism—is the real thing.

Tetzei—"you [shall] go out." The Talmud teaches that *tetzei* means "go out and take the battle to the enemy." Don't wait for them to come to you on your own turf. The text understands the devastating effects of war fought on one's home turf, and it is anxious regarding those realities.

This attack mentality differs from the defense mentality. When you are on defense, you are wary, anxious, suspicious and static. You wait for the other shoe to drop. You build higher and higher walls, but you know that you can never build them high enough. The enemy will always figure how to build them even higher, how to scale the walls you have built, or how to find the hidden weaknesses that will allow them to push through your defenses. The attack mentality is brave, determined, optimistic, ferocious, and constantly inventive. The attack mentality is how we raise our boys in Israel to be men. It's charismatic; the commander is first into battle rather than hiding in command central. But the attack mentality is also abrasive, *chutzpahdik* (Yiddish, "gutsy") and falsely invincible. Therefore, it is also tragic. But there is no other way.

La-milchamah—"to war." Not "to battle." A battle is episodic; it is fought, and then it is over. Our war is constant; it just goes on, with only variations in intensity. When we send our sons out, they go into a combat condition that has no end. Therefore, we have to be even more committed to both winning and to finding the prospect of peace.

Al oyvecha—"against your enemies." I return to my opening story. In responding to my student regarding the value of the life that he is charged to take, we turned to Maimonides. In the *Mishneh Torah*, he outlines what is to be done, based on the verse uttered by the priest anointed for battle, "Let not your courage falter" (Deuteronomy 20:3). Maimonides explains:

> Who is "the man who fears and is soft in his heart"? This refers to one who does not have the heart and the fortitude to stand in the throes of battle. But once he enters the throes of battle, he should depend upon the Hope of Israel and its Savior in dire straits. He should know that it is for the unification of the Name that he wars. He should put his soul into His Hand and not be afraid, nor be panicked and he should not think of his wife and not of his children. Rather, he should wipe their memory from his heart and should turn away from any distraction [but rather turn] to battle. And anyone who begins to think and to worry during battle and thereby upsets himself violates a negative prohibition, as it says, "Let not your courage falter...." Furthermore, all Jewish blood (spilled) is on his head. If he does not overcome (himself) and does not fight with all his heart and soul, it is as if he shed the blood of them all...."
>
> (*Mishneh Torah, Hilchot Melachim* [Laws of Kings] 7:15)

We pause. My student closes his eyes, as if searching for the deeper meaning of that teaching. Wordlessly, he absent-mindedly inclines slightly forward, lightly touching his fore- and middle finger to his right temple. He is ready. The next day he assumes his new career, in the service of the Jewish people.

U'netano Adonai Elokeikha b'yadecha—"And the Lord your God delivers them into your power." Once the battle is finished, the rules change. Our sons learn that the vanquished enemy is also made *b'tzelem elokim*, "in the image of God." Therefore, we have direct obligations to protect and to care for him. Most important, we must not let our "attack mentality" run wild.

Our Torah verse continues, and it introduces us to the biblical character known as the beautiful and desirable woman who is captured in the midst of war. The Torah describes a process of "taking" her. As the victor brings her into his house, she shaves her head, pares her nails, and mourns and cries for her father and mother for a month. The intention of the Torah is to render her initially undesirable, so that the Israelite soldier will come to his senses and let her go. If he does not, then "after that you may come to her and possess her, and she shall be your wife." She has earned both full status and her own sense of integrity: "Then, should you no longer want her, you must release her outright. You must not sell her for money; since you had your will of her, you must not enslave her" (Deuteronomy 21:11–14).

The Torah does not assume that lofty exhortations can curb the needed "attack mentality." Instead, it provides mechanisms that will surround and tame that mentality itself. The resolution is not perfect; every halachic process embodies a tension between either opposing principles, or principles and reality. Rather, the halachic process respects the fact of human emotions, as we move ourselves toward respect and protection of the other.

Over the centuries, these teachings have imposed many social controls upon Jewish men. Some of those controls have emerged through the army. The IDF, of course, would view the implementation of the Torah's laws regarding a woman captive as a severe human rights violation. Other controls are educational; most are familial. Judaism understands the tension; on the one hand, it maintains the "attack mentality" needed for victory and survival, and on the other hand, it demands a sense of *menschlichkeit* (Yiddish, "human decency"), which makes survival worthwhile.

V'shavita shivyo—"and you take some of them captive"; literally, "and you shall capture him as a captive." The double use of "capture/captive" (*shavitah/shivyo*) refers reflexively to the double capture that our sons endure. By holding the other in captivity, they are also captured. They are in the dual captivity of their own "attack mentality" and their own *menschlikhheit*—both of which we, parents and teachers, have evoked and demanded. The loss of either one of these qualities would spell disaster—physical and moral—for both them and for the nation. Can they be kept in balance? Yes, there is tension. But the nature of people, situations, and struggle renders all of this to be a dynamic tension.

We call upon our sons to make extraordinary moral decisions, *al ha-makom*—on one foot. These decisions often have life-and-death consequences. Two short stories:

First story: A Pardes student entered an IDF combat unit and was stationed at a border crossing. A group of Palestinian laborers with work papers who crossed into Israel every day were ordered to strip for a search before they would be allowed to enter Israel proper—in the broiling sun. This went on for a week, until my student could no longer tolerate this affront to human dignity. He articulately protested this treatment to his captain, within earshot of the workmen. The next day, when the work crew showed up at the crossing, the captain once again ordered a search. One of the workmen was found with a significant amount of explosives taped to his body.

Second story: My son and his group were guarding a blockade crossing outside Nablus (in the West Bank), a hotbed of radicalism, where a strict curfew is enforced. Late one night, a car approached. The driver was a man with papers stating that he was a medical doctor. He had a problem. He was called out of a wedding in village A to attend to a man in village B. Now his wife and kids were stranded in village A, and he wanted to take them home. The rules are clear; it is forbidden. The soldiers consulted with each other, took his papers, and allowed him a quick but doable period to get back. Their actions put them in danger of court-martial, and worse. The doctor returned with his family, the soldiers returned his papers to him, and the doctor got his family home.

What would you or I have decided, in these rather simple occurrences, which contain so much moral weight and ambivalence? Making those decisions in real split-second time creates an instant pull between the dual "attack" and *menschlichkeit* mentalities. In the end, it's a man's job, and I honor those who have to make those decisions.

Ki tetzei—"when you go out": they deserve that we empathetically go out with them to the danger—existential and moral.

כי תבוא

Ki Tavo

Until This Very Day

RABBI SIDNEY SCHWARZ, PhD

You have seen all that the Lord did before your very eyes in
the land of Egypt, to Pharaoh and to all his courtiers and
to his whole country: the wondrous feats that you saw
with your own eyes, those prodigious signs and marvels.
Yet to this day the Lord has not given you a mind to understand or eyes to see or ears to hear. (Deuteronomy 29:1–3)

It is perfectly true, as philosophers say, that life must be
understood backwards. But they forget the other proposition, that it must be lived forwards. And if one thinks
over that proposition it becomes more and more evident
that life can never really be understood in time simply
because at no particular moment can I find the necessary
resting place from which to understand it—backwards.
(Søren Kierkegaard, nineteenth-century Danish philosopher)

RABBI SIDNEY SCHWARZ, PhD, is founder and president of PANIM:
The Institute for Jewish Leadership and Values and founding rabbi of Adat
Shalom Reconstructionist Congregation in Bethesda, Maryland. He is
author of *Finding a Spiritual Home: How a New Generation of Jews Can
Transform the American Synagogue* and *Judaism and Justice: The Jewish
Passion to Repair the World* (both Jewish Lights).

I don't know when the publishing industry came up with the gimmick of producing books with alternate endings. Nonetheless, it seems to have gained in popularity. A long-running comedy whodunit at the Kennedy Center takes suggestions from the audience, and the cast is versatile enough to craft out of those suggestions a different ending to each show. I notice that many of my DVD rentals now offer alternate endings to movies, a choice denied to those who saw it in the theater at full price.

A recent reading of *Ki Tavo*, specifically Deuteronomy 29:1–8, made me consider that maybe the Bible was the first book in history to come up with the alternate ending gimmick. It suggests a whole new marketing strategy for the best-selling book of all time!

Here is the context: Moses is giving his final orations before he passes away and the children of Israel enter the Land of Israel under the leadership of Joshua. Most of the portion of *Ki Tavo* is taken up with a juxtaposition between two scenarios. In one, the children of Israel obey God's covenant, and they receive abundant blessings. In the second scenario, Israel disobeys the covenant, and Moses recounts a list of curses that would be the consequence of such a choice. The implication of the chapter is that there is a direct correlation between behavior and consequences, the biblical theme of reward and punishment. Now this theme raises huge problems for believers for, as we know both from history and from our own lives, sometimes bad fortune follows good behavior, and good fortune follows bad behavior. Hold this thought. We'll come back to it.

The portion ends with a deliciously ambiguous passage that centers on the three Hebrew words *ad ha-yom ha-zeh*, "until this day" (Deuteronomy 29:3). The only way to do this phrase justice is to offer two loose translations of the section (Deuteronomy 29:1–3) and then to reflect on the lesson that we might draw from the contrast.

Version A: "You [the children of Israel] witnessed the redemptive acts of God bringing you out of Egypt, the revelation of Torah at Mount Sinai, and how you were sustained during your long journey through the wilderness. Yet until this day, you just don't seem to understand the larger purpose of this drama in which you have been primary actors."

Version B: "You [the children of Israel] witnessed the redemptive acts of God bringing you out of Egypt, the revelation of Torah at Mount Sinai, and how you were sustained during your long journey through the wilderness. You were primary actors in this story, but you did not seem to understand the larger purpose of these events until this day."

Standard translations of the Bible follow the intent of version A and actually attribute to God the fact that the Israelites seem not to have "a mind to understand or eyes to see or ears to hear" (Deuteronomy 29:3). Maimonides uses this verse to launch into an argument in favor of free will. Yet the Hebrew can legitimately yield version B as well as version A. Version B suggests that at this moment, when Moses is about to die and the Israelites are about to enter into the land that God promised to their ancestor Abraham, they finally come to understand what all these events mean and their role in it.

What lessons can men draw from the passage? Life is a lot like a book with a choice of endings. It might be a comforting thought except that, in truth, it is extraordinarily hard to make wise choices when we are actors in our own life dramas. Rare is the man who has the capacity to see his actions "from the balcony" as an objective observer might. We want to do the right thing, but much gets in the way—ego, ambition, selfishness, insecurity, avarice, to name but a few. Our tradition would call these influences on our psyche and behavior our *yetzer ha-ra*, our "evil inclination." Somewhat disconcertingly, the Rabbis believed that the evil inclination was stronger than the good inclination. It is not impossible to overcome the *yetzer ha-ra*, but it is also not easy.

Let's look at three "case studies" to better understand this phenomenon.

First: A teenager, eager to impress a girl in his class who is dating a member of the football team, decides that he needs to show a bit of macho to win her over. He becomes obsessed with weight training in an effort to bulk up his slight frame. He begins to spend every extra hour of his free time in the gym, and his bedroom floor is filled with bodybuilding magazines. A year goes by and he has added some muscle to his frame. Yet the girl still does not give him a second look. The boy's parents, aware of their son's flair for writing, which he has all but given up in his pursuit of perfect pectoral muscles, beseech him fruitlessly to focus on his true gifts.

Second: A young man is in his final year at an Ivy League law school. He has always wanted to find a way to be an advocate for the most vulnerable members of society. He has made inquiries about two jobs that have him very excited. One would put him in a public defender's office, where he would defend prisoners who cannot afford their own legal counsel. The other job would be in a nonprofit organization that advocates for rights of victims of human rights abuses around the world. The young man's father is a senior partner in a prestigious law firm and continues to tell his son not to "waste" his potential in these "do-good" causes. Take one of the offers you are getting from Wall Street law firms, he argues, and advance the causes you believe in through charity work, just as I have done. The son, wanting to please his father and finding it hard to refute his father's logic and role model, takes a job with a Wall Street firm. Only after his father's death, twenty years later, does he have the courage to leave the private practice of law and to pursue his real passion.

Third: A middle-aged man is an extraordinarily successful entrepreneur. He is married with three children and, when viewed from the outside, leads a storybook life—beautiful home, exotic vacations, a contributor to high-profile charities, highly respected in the community. Yet his ego is driven by his ability to create the next business and make it even more successful than the last. His competitive drive and ability to work fourteen-hour days, seven days a week, make him the envy of many of his male peers. Yet his family relationships are in shambles. He has taken his wife for granted and missed virtually every milestone event in his children's lives for work-related travel and meetings. Now he is age fifty-five, his youngest child has moved on to college, and his wife decides to leave him for another man who has shown her attention and was recently widowed. The entrepreneur has another great business idea and, now, little to hold him back in pursuing it. Yet it seems somehow less alluring.

Many of us will identify with at least one of the above story lines. We can cite dozens more such vignettes from the pages of our own life's storybook. The reader of the vignettes will see them as clichéd, the "wise" choices patently obvious. Yet how many of these vignettes are we actually living out right now, the "wise" choices eluding us? In each vignette, the protagonist does not have the eyes to see, the ears to hear, or the insight to understand the consequences of his choices ... until this day. We can see the potential in each story for the protagonist to wake up and make the wise choice. We can also understand how the self-delusion, of which we are all so immensely capable, can condemn us to chasing false Gods, be it a partnership in a Wall Street law firm, wealth, or great pectorals.

And here is the crux of the matter. Søren Kierkegaard observed that life is lived forward but understood backwards. Often, we live our lives at such a frenetic pace that it is impossible to gain the perspective necessary to understand the possible consequences of the decisions that we make. The Bible would have us believe that bad choices lead to a cursed life, and good choices lead to a blessed life. Would that it be so simple!

Our ability to justify our own behaviors, no matter how dysfunctional they might be, is enormous. A person can have a trait that results in an inability to make or keep friendships. That person can even articulate what that trait might be. And yet they find it hard to break a pattern of a lifetime and, more often than not, will repeat the behavior notwithstanding the negative consequences. We need only look at the list of sins in the Yom Kippur liturgy to see how many bad choices we repeat, year after year. The list is even longer for those of us who attend synagogues that add to the traditional liturgy a contemporary version of the *Al Chet* prayer.

Judaism does suggest that even though bad choices might yield short-term gains that others may envy, the key to a fulfilled life lies in making the wise choices. Each of us lends our own interpretation to the three words *ad ha-yom ha-zeh*, "until this day." If we cannot find life partners, spiritual guides, therapists, or our inner voice to help us see the negative consequences of the choices that we are making daily, we will continue to make those mistakes even until this very day (and beyond).

But the *parashah* offers another scenario. Imagine yourself being able to take a step back from the life you are leading. Maybe this step back will be aided by the observance of a true Shabbat, some meditation, a sabbatical, or, God forbid, a tragedy. If we can achieve a Kierkegaardian glimpse of what our life looks like with 20/20 hindsight, it just might reveal a different ending to our story. And if we get to such a place, we might say,: "I really did not understand what I was doing with my life and the impact it would have on me and on others, until this very day. But now I see it. And I will choose a different path."

If life is like a book with alternate endings, maybe religion is a device to allow us to sneak a peak at the choices before we stumble into the wrong ending.

נצבים

Nitzavim

A Few Choice Gifts

RABBI HOWARD AVRUHM ADDISON

I call heaven and earth to witness against you this day: I
have put before you life and death, blessing and curse.
Choose life—if you and your offspring would live....
(Deuteronomy 30:19)

Tonight I walk by the mirror
in my father's green shirt
that I am wearing for the first time.... (Tom Daley, "Legacy")[1]

Fathers and children. Chains of transmission. What garments shall
we bequeath to our sons and to our daughters who come after us?
Will they brighten our children's days and warm their nights? Will
they be shabby and frayed or sewn sturdy even where patched? Will
they buoy their spirits or just burden their bodies? What will our

RABBI HOWARD AVRUHM ADDISON teaches humanities at Temple
University in Philadelphia, Pennsylvania, and serves as rabbi of
Congregation Melrose B'nai Israel Emanuel in Cheltenham, Pennsylvania.
A founding teacher of *Lev Shomea*, the first institute for training spiritual
directors in the Jewish tradition, he is author and co-editor of several
books on Kabbalah, personality type, and traditions of spiritual guidance,
including *Enneagram and Kabbalah: Reading Your Soul* and *Jewish Spiritual
Direction: An Innovative Guide from Traditional and Contemporary Resources*
(both Jewish Lights).

descendants think when they wear them for the first time—and the times after that? And what will they think when they think of us?

Nitzavim finds the Israelites on the eastern bank of the Jordan River just prior to Moses's death. Having listened to the curses detailed in *Ki Tavo*, the modern Orthodox commentator Rabbi Samson Raphael Hirsch imagines our ancestors' despair as they wonder, can we achieve God's standards of sacred living or withstand the punishments that come with failure? To this Moses replies, "*Atem nitzavim*—you're still standing!" You have endured the perils of a forty-year journey through the wilderness and flourished; therefore you can take heart that you and your descendants can likewise endure whatever the future may bring.[2]

Nitzavim pictures all strata of Israelite society, including those living and those yet to be born, entering into a renewed covenant with God. With striking imagery the Torah describes the destructive alienation that can result from self-inflation and turning from God. Through a wordplay on the Hebrew verb *lashuv*, "to turn," we learn how Israel and God will ultimately be reconciled through an intricate divine-human dance of repentance (*teshuvah*) and return. As the portion nears its end, it calls us to lovingly and reverently cleave to God, assuring us that divine guidance is not distant and unattainable, but near to us indeed.

Perhaps the most compelling challenge in this entire *parashah* comes in its penultimate verse: "I call heaven and earth to witness against you this day: I have put before you life and death, blessing and curse. Choose life—if you and your offspring would live" (Deuteronomy 30:19).

The scope of meaning that our interpretive tradition ascribes to the phrase "choose life" can be as contradictory as it is far-ranging. In the Jerusalem Talmud, Rabbi Ishmael claims that this is a call to learn a vocation that can support you and your family in this world.[3] The twelfth-century kabbalistic work *Sefer Ha-bahir* ("The Book of Brilliance") asserts that these words call us to abandon the preoccupations and pleasures of this world and seek eternal life through accepting the yoke of the divine commandments.[4] The *Sefer Avodat*

Ha-kodesh ("The Book of Sacred Service") imagines two paths lying in front of the listener, who is free to choose either course, immune from any coercive powers that might be found in heaven or upon earth.[5]

Yet what special imperative might the rejoinder to the charge "choose life" mean for those of us who take the task of generativity seriously? What kind of life-giving choices should we as men make "if we and our offspring would live"? What life-affirming legacies might we model and then pass on that our children might wish to carry them forward? I believe that some of the answers may be found within the passages of *Nitzavim* itself.

The first of these gifts, the will to persevere, can be found at the very beginning of the *parashah*. As mentioned above, Moses reminded the people that they were still standing despite or perhaps because of the many trials they had undergone in the wilderness. Those moments of failure and losses of faith did not come without cost, but they ultimately prepared a former slave people to assume the challenges of entering the Promised Land as God's covenant folk. Observers as diverse as Mark Twain and Friedrich Nietzsche have marveled at the subsequent ability of our people to persevere and even flourish amidst centuries of statelessness and tragedy dating back to our first exile to Egypt, our enslavement, ultimate liberation, and journey to Eretz Yisrael.[6]

How might fathers bequeath the gift of perseverance? Let me offer an example. Sylvia Kinzer Blanchfield, a child of the post–World War II "baby boom," took accelerated courses in mathematics and science during her school years. The encouragement she received from her father in part inspired her 2002 doctoral dissertation entitled "The Relationship between Fathers and Their Gifted Daughters That Supports Giftedness: A Grounded Theory" (Iowa State University, Ames, Iowa). Her interviews with women college students and their fathers revealed that "fathers who held high expectations of their daughters and who provided encouragement, advocacy, and guidance, had daughters who demonstrated perseverance, and persistence, with a sense of equanimity across the tasks of their lives."[7]

A second gift of life we might transmit is the potency of *teshuvah*, repentance and transformation, the realization, amidst failure and despair, that things need not be as they are now. It is no surprise that *Nitzavim*, with its emphasis on *teshuvah*, is always read on the Shabbat prior to Rosh Hashanah. As we enter the penitential season, it teaches us that if we prayerfully turn our hearts toward God and are willing to persevere, taking the concrete, often difficult steps of confession, restitution, and reconciliation, we might return from even the outer reaches of alienation.

The fourth edition of *Alcoholics Anonymous* recounts the story of a pilot who endured firing, decertification, and imprisonment because his alcoholism led him to fly while intoxicated. In striking detail, we learn how this man turned toward God and painstakingly rebuilt his life, step by step. By turning toward God through the support of AA and loved ones, he was able to regain his standing in the pilots union following years of sobriety. Among the many blessings in his current life, he counts the gift of a son's similar recovery as most precious. "Today one of my sons has more than three and a half years of sobriety, after nearly losing his life to alcohol and drugs. He is truly one more miracle in my life, for which I am so deeply grateful."[8] While genetics and negative role modeling certainly played a role in the son's addiction, we can also be certain that the example of this father's *teshuvah* was invaluable in motivating his son to "choose life" as well.

Desire and passion are not words we usually associate with religious virtue. Yet our High Holy Day liturgy praises God, who *chafetz chayim*, "who desires life."[9] The Book of Ecclesiastes bids us to live passionately, proclaiming: "Whatever it is in your power to do, do with all your might ..." (Ecclesiastes 9:10). Along these lines, Rabbi Mordechai Joseph Leiner of Izbica interpreted the verse "Then the Lord your God will open up your heart and the hearts of your offspring to love the Lord your God with all your heart and soul, in order that you may live" (Deuteronomy 30:6) to indicate that God doesn't want us to neutralize our passion, but to channel it into the service of committed, ethical, godly living.[10] Only thus, claimed this nineteenth-century Hasidic master, can we model an engaged, sanctified life that can enliven both us and our descendants.

A wise psychotherapist told me that when his children were young, he would only allow them to watch one family-themed television show—*The Addams Family*, a campy horror spoof. When I expressed surprise, he told me to consider the following: the differences of all the family members were both accepted and respected (and boy, were they different!), and it was the only show on television in which the two parents were passionately devoted to each other and not ashamed to openly express that love in front of their children.

My friend went on to tell me that the best gift one can give one's children is to engage life and, despite its grinds, to be unafraid to model a loving relationship. Such modeling conveys a message louder than words that passion and love can be available to them as well within the bonds of sanctified commitment.

One additional legacy that we might bequeath our children is the ability to extract good from evil. This, wrote Rabbi Moses Chaim Ephraim of Sudilkov, grandson of the Baal Shem Tov, is the true meaning of the verse "I have put before you life and death, blessing and curse" (Deuteronomy 30:19). Since everything comes from God, true blessing is the ability to trace every occurrence back to its divine origin, to identify and actualize godliness even in seemingly cursed situations.[11]

I once heard a story about a man who was the most reliable, devoted parent in his town. Most of his neighbors were surprised, since he had been raised by a single father who was often drunk and rarely employed. When asked how his life had come to deviate so radically from his dad's, the man replied, "No matter how bad things were, what I remember most is my father coming to my bedside every night and tenderly saying, 'I love you.' Somehow it made our tough times more bearable and has motivated me, albeit in a much more responsible way, to convey that same tender love to my children."

What mantle shall we pass down to our children? It should be woven of persistence and the possibility of transformation through *teshuvah*. It should be woven passionately with the realization that through the alchemy of spirit, even what seems to be rotting straw can be spun into golden threads. It certainly cannot be purchased ready-made, but must be sewn throughout years of active involvement, with all the trial and error that implies. *Nitzavim* promises us that the godliness we'd seek for ourselves and model for our children is as near as our hearts and our tongues, but only if we're willing to act (Deuteronomy 30:11–14). As Robert Fulghum teaches, "Don't worry that they [your children] don't listen to you; worry instead that they are always watching you."[12]

A final note: Our garments of life can only be passed on with the knowledge that our children must make their own alterations. Neither dogmatism nor the frustration of our own disappointments can be allowed to change these cloaks of legacy into straightjackets that will be resentfully cast aside. Their means of transmission to our daughters might, in some ways, need to differ from how we convey them to our sons. But if that transmission is done with integrity and thoughtful attention, then hopefully those who come after us will bless us, no matter what color shirt we wear and lovingly leave behind.

‏וילך‎
Vayelech

How to Succeed at Failure

RABBI HAROLD S. KUSHNER

Moses went and spoke these things to all Israel. He said
to them: "I am now one hundred and twenty years old, I
can no longer be active. Moreover, the Lord has said to
me, 'You shall not go across yonder Jordan.'"

(Deuteronomy 31:1–2)

"We teach people how to fail."

The words were spoken by the dean of an MBA program at a
major university. His point was that business executives can learn a
lot by studying the success stories of major companies, but they
would learn more by studying their failures. How did they respond
to frustration and disappointment? How did they react when things
did not turn out as they hoped they would?

As we come to the last pages of the Torah, the last days of
Moses's life, we see him coping with the final, and perhaps most
crushing, disappointment of his life, and there are lessons many of
us can learn from the way he handled it. The people who have been
burdening him with their complaints for forty years are about to
enter the Promised Land, but he will never get to set foot in it.

RABBI HAROLD S. KUSHNER is rabbi laureate of Temple Israel in
Natick, Massachusetts. He is author of several best-selling books on find-
ing the spiritual resources to cope with life's problems, most notably *When
Bad Things Happen to Good People*.

Ostensibly God is punishing him for what seems to have been a minor infraction, hitting a rock to make it gush forth water instead of speaking to it as God had told him to do (Numbers 20:2–13).

The punishment seems so disproportionate to the offense. I have always found the key to understanding it in two details. First, Moses seems to be reenacting an earlier miracle where he struck a rock and brought forth water. Like many older people, he seems to assume that what worked for him years ago in different circumstances would work just as effectively now. In that way, without in any way diminishing the greatness of his earlier leadership, he raises doubts about his fitness to be a leader tomorrow. Secondly, when he says to the people who are crying for water, "Listen, you rebels" (Numbers 20:10), he betrays the fact that he is burned out. He has been putting up with their complaints and disobedience for too long and has lost patience with them. At times, he seems not to realize that the people he is speaking to forty years after the Exodus are not the same people he led out of Egypt. He is now dealing with their children and grandchildren. God's response can be seen not as a punishment but as a recognition of how much Moses has changed and how the people's needs have changed. I can imagine God saying to Moses, "You were the perfect leader to bring this people out of Egypt, lead them across the sea and guide them to Sinai. But you are not the right man to lead them into battle to settle the land of Canaan. You are tired, you are worn out, and you are too tied to the solutions of the past. Israel needs a younger man, a warrior, to do that."

How does Moses respond? His first response is an impressively unselfish one. Told that he will die in the wilderness before the people enter Canaan, his concern is that God replace him with a worthy successor. "Let the Lord, Source of the breath of all flesh, appoint someone over the community who shall go out before them and come in before them, and who shall take them out and bring them in [that is, who will lead them in battle], so that the Lord's community may not be like sheep that have no shepherd" (Numbers 27:16–17).

By the beginning of the Book of Deuteronomy, Moses has come to focus more on his own fate and his own feelings. He complains about the unfairness of God's decision and pleads for a reconsideration (Deuteronomy 3:24–26). He chastises Israel for causing God to be upset with him (Deuteronomy 4:21). Then by the time we read these last chapters of the Torah, he seems to have accepted his fate.

But at least some of the sages wonder if Moses really did come to terms with God's decision, perhaps speculating as to how they would react in similar circumstances. The Torah almost exclusively describes events without speculating about the emotions of the people involved, leaving that to the reader's imagination. The midrash typically steps in to fill the void. In the case of Moses's final days, one midrash (*Devarim Rabbah* 9:9) pictures Moses saying to God, "All right, I can accept the fact that I would not be the best person to lead Israel in battle. But can't I enter the Promised Land without being the leader? I don't have to be a general; I could be a private in Joshua's army." God says to him, "Is that what you really want? You may find it harder than you think." But Moses persists and God agrees. Moses steps aside and Joshua becomes the people's leader. The first time Joshua goes into the Tent of Meeting to receive the word of God, Moses is waiting for him outside and says as he leaves, "How did it go? What did God say to you?" Joshua replies, "Excuse me, but when you went in to speak to God, did you ever tell me what He said?" At that point, Moses turns to God and says, "Take me now. I don't want to spend the rest of my life jealous of my successor."

The author of that midrash had no idea how Moses felt at that moment more than a thousand years earlier, but he could imagine how he himself would have felt. It is hard for an older man to give up a position of prestige and authority that he has held for much of his adult life, a position that has defined him, empowered him and earned him the respect and admiration of others. It may be hard for him to admit that another, younger man can do the job better. And he often finds himself haunted by the question, without my job, who am I?

This has become an even more serious issue in recent years. For one thing, people are living longer. We have added thirty years to the average life span in the last two generations. That is a long stretch of time to fill when one no longer has a job to do or an office to go to. In addition, the rapid rate of change in so many areas of life, coupled with economic considerations, has put pressure on many organizations, from large and small corporations to professional sports teams, to look to replace expensive seasoned veterans with hungry young newcomers.

It has been said that whereas women's souls are nourished by relationships, men's souls are nourished by achievement. Where then does a man go to sustain his soul when he has been asked to leave the arena of achievement with which he is most familiar and for which he is most qualified? Too many of us cling desperately to positions of importance even when it has become clear to everyone else that age and changing conditions have rendered us less than ideal leaders. Some of us leave but don't really leave, standing in the wings and criticizing our successor. And too many of us die shortly after retirement or separation (even as Moses does), as if we were saying, "Without my job, without my title and office, without people coming to me for guidance, do I really exist?"

How does the man who has come to regard himself as indispensable survive being told that he is in fact dispensable? Perhaps the first thing he can do is realize that he need not define himself totally by his work. When the Torah commands us to do no work on the festival days, part of the message is the challenge of forcing us to discover who we are without our work. One thing a person in that position can do is turn to the one area in his life where he is truly irreplaceable, his family. For a man to say, "Without my job, I am nothing," is to dismiss the importance of his ties to a wife, children, and grandchildren. For a man leaving a job by choice or by necessity to say, "No one needs me anymore," is to lose sight of the people who have always needed him and still need him and for whom he can now be more accessible.

Secondly, he can find things to do in his community as a volunteer, tutoring, helping out at a local synagogue or social service agency, sharing the wisdom born of experience with those who would benefit from it.

Third, he now has the leisure to go back and fill in all the parts of his life that he neglected while he was busy being indispensable at work. It was Carl Jung's theory that society distorts people, leading them to overdevelop the parts of their personality that society finds useful and neglect the rest. The years of leisure that come our way when our working years are ended can be a time to develop all the parts of our lives that we never had time for.

Additionally, a man can be reminded that when the Academy Awards are given out every spring, not everyone vies for the Best Actor award. Many performers are thrilled to be nominated for Best Actor in a Supporting Role. Once he gets used to the change, a man who has always been in charge might very well come to appreciate the advantages of no longer being the person responsible for all the decisions. Life is less pressured. It becomes easier to take a vacation, take up a hobby. Insoluble problems are now somebody else's headache.

And finally, he can realize that, even if it wasn't his choice to give up his position of prestige and authority, it will be his choice as to how he responds to the decision. He can choose to feel bitter, resentful, unwanted. He can choose to complain and undermine. Or he can choose to feel liberated, free to write a new chapter in his autobiography. He can respond as Moses did, blessing his successor, blessing the people whom he had once led and would now no longer lead, and looking back in satisfaction, singing the praises of God, who gave him the ability and the opportunity to do so much in his life.

A Time to Go

ARIEL BEERY

**The Lord said to Moses: "The time is drawing near for
you to die. Call Joshua and present yourselves in the
Tent of Meeting, that I may instruct him."**
(Deuteronomy 31:14)

Looking over the assembly, a cold shudder must sweep through
Moses as he says these words (a paraphrase of Deuteronomy 31:2):
"One hundred and twenty years am I today, and I will not be allowed
to come and go any longer, since the boss told me that I am not
allowed to keep going with you." Promoted into retirement just
before the project he has worked on for forty years comes to fruition,
the courage to stand before others and say these words is unfathomable. No, this time Moses does not choose to argue, as he did in
the past. No, Moses does not decide to lash out and take the ship
down with him. He understands the first rule of Jewish leadership:
It's not all about you.

Many who aspire to become leaders do so out of the belief of
entitlement; feeling smarter, stronger, faster than others, these candidates seek to garner the trust of others by proving that they are the

ARIEL BEERY is founder and codirector of PresenTense, an international
grassroots network building the infrastructure for Jewish social entrepre-
neurs to pioneer new frontiers for the Jewish people in the twenty-first
century.

ones who can solve the challenge ahead. They accept applause with smiles and self-congratulations, and they stand tall when someone mentions their name in praise.

Moses, on the other hand, understands that Jewish leadership is a burden to carry and not a prize that goes to the victor. God doesn't choose the strongest or the fastest. God doesn't choose Abraham for his riches in Haran; God doesn't confer the new name "Israel" upon Jacob until he has sent all his goods to Esau and humbles himself before him; God doesn't choose Joseph until he is in the depths of the dungeon. Jewish leadership, therefore, is the acceptance that in this world of *havel havalim* ("vanity of vanities" [Ecclesiastes 1:2]) we might be asked to choose the collective over ourselves, even when it means giving up our own chance at contented happiness.

The task of the Jewish leader, therefore, is not to finalize the project and not to accomplish the mission—but rather to build the platform and create the structure that will enable other leaders to arise and continue to better the Jewish people. Moses learns this important lesson twice: first from Jethro, and now directly from God. Moses is not to lead the people into the Promised Land; his role is to build the people and provide them with the infrastructure to lead themselves.

"You might not complete the task," we read in *Pirkei Avot* (Ethics of the Fathers), "but neither are you free to avoid it" (2:12). On that day, looking over the Land of Israel, Moses sees that his obligation is complete. "Joshua will go before you," he tells his people—and then he leaves the scene and disappears, alone.

האזינו
Haazinu

Ask Your Father

Craig Taubman

Remember the days of old,
Consider the years of ages past;
Ask your father, he will inform you,
Your elders, they will tell you. (Deuteronomy 32:7)

It is very good—even smart—to seek the advice of one's father. And I know it happens, but just not in my family. My son (like his father) spent much of his time ignoring his father's pearls of wisdom. I think it is in the Taubman family DNA to prove to the previous generation just how much we have improved on the gene pool we were given at birth.

My guess is that it was in the biblical DNA as well. The reminder "to remember the days of old, consider the years of ages past" (Deuteronomy 32:7) suggests that the kids of the Bible were just like kids today. They, too, needed gentle reminders to look past themselves and open up their minds and hearts to the people on whose shoulders they stood. As smart as we may be as children, none of us invented the wheel.

"Ask your father, he will inform you, your elders, they will tell you" (Deuteronomy 32:7). The text instructs children, at any age, to

---

CRAIG TAUBMAN has been a musical inspiration to the Jewish community for over thirty years. His magical and enchanting music brings to life the joy and spirit of the Jewish heritage, bridging traditional Jewish themes and ancient teachings with passages of contemporary Jewish life.

seek the advice of their parents—obliging the younger generations to seek the wisdom of those who preceded them. What happens when the children are not willing to listen to the advice? One of my favorite parenting stories comes from the Hasidic tradition. It speaks of a father who comes to his teacher, the Baal Shem Tov, with a problem concerning his son. He complains that his son is forsaking Judaism and all that he had taught him. What should he do? The Baal Shem Tov answers, "Love him more."

My parenting rebbe is my wife, who has taught me some wonderful lessons:

1. You cannot expect your children to listen to you if you do not listen to them.
2. You cannot expect to listen to them if you are not interested in them.
3. You cannot be interested in them if you do not celebrate them.

The key to all three of these lessons is being present in the moment. And this requires that we listen. My aunt Ruth would say, "God gave us two ears and one mouth so we would listen twice as much as we speak." All of this is great wisdom; the challenge is to follow it. I know this firsthand, for while I quote my wife, she constantly reminds me that it would be far better if only I would actually listen to her more!

"Give ear, O heavens, let me speak; let the earth hear the words I utter!" (Deuteronomy 32:1). *Haazinu* reminds us to listen. In fact, *haazinu* literally means "to give ear." And when we truly listen, we are living lives of grace and humility. My generation, or yours, may be able to "do it" faster, smarter, or even better than those who came before us. That does not mean that we are better. The Israeli poet Abba Kovner wrote that our challenge is "to remember the past, to live the present, to trust the future." We do not live in a vacuum. The generations that precede us and those that will follow us can only be a part of us when we invite them in.

We are obliged to look back, open ourselves up, and listen to the wisdom of our roots. The blessing is when we are able to add our own links to the chain, building on the inheritance left to us, and passing it on to future generations.

May we be blessed to listen to the songs of yesterday, sing the songs of today ... and trust that new songs will be written for tomorrow.

וזאת הברכה
Ve-zot Ha-brachah

A Farewell Kiss from God

Rabbi Levi Weiman-Kelman

Moses was a hundred and twenty years old when he died; his eyes were undimmed and his vigor unabated.

(Deuteronomy 34:7)

We think of death as the end. *Ve-zot Ha-brachah* is the final portion of the Torah; it is all about endings. As in "real life," here, too, death appears to be the ultimate finality. This portion contains the final words of Moses our teacher and describes his death. However, the Jewish tradition cannot give death the last word. *Ve-zot Ha-brachah* is only read on Simchat Torah, the festival that celebrates the Torah reading cycle (and not as a weekly Shabbat Torah portion). Immediately after reading the last verse of Deuteronomy, we roll the Torah scroll back to the beginning—to *Bereshit*, Genesis chapter 1, verse 1. We celebrate the cycle of Torah reading and the cycle of life. We don't remain stuck in the mourning for Moses. We celebrate the great beginning. (On Simchat Torah we read only the beginning of Genesis. The whole portion is read on the following Shabbat.)

RABBI LEVI WEIMAN-KELMAN is rabbi of Kehillat Kol HaNeshama in Jerusalem, and was ordained at the Jewish Theological Seminary in 1979. He teaches prayer and liturgy at the Hebrew Union College–Jewish Institute of Religion. He is an active member of Rabbis for Human Rights and is deeply committed to interfaith dialogue. Rabbi Weiman-Kelman is married to Paula, a documentary filmmaker and they have three grown children.

These are the last words of our teacher Moses. His death casts a shadow over the whole portion. It gives us the opportunity to compare it to other biblical deaths and to contemplate our own mortality. The Torah purposely presents Moses's death to emphasize his mortality. Rather than present Moses as a superhuman leader, we are reminded that our greatest leader was indeed human, mortal.

The text gives us two tantalizing descriptions of Moses at the time of his death: *lo chahatah eino ve-lo nas leichoh*, "his eyes were undimmed and his vigor unabated" (Deuteronomy 34:7). The Hebrew *leich* (vigor) comes from the word for moisture and implies freshness. What a fantasy—at the age of 120, Moses kept his eyesight, and he stayed juicy! Yet at the beginning of Deuteronomy 31, Moses acknowledges that his powers are fading.

The text has a hard time acknowledging that Moses has aged. It is easy to identify with this. As we men get older, sometimes it feels as if our bodies betray us. Why do we need glasses, hearing aids, pacemakers, and Viagra? Western culture is committed to creating the illusion that we can defy death and aging. Everything about modern Western culture invites us to ignore death. We pretend not only that we live forever but also that we can avoid aging.

Judaism (and all serious spiritual disciplines) demands an awareness of mortality and aging. On a daily basis, the Jewish prayer book demands that we acknowledge our mortality. Among the prayers that open the morning service, we say, "My God the breath/spirit You have given me ... You breathed it into me, You keep it safe within me, and one day You will take it from me." This reality does not lead to despair. The prayer continues, "As long as my breath/spirit is within me I thank You."

There is a striking (and disturbing) midrash about the patriarchs, Abraham, Isaac, and Jacob. Abraham demanded aging. Before Abraham people didn't age. Abraham pointed out to God that people couldn't distinguish between the young and old. "Crown people with age so they will know whom to honor," suggested Abraham. "I swear you are right!" said God, "and it starts with you!" "Abraham was now old" (Genesis 24:1)—this is to teach us that Abraham brought aging into the world. This is the first time the word *zaken*, "aged," appears in the Torah.

Isaac demanded physical suffering: "If a person dies without suffering (in this world) he will face harsh judgment (he will have to suffer as atonement in the next world). If he suffers (in this world) it will be easier for him (in the next world)." "I swear you are right!" said God, "and it starts with you!" "Isaac was old and his eyes were too dim to see" (Genesis 27:1)—this is to teach us that Isaac brought physical suffering into the world. This is the first description of a physical disability in the Torah.

Jacob demanded illness: "If a person dies without illness (to remind him of his mortality), he won't make things right between his children. If a person gets sick, he will make an effort to bring reconciliation between his children." "I swear you are right!" said God, "and it starts with you!" "Joseph was told, 'Your father is ill'" (Genesis 48:1)—this is to teach us that Jacob brought illness into the world. This is the first time the word *choleh*, "ill," appears in the Torah (midrash, *Bereshit Rabbah* 65).

This teaching challenges us to view aging, suffering, and illness as gifts that the patriarchs demanded from God. This is totally counterintuitive. We spend so much time, energy, and money to erase, reverse, or ease the natural consequences of aging. Judaism certainly embraces medical intervention to relieve suffering, but wisdom allows us to discover the right balance. At some point we are called to accept the challenges that come with aging and seek out the blessings they may contain. We are so used to being in control and taking care of others. Perhaps we can find blessing in acknowledging our limitations and finally let others take care of us.

It is impossible to read *Ve-zot Ha-brachah* without hearing echoes of the whole Torah especially the Book of Genesis. Like Jacob on his deathbed (Genesis 49), Moses has words of blessing for each of the twelve tribes. Unlike Jacob, Moses's words are uniformly positive. As Jacob confronts his own mortality, his bitterness and pessimism are expressed as his farewell to his sons. Moses's life has also been filled with disappointments and failures, yet he is blessed to end his life by truly blessing others.

Genesis is filled with God's blessings. God blesses the creatures that were created on the fifth and sixth days of creation. God blesses the human as well. On the seventh day God blesses the Shabbat day. The Book of Genesis ends with Jacob blessing his sons. In this final portion of the Torah we note that the divine role of blessing has been transferred to the hands of humans as Moses blesses the people of Israel.

The Torah presents us with an ideal—to end our lives filled with blessing and no bitterness. Our lives are so goal oriented. This can easily lead to disappointments and frustrations. It is a real blessing to be able look back on our lives and accept. Then we can pass on our dreams and hopes to the next generation without conveying judgment.

Moses so dominates the last four books of the Torah, yet his death is reported in twelve concise verses. The first word sets the stage: *va-yaal*, "went up" (Deuteronomy 34:1)—Moses ascends Mount Nebo. Other deaths are described in the Torah as descending into Sheol (a vague, undefined netherworld). Moses's death is characterized as an ascent, which echoes his ascent to Mount Sinai to receive the Torah.

These verses are bittersweet because they are a painful reminder of the price of leadership. Moses, who has led the people to the Land of Israel, will not enter Israel. He lost his temper and struck the rock when he was commanded to speak to it. Before Moses's death, God shows him a panorama of the Land of Israel.

For modern Israelis, privileged to live in Israel, these verses depict places that are part of our day-to-day landscape: Dan (on the northern border), the Negev (south), the date palms of Jericho (east), and the (Mediterranean) Sea (west). As I read of Moses's death, I marvel: how is it that I am privileged to achieve that which was denied to Moses? Today any Jew can achieve what Moses yearned for—to set foot in the Land of Israel.

That Moses is allowed to see the land is, according to the Talmud, proof of the power of prayer. "*Va'etchanan*, and I prayed ...

let me see the good land" (Deuteronomy 3:23–25). "Rabbi Eliezer said: Prayer is greater than good deeds. Who was greater in deeds than Moses our teacher? Yet his wish (to have his punishment eased and to see the land) was granted only when he prayed ..." (Talmud, *Berachot* 32b). Rabbi Eliezer emphasizes the power of prayer to move God. Compare this to when Moses and the children of Israel stood at the Sea of Reeds. The raging sea was before them and the Egyptians behind them. Moses began to pray. The Lord said to Moses, "Why do you cry out to Me? Tell the Israelites to go forward. And you lift up your rod...!" (Exodus 14:15). He does, and the sea splits and the people are saved. Poor Moses—at the Sea of Reeds it was right to use his staff; in the desert it was a tragic mistake! I imagine Moses looking at the vista of the land he will not enter and assessing his past actions. You try and learn from your mistakes, yet sometimes it feels like the rules keep changing!

Moses dies with a title—*eved Adonai*, "the servant [or slave] of the Lord" (Deuteronomy 34:5). Moses, who took the people of Israel out of Egyptian slavery, is known as God's servant. According to the medieval commentator Ibn Ezra, this reflects Moses's total acceptance of the divine decree of his death. He is a submissive servant.

Other Rabbinic voices fill in the terse text. In the midrash *Devarim Rabbah* (11:10), Moses does not approach death willingly or submissively. When God informs Moses that the time of his death has come, Moses stalls. He asks for the chance to bless the people of Israel before his death. God agrees. He blesses them with a general blessing, but when he realizes that means that his time is up, he decides to bless each tribe separately. This adds a level of emotional intensity to these poetic blessings. Each blessing gives Moses a little more time; each one brings his own death closer. After he has run out of blessings, Moses pleads with God: if he cannot enter the land as the leader, perhaps God will allow him to enter the land as a beast that can graze on the land of Israel or as a bird that can fly over the land?

The midrash presents Moses as a man unwilling to accept his fate, wanting desperately to hang on, anyway he can. So much of our lives demands that we plan for ourselves and for others. At some point, we are called to let go. We must accept what we have accomplished and our limitations, our failures, our disappointments. We might be blessed with a glimpse of where our accomplishment will lead, but after we die, it is out of our hands. As it says in Psalm 146:4, "His breath departs; he returns to the dust; on that day [of death] his plans come to nothing."

Moses offers to step aside to let Joshua take over the leadership of the Jewish people. Perhaps, he hopes, God will allow him to enter the land as Joshua's assistant. The midrash describes God commanding the people to accept Joshua's authority. Moses attends a session where God speaks to the people through Joshua. Afterward he asks Joshua what God told him. Joshua answers, "Did you share that kind of information with me when I was your assistant?" Moses cries out, "Better a hundred deaths than a single pang of envy. Master of Infinity! Until now I sought life. But now my soul is surrendered to you!" Moses accepts his death.

This is a serious challenge for those of us in positions of authority and influence, used to running our own businesses or institutions. We tend to overidentify with our jobs. Choosing a successor is important to ensure that our institutions will survive our departure. No one is indispensable. If we care about what we have built, we must overcome our narrow ego needs and imagine our institutions without us.

Moses asks that his bones be brought to Israel (as Joseph's bones were to be brought as well). Even that request is denied. Moses dies outside of Israel, and he is buried in an unspecified location on Mount Nebo. Moses's name does not appear in the traditional Passover Haggadah, the holiday that celebrates the Exodus that he led. There was a fear that Moses might become the object of a hero worship that could lead to idolatry. There is no gravesite shrine that could distract people from authentic Jewish worship.

"Moses the servant of the Lord died there, in the land of Moab *al pi Adonai*" (Deuteronomy 34:5). *Al pi Adonai* means, literally, "by the mouth of God." The simple meaning is that his death is according to divine decree. The midrash understands these words to mean "with a kiss from God." This echoes the creation of Adam: "[God] blew into his nostrils the breath of life, and man became a living being" (Genesis 2:7). The tradition offers this incredible image of human life that begins and ends with intimacy with the Divine. Adam is brought to life with a divine exhalation—or perhaps the first human inhalation is really a *divine* exhalation. Moses dies with a divine kiss.

As you read these final words of the Torah, get ready to start again with the opening words of Genesis. May your life be like the Torah—framed by the intimate experience of the living God.

Rabbinic Commentators, Literary Figures, and Texts Noted in the Book

Auerbach, Erich: Philologist and literary scholar; Germany (1892–1957).

Avot d'Rabbi Natan: Post-Talmudic commentary on *Pirkei Avot* (the Ethics of the Fathers).

Baal Shem Tov (Israel ben Eliezer): Founder of Hasidism, also known as the BESHT; Poland (c. 1700–1760).

Bachya, Rav: Preacher, commentator, and mystical teacher; Spain (thirteenth century).

Bialik, Chaim Nachman: Modern Hebrew poet; Israel (1873–1934).

Borowitz, Eugene B.: Contemporary Jewish theologian and educator, leader of liberal Judaism; United States (born 1924).

Buber, Martin: Modern Jewish theologian; Austria, Germany, Israel (1878–1965).

Eyebeschutz, Jonathan: Talmudist and halachic authority; Poland, Prague (1690–1764).

Frankl, Victor: Holocaust survivor, psychiatrist, and philosopher, best known for his book *Man's Search for Meaning*; Austria (1905–1997).

Heidegger, Martin: Modern philosopher; Germany (1889–1976).

Heine, Heinrich: Journalist, essayist, and poet; Germany (1797–1856).

Hirsch, Samson Raphael: Foremost exponent of early modern Orthodoxy; Germany (1808–1888).

Hobbes, Thomas: Early modern philosopher, known principally for his book *Leviathan*, in which he lays out a theory of social contracts; England (1588–1679).

Ibn Ezra, Abraham: Biblical commentator, poet, and philosopher; Spain (1089–1164).

Kovner, Abba: Holocaust resistance fighter and poet; Lithuania, Israel (1918–1987).

Lessing, Gotthold Ephraim: Writer, philosopher, and dramatist; Germany (1729–1781).

Luzzatto, Samuel David: Jewish philosopher and biblical commentator; Italy (1800–1865).

Maimonides (Rabbi Moses ben Maimon; also known by his initials, Rambam): Jewish philosopher, codifier of Jewish law, and physician; Spain, Egypt (1135–1204).

Mann, Thomas: Novelist, essayist, and social critic; Germany (1875–1955).

Mendelssohn, Moses: Jewish philosopher, considered the founder of modern Jewish thought; Germany (1729–1786).

midrash, midrashim: Literally, "searching out"; Rabbinic commentaries on biblical texts, consisting of legends and homilies. "Midrash" or "the midrash" refers to the body of literature; a "midrash" (plural, midrashim) refers to a particular teaching.

Midrash Rabbah: The major collection of midrashim, compiled in the Land of Israel after the fifth and sixth centuries CE, though based on earlier teachings. It consists of midrashim based on the books of the Torah— *Bereshit* (Genesis) *Rabbah, Shemot* (Exodus) *Rabbah, Vayikra* (Leviticus) *Rabbah, Bemidbar* (Numbers) *Rabbah,* and *Devarim* (Deuteronomy) *Rabbah*—as well as on the five scrolls of the Writings—*Shir Ha-shirim* (Song of Songs) *Rabbah, Rut* (Ruth) *Rabbah, Eichah* (Lamentations) *Rabbah, Kohelet* (Ecclesiastes) *Rabbah,* and *Esther Rabbah.*

Mishnah: The classic code of postbiblical Jewish law, compiled in Israel circa 200 CE by Rabbi Judah Ha-nasi (Judah the Prince).

Mishneh Torah: The legal code composed by Maimonides.

Pirkei Avot: "The Ethics of the Fathers," the section of the Mishnah that consists mostly of ethical maxims.

Pirkei d'Rabbi Eliezer: Collection of midrashim, eighth century CE.

Plaut, W. Gunther: Contemporary Reform congregational rabbi, communal leader, and biblical commentator; Germany, Canada (born 1912).

Ramban (Rabbi Moses ben Nachman, Nahmanides): Medieval Jewish theologian and mystic; Spain (1194–1270).

Rashbam (Rabbi Samuel ben Meir): Biblical commentator and Talmudist, the grandson of Rashi; France (c. 1085–c. 1158).

Rashi (Solomon ben Isaac): The preeminent Jewish commentator on Bible and Talmud; France (1040–1105).

Sefer Ha-bahir: Anthology of mystical writings, constituting one of the principle layers of the *Zohar*; composed in France and Spain, probably in the early thirteenth century.

Shulchan Aruch: The classic and authoritative code of medieval Jewish law, edited by Rabbi Joseph Caro in Safed, Israel, in the sixteenth century.

Sifrei Bemidbar: A midrash on the halachic (legal) material in the Book of Numbers (*Bemidbar*).

Sifrei Devarim: A midrash on the halachic (legal) material in the Book of Deuteronomy (*Devarim*).

Soloveitchik, Joseph B.: Scholar and philosopher, considered the preeminent sage of modern Orthodoxy; Russia, United States (1903–1993).

Tanchuma: Collection of midrashim, third century CE.

Tanna d'bei Eliyahu: A midrashic work, consisting of moral precepts; date of authorship unclear, between third and tenth centuries CE.

Targum Yerushalmi: An Aramaic translation and interpretation of the Torah, of uncertain authorship, but apparently well known as early as the first to fourth centuries CE.

Torah Temimah: A commentary on the Torah that cites all quotes of a particular verse in Rabbinic literature; compiled by Rabbi Baruch Epstein, Russia (1860–1941).

Vilna Gaon (Elijah ben Solomon): Talmudist, halachist, and mystic, considered one of the most influential rabbinic authorities in Jewish history; Vilna, Lithuania (1720–1797).

Yalkut Shimoni: A midrashic anthology, compiled in Germany, most likely in the thirteenth century.

Zohar: The cardinal text of Jewish mysticism, organized as a running commentary on the Torah and other books of the Hebrew Bible, compiled in Spain in the thirteenth century.

Notes

Introduction

1. Among them, Ellen Frankel's *Five Books of Miriam: A Woman's Commentary on the Torah* (New York: Harper One, 1997); *The Women's Torah Commentary: New Insights from Women Rabbis on the 54 Torah Portions* (Woodstock, Vt.: Jewish Lights, 2000) and *The Women's Haftarah Commentary: New Insights from Women Rabbis on the 54 Weekly Haftarah Portions, the 5 Megillot and Special Shabbatot* (Woodstock, Vt.: Jewish Lights, 2004), both edited by Rabbi Elyse Goldstein; and *The Torah: A Women's Commentary*, edited by Dr. Tamara Cohn Eskenazi and Rabbi Andrea Weiss (New York: URJ Press, 2007). There have also been numerous "premodern" Torah commentaries that were intended primarily for a female audience, such as the classic *Tzenah Urena*, which was written in Yiddish.
2. Sylvia Barack Fishman and Daniel Parmer, *Matrilineal Ascent/Patrilineal Descent: The Growing Gender Imbalance in American Jewish Life* (Maurice and Marilyn Cohen Center for Modern Jewish Studies) (Boston: Brandeis University, 2008), p. 1.
3. Sylvia Barack Fishman, "Transformations in the Composition of American Jewish Households," Jerusalem Center for Public Affairs, http://www.jcpa.org/cjc/cjc-fishman-f05.htm.
4. Fishman and Parmer, p. 5.

Bereshit/Genesis

Bereshit • Rabbi Sheldon Zimmerman

1. The sound and use of words call our attention to the narratives containing them. Since Torah stories were heard and not read by the vast majority of people assembled (at most only the reader had a written text), sounds are crucial and draw attention to other words with similar sounds. We hear a word or words used again and our attention is heightened. In a class on midrash, our teacher and *rav* Dr. Eugene Borowitz called this the "boing theory." We hear the sound(s), and our attention becomes focused. We can then learn from both contexts about each of them.

2. The Rabbis in the midrash, as well as the traditional commentators, try to understand Ishmael's playing in a negative way. There is no evidence for that interpretation in the text.

3. Some even believe that the angel spoke too late to prevent an eager Abraham from sacrificing his son. Isaac dies and is then resurrected. Remnants of this view remain in the traditional Rosh Hashanah liturgy. Also see Shalom Spiegel, *The Last Trial: On the Legends and Lore of the Command to Abraham to Offer Isaac as a Sacrifice* (Woodstock, Vt.: Jewish Lights Publishing, 1993).

4. The silence of the text is most telling. Isaac is not mentioned.

5. The Rabbis rarely, if ever, try to see something positive in Esau's behavior. They almost always favor Jacob and express mistrust over Esau. See the midrash *Bereshit Rabbah* 78 and *Avot d'Rabbi Natan* 34. I see this text and Esau's behavior as I see Ishmael's actions. The cast-out brother and the less-loved brother move toward reconciliation and can be more positively seen as their brothers' keepers.

6. The use of *achi*, "my brother," demands that we pay attention.

7. The text also reads "you shall not see my face," reminding us of the words that Jacob utters when he reconnects and reconciles with Esau: "To see your face is like seeing the face of God" (Genesis 33:10). The stage is being set. Once again, the words call us to attention.

Noach • Rabbi John Moscowitz

1. *Midrash Tanchuma, Noach.*

2. Karen Armstrong, *In the Beginning: A New Interpretation of Genesis* (New York: Ballentine Books, 1997), p. 41.

3. Sigmund Freud, *The Interpretation of Dreams*, trans. A. A. Brill (New York: Random House, 1950), pp. 98–99.

4. Sigmund Freud, *Civilization and Its Discontents* (New York: W. W. Norton & Company, 1961), p. 50.

5. Leon Kass, *The Beginning of Wisdom* (New York: Free Press, 2003), p. 204.

6. *Midrash Rabbah: Genesis* (Oxford, 1977), p. 209.

Vayera • Dr. Sander L. Gilman

1. Erich Auerbach, *Mimesis: The Representation of Reality in Western Literature* (Garden City, N.Y.: Doubleday, 1957), p. 19.

2. Joseph B. Soloveitchik, *Divrei Hashkafa*, ed. Moshe Krone (Jerusalem: World Zionist Organization, 1992), p. 255.

3. Lippman Bodoff, *The Binding of Isaac, Religious Murders, & Kabbalah: Seeds of Jewish Extremism and Alienation?* (New York: Devora Publishing, 2005).

4. Wilfred Owen, "The Parable of the Old Man and the Young," in *The Complete Poems and Fragments*, vol. 1, *The Poems*, ed. Jon Stallworthy (London: Chatto & Windus, 1983), p. 151.

5. Martin Heidegger, "Conversation on a Country Path about Thinking," in *Discourse on Thinking*, trans. John M. Anderson and E. Hans Freund (New York: Harper and Row, 1966), p. 61.

6. Woody Allen, *Without Feathers* (New York: Warner Books, 1975), p. 137.

Toldot • Rabbi Peter S. Knobel

1. *The Torah: A Modern Commentary*, rev. ed., ed. W. Gunther Plaut (New York: URL Press, 2005), p. 188.

Vayishlach • Dr. Norman J. Cohen

1. Much of this *devar Torah* is based upon material in chapter 4 of my book, *Self, Struggle and Change: Family Conflict Stories in Genesis and Their Healing Insights for Our Lives* (Woodstock, Vt.: Jewish Lights Publishing, 1995), pp. 95–124.

2. The word *yippareidu* clearly breaks up a pattern in the Hebrew of four phrases of three beats each. It sticks out and as such seems to be a thematic key.

3. The root of the word for wrestling used here is *avak*, which literally means "dirt" or "dust." It is also very similar in sound to the name Yaakov and to Yabbok.

4. They tore each other apart in the womb—*va-yitrotzatzu* (Genesis 25:22), from the verb *ratzatz*. Now Esau runs toward Jacob (*va-yarotz* [Genesis 33:4]), from the similar verb, *ratz*.

5. The wordplay between *machaneh* (camp), mentioned several times, *chen* (favor), and *minchah* (gift) stresses that one can move from a defensive posture to reestablishing relationship.

6. Esau accepted Jacob (*va-tirtzeni*) (Genesis 33:10). The root *ratzah* is similar to *ratzatz* (struggle) and *ratz* (run), which were used before. The movement is from struggle and conflict, to running toward each other, to acceptance.

Miketz • Joel Lurie Grishaver

1. Frank Pittman, *Man Enough: Father, Sons, and the Search for Masculinity* (New York: G. P. Putmam's Sons, 1993), p. 34.

2. Ibid., p. 34.

Bo • Rabbi Joseph Black

1. Cf. Midrash, *Shemot Rabbah* 13:3; Rashi on Exodus 7:3.

Beshalach • Cantor Jeff Klepper

1. Midrash, *Shir Ha-shirim Rabbah* 1:65.

Vayikra • Rabbi Joseph B. Meszler

1. See Frank Pittman, *Man Enough: Fathers, Sons, and the Search for Masculinity* (New York: Berkley Publishing Group, 1993), pp. 233–36.

2. The tradition of writing a small letter *aleph* for the Hebrew word *vayikra* is maintained in many editions of the Torah in book form as well, not just the scroll.
3. This is the theory of Rabbi Moses Chaim Luzzatto (seventeenth century).
4. Victor Cohen, *The Soul of the Torah: Insights of the Chasidic Masters on the Weekly Torah Portions* (Northvale, N.J.: Jason Aronson, 2000), pp. 185–186.

Shemini • Rabbi Stephen S. Pearce

1. Howard Thurman, "For a Time of Sorrow," in *Meditations of the Heart* (New York: Harper and Brothers, 1953).

Emor • Rabbi Simkha Y. Weintraub

1. Baruch A. Levine, *The JPS Torah Commentary: Leviticus* (Philadephia: Jewish Publication Society, 1989), p. 143.
2. P. C. Rosenblatt, R. Walsh, and D. A. Jackson, *Grief and Mourning in Cross-cultural Perspective*, Human Relations Area File Press, 1976, chap. 5.
3. W. Stroebe and M. S. Stroebe, *Bereavement and Health* (Cambridge: Cambridge University Press, 1987).
4. After the bombing of an Iraqi air-raid shelter in the 1991 Gulf War, one report described a group of boys overcome by grief in the hospital court-yard beating their heads against a wall until they bled, screaming "Gone! Gone!" (A. Rojo, "Corpses seemed shrunk by the heat of bunker fire," *The Guardian*, February 14, 1991, p. 1).
5. Indeed, one reason that scholars have offered for the biblical ban on destroying the "corners" of the beard was that it was intended to differentiate the Israelites from other peoples; in the ancient world, the manner of shaving, cutting, curling, and grooming hair and beard distinguished different peoples from one another. Others have suggested that shaving specific areas of the face was associated with certain pagan cults, or symbolized those who ministered to foreign gods, so this ban is to be seen within the context of opposing pagan practices ("Beards and Shaving," *Encyclopaedia Judaica*, vol. 4, columns 356–58).
6. Meir Soloveichik, "Why Beards?" *Commentary*, February 2008, pp. 41–44.
7. Leon R. Kass, *The Beginning of Wisdom: Reading Genesis* (New York: Free Press, 2003), p. 626.
8. Soloveichick, "Why Beards?" p. 42.
9. Bringing to mind the words of William Shakespeare (1564–1616): "He that hath a beard is more than a youth, and he that hath none is less than a man" (*Much Ado about Nothing*).
10. The Jerusalem Talmud offers this connection between the beard and God's love for the people of Israel: "It is the custom among men when they appear before a court of justice to put on black clothes, and to let their beard grow long because of the uncertainty of the verdict. The people of Israel do not act so. On the day when the judgment opens (Rosh Hashanah), they are clad in white and shave their beards; they eat and

drink and rejoice in the conviction that God will do wonders for them ..."
(Jerusalem Talmud, *Rosh Hashanah* 1:3).

11. Soloveichik, "Why Beards?" p. 42.

12. See Mark J. Zucker, "Raphael and the Beard of Pope Julius II," *The Art Bulletin*, vol. 59, no. 4 (December 1977), pp. 524–33.

13. See Guilielmus Durandus, *Rationale Divinum Officiorum: The Foundational Symbols of the Early Church, Its Structure, Decoration, Sacraments and Vestments* (Louisville, Ky.: Fons Vitae, 2007).

14. "Beards and Shaving," *Encyclopaedia Judaica*.

15. See C. M. Horowitz, *Toratan shel Rishonim*, vol. 1 [1881], p. 29, and vol. 2 [1881], p. 18.

16. See the *Bah* (the *Bayit Hadash*, the classic commentary by the seventeenth-century Polish scholar) on the *Shulchan Aruch, Orach Chayim* 53.

17. *Be'er Heitev, Yoreh De'ah* 181:5.

18. See *Noda B'Yhudah, Mahadura Tinyana, Yoreh De'ah* 80.

19. From a strictly traditional point of view, what was forbidden was the removal of the hair of the beard using a single-edged razor. Utilizing chemical (depilatory) means, scissors, or an electric shaver (with two or more cutting edges) were all permitted. In fact, from a very specific, technical understanding of the commandment, even the single-edged razor shaving was only forbidden concerning five parts of the face—but since differences of opinion arose concerning what/where precisely these points are, the practice developed not to use a single-edged razor at all. Despite these attitudes and restrictions, to trim the beard and/or have a haircut in honor of Shabbat and the festivals is generally regarded as a pious duty.

It should be noted that in terms of the state government's ruling authorities, the Jews simply could never get it quite right. Certain rulers, among them the harsh and despotic Nicholas I of Russia (1796–1855) tried to force the Jewish population to cut off their beards and earlocks, whereas others, such as Maria Theresa of Austria (1717–1780) ordered Jews to keep their beards so as to be easily singled out as an alien element by Christian neighbors!

Behar (25:10–26:2)–Bechukotai • Rabbi Mike Comins

1. Especially in ancient times, but even today, some of the crops will grow without cultivation in the coming year. Orchards only suffer from the lack of pruning and irrigation.

2. Sinai, here, is called Horeb.

3. Jacob prefers to dwell with the women, in the tents; see Genesis 25:27.

4. The Jabbok River, just south of the Golan Heights, runs east-west and feeds the Jordan River. Jacob comes from Paddan-aram in the north. Esau, who sojourns in Seir/Edom, also east of the Jordan, is coming from the south. When Jacob moves his camp across the river, he likely moves them from the northern bank to the southern, leaving him on the northern bank—the direction in which he would run.

5. The midrash likens Jacob to a captain who leaves his ship last. But Rashi's grandson, Rashbam, gives us the simple meaning of the text in Genesis 32:25: "'Jacob was left alone'—in order to flee a different route, where he intended to avoid Esau. 'And wrestled an angel with him'—so that he would not be able to flee." This interpretation is appropriate to Jacob's character. He has fled twice before—once from Esau, once from Laban.

6. Most interpreters understand the *ish* to be an angel. Following Jack Miles, however, I think the man is Esau himself, the master tracker, who has gone out ahead of his army to reconnoiter. There, he discovers Jacob preparing to run. But twenty years more mature, he is no longer interested in killing his little brother. Instead, he gives him the gift of a fight! (Jack Miles, *God: A Biography* [New York: Knopf, 1995], p. 73; I am grateful to Rabbi Mordecai Finley for bringing this interpretation to my attention.)

7. The *ish* blesses Jacob with his new name, Israel, because "you have struggled with God and people, and you were able" (Genesis 32:28).

Pinchas • Rabbi Tony Bayfield

1. W. Gunter Plaut, *The Torah: A Modern Commentary* (New York: UAHC Press, 1981), p. 1195.
2. Ibid.
3. Samson Raphael Hirsch, *The Pentateuch with Translation and Commentary* (New York: Judaica Press, 1962), *ad loc.*
4. Baruch Epstein. Quoted in Nehama Leibowitz, *Studies in Bamidbar* (Jerusalem: World Zionist Organizations, 1980), p. 330.

Mattot • Doug Barden

1. Allan C. Tuffs, *And You Shall Teach Them to Your Sons: Biblical Tales for Fathers and Sons* (New York: UAHC Press, 1997), p. 2.

Ekev • Rabbi David B. Rosen

1. Harold Kushner, in *Etz Hayim: Torah and Commentary*, ed. David L. Lieber (New York: Rabbinical Assembly, 2001), p. 1040.
2. Henry Ward Beecher, *Life Thoughts Gathered from the Extemporaneous Discourses of Henry Ward Beecher*, ed. Edna Dean Proctor (Whitefish, MT: Kessinger Publishing, 2003), p. 116.

Re'eh • Rabbi David J. Gelfand

1. Victor Frankl, *Man's Search for Meaning*.
2. Dennis Prager, *Happiness Is a Serious Problem: A Human Nature Repair Manual* (Harper Paperbacks, 1998), p. 47.

Nitzavim • Rabbi Howard A. Addison

1. See http://www.webdelsol.com/Perihelion/Daleypoetry.html.
2. Samson Raphael Hirsch, *The Pentateuch: Translation and Commentary*, vol. V, Deuteronomy, trans. Isaac Levy (Gateshead, England: Judaica Press, 1976), pp. 586–87.

3. Jerusalem Talmud, *Pe'ah* 3:1.
4. *Sefer Ha-bahir* 51.
5. *Sefer Avodat Ha-kodesh* 2:30.
6. Mark Twain, "Concerning the Jews," *Harpers Magazine*, March 1898; the text can be found at http://www.fordham.edu/halsall/mod/1898twain-jews. Friedrich Nietzsche, *Beyond Good and Evil*, sec. 251, 1886, in Walter Kaufmann, ed., *Basic Writings of Nietzsche* (New York: The Modern Library, 1968), p. 377.
7. See http://www.wallawalla.edu/westwind/archives/fall02.
8. "Grounded," *Alcoholics Anonymous*, 4th ed. (New York: Alcoholics Anonymous World Services, 2002), pp. 522–30.
9. *The Complete Art Scroll Machzor: Rosh Hashanah* (Brooklyn: Mesorah Publications, 1985), p. 65.
10. *Mei Ha-shiloach* on *Nitzavim*.
11. *Degel Machaneh Ephraim* on *Terumah*.
12. Robert Fulghum, *It Was On Fire When I Lay Down on It* (New York: Villard Books, 1989), p. 104.

Glossary

Akedah: Literally, "the binding"—the near-sacrifice of Isaac on Mount Moriah by his father, Abraham (Genesis 22).

aliyah: Literally, "ascent." The act of emigrating to the State of Israel. It can also mean the honor of being called to say the blessings over the reading of the Torah.

Amidah: Literally, "the standing prayer." The eighteen (or nineteen prayers) that constitute the main body of Jewish liturgy; also known as the *Tefilah* and the *Shemoneh Esreh*.

bar/bat mitzvah: The ritual coming of age of a Jewish boy or girl, observed at thirteen years old.

bikkur cholim: The mitzvah of visiting the sick.

brit milah: Ritual circumcision, held on the eighth day of a Jewish boy's life.

cheshbon ha-nefesh: Literally, "soul account." The process of introspection that leads to *teshuvah* (repentance).

Chumash: The Five Books of Moses (Pentateuch or the Torah), consisting of Genesis, Exodus, Leviticus, Numbers, and Deuteronomy; any volume containing the same.

chutzpah: Audacity or gall.

daven: The act of praying (Yiddish).

devekut: Literally, "cleaving." In Jewish mysticism, the sense of intimacy with God.

El Shaddai: God Almighty, an ancient biblical epithet for God.

hachnasat orchim: Literally, "welcoming guests"; the mitzvah of offering hospitality.

halachah: Literally, "the way to go." Jewish law.

haredi, haredim: Ultra-Orthodox Jews.

Hasid: Literally, "pietist." An adherent of the mystical sect of ultra-Orthodox Jews who believe in the service of God through utter joy and contemplation.

hesder: An Israeli program that combines traditional Jewish yeshiva learning with military service.

hitlahavut: Literally, "to be on fire." In Jewish mysticism, the sense of religious ecstasy and enthusiasm; it often marks Hasidic devotion.

IDF: The Israel Defense Forces, also known as Tzahal.

kohanim (**singular,** *kohen*): Ancient Jewish priests, and those who believe themselves to be descended from them.

menschlichkeit: Human decency, as exhibited by a mensch (literally, "a man," or any human being with depth) (Yiddish).

mishkan: The ancient desert tabernacle.

mitzvah (plural, mitzvot): A commandment or obligation of Jewish life.

Molech: The ancient Canaanite god who was worshiped through child sacrifice.

parashah: The Torah portion of the week (also, *sedra*). The Torah is read consecutively, from the beginning of Genesis (*Bereshit*) to the end of Deuteronomy (*Devarim*), on each Shabbat of the Jewish year, as well as on Mondays, Thursdays, and holidays.

p'shat: The "simple" or literal sense of the meaning of a biblical text.

rebbe: A spiritual leader of a Hasidic dynasty.

sefirot: The emanations of God in the world, consisting of the different aspects of the divine personality, as taught in Jewish mysticism.

Shechinah: The mystical feminine Presence of God.

tallit: Jewish prayer shawl.

tzaddik: A righteous person.

Yamim Noraim: Literally, "the awesome days." The Jewish High Holy Day season of deep personal and spiritual introspection. It includes Rosh Hashanah, the Jewish New Year, and culminates with Yom Kippur, the Day of Atonement.

Yizkor: Literally, "let (God) remember." The memorial service that is held on Yom Kippur and other festivals.

Bibliography and Suggestions for Further Reading

Torah Commentaries and Useful Books about the Hebrew Bible

Alter, Robert. *The Five Books of Moses: A Translation with Commentary*. New York: W. W. Norton, 2008.

Cohen, Norman J. *Self, Struggle & Change: Family Conflict Stories in Genesis and Their Healing Insights for Our Lives*. Woodstock, Vt.: Jewish Lights, 1996.

———. *Voices from Genesis: Guiding Us through the Stages of Life*. Woodstock, Vt.: Jewish Lights, 2001.

———. *The Way Into Torah*. Woodstock, Vt.: Jewish Lights, 2004.

———. *Hineini in Our Lives: Learning How to Respond to Others through 14 Biblical Texts and Personal Stories*. Woodstock, Vt.: Jewish Lights, 2005.

———. *Moses and the Journey to Leadership: Timeless Lessons of Effective Management from the Bible and Today's Leadership*. Woodstock, Vt.: Jewish Lights, 2008.

Fields, Harvey J. *A Torah Commentary for Our Times*. 3 vols. New York: UAHC Press, 1990–93.

Gillman, Neil. *Traces of God: Seeing God in Torah, History and Everyday Life*. Woodstock, Vt.: Jewish Lights, 2008.

Hertz, J. H. *The Pentateuch and Haftorahs: Hebrew Text English Translation and Commentary*. New York: Soncino Press, 1960.

Kass, Leon R. *The Beginning of Wisdom: Reading Genesis*. New York: Free Press, 2003.

Kushner, Lawrence, and David Mamet. *Five Cities of Refuge: Weekly Reflections on Genesis, Exodus, Leviticus, Numbers, and Deuteronomy*. New York: Schocken, 2003.

Leibowitz, Nehama. *Studies in Bereshit (Genesis)*. 4th ed. Jerusalem: World Zionist Organization, Department for Torah Education and Culture in the Diaspora, 1980. (Other commentaries in this series cover the other books of the Torah: Exodus, Leviticus, Numbers, and Deuteronomy.)

Levine, Baruch. *The JPS Torah Commentary: Leviticus*. Philadelphia: Jewish Publication Society, 1989.

Lieber, David L. *Etz Hayim: Torah and Commentary*. New York: Rabbinical Assembly, 2002.

Milgrom, Jacob. *The JPS Torah Commentary: Numbers*. Philadelphia: Jewish Publication Society, 1990.

Plaut, W. Gunther. *The Torah: A Modern Commentary*. New York: UAHC Press, 1981.

———, ed. *The Torah: A Modern Commentary*. Rev. ed. New York: URJ Press, 2005.

Salkin, Jeffrey K. *Righteous Gentiles in the Hebrew Bible: Ancient Models for Sacred Relationships*. Woodstock, Vt.: Jewish Lights, 2008.

Sarna, Nahum M. *JPS Torah Commentary: Genesis*. Philadelphia: Jewish Publication Society, 1989.

———. *The JPS Torah Commentary: Exodus*. Philadelphia: Jewish Publication Society, 1991.

Tigay, Jeffrey S. *The JPS Torah Commentary: Deuteronomy*. Philadelphia: Jewish Publication Society, 1996.

Zornberg, Avivah Gottlieb. *The Beginning of Desire*. Philadelphia: Jewish Publication Society, 1995.

———. *The Particulars of Rapture: Reflections on Exodus*. New York: Doubleday, 2001.

Books about Gender That Are Particularly Useful for Exploring Issues of Jewish Masculinity

Barden, Doug. *Wrestling with Jacob and Esau: Fighting the Flight of Men*. New York: Men of Reform Judaism, 2005.

Boyarin, Daniel. *Unheroic Conduct: The Rise of Heterosexuality and the Invention of the Jewish Man*. Contraversions: Critical Studies in Jewish Literature, Culture and Society 8. Berkeley: University of California Press, 1997.

Brod, Harry, ed. *A Mensch among Men: Explorations in Jewish Masculinity*. Freedom, Calif.: Crossing Press, 1988.

Cantor, Aviva. *Jewish Women, Jewish Men: The Legacy of Patriarchy in Jewish Life*. San Francisco: HarperCollins, 2005.

Faludi, Susan. *Stiffed: The Betrayal of the American Man*. New York: HarperPerennial, 2000.

Fishman, Sylvia Barack, and Daniel Parmer. "Matrilineal Ascent/Patrilineal Descent: The Growing Gender Imbalance in Contemporary Jewish Life." Waltham, Mass.: Cohen Center for Modern Jewish Studies, Brandeis University, 2008.

Gilman, Sander. *The Jew's Body*. New York: Routledge, 1991.

Goldberg, Herb. *The Hazards of Being Male: Surviving the Myth of Masculinity*. Wellness Institute, 2000 (originally published in 1976).

Grishaver, Joel Lurie. *The Bonding of Isaac: Stories and Essays about Gender and Jewish Spirituality*. Los Angeles: Aleph Design Group, 1997.

Holzman, Michael. *The Still Small Voice: Reflections on Being a Jewish Man*. New York: URJ Press, 2007.

Kimmel, Michael S. *Manhood in America: A Cultural History*. New York: Oxford University Press, 2005.

Meszler, Joseph B. *A Man's Responsibility: A Jewish Guide to Being a Son, a Partner in Marriage, a Father and a Community Leader*. Woodstock, Vt.: Jewish Lights, 2008.

Olitzky, Kerry M. *From Your Father's House: Reflections for Modern Jewish Men*. Philadelphia: Jewish Publication Society, 1999.

Person, Hara, et al., eds. *The Gender Gap: A Congregational Guide for Beginning the Conversation about Men's Involvement in Synagogue Life*. New York: URJ Press, 2007.

Peskowitz, Miriam B. *Spinning Fantasies: Rabbis, Gender and History*. Berkeley: University of California Press, 1997.

Peskowitz, Miriam B., and Laura Levitt, eds. *Judaism since Gender*. New York: Routledge, 1996.

Pitzele, Peter. *Our Fathers' Wells: A Personal Encounter with the Myths of Genesis*. New York: HarperCollins, 1996.

Salkin, Jeffrey K. *Searching for My Brothers: Jewish Men in a Gentile World*. New York: Putnam, 1999.

Shapiro, Rami M. *Embracing Esau*. New York: Signet, 1977.

Tuffs, Allan C. *And You Shall Teach Them to Your Sons: Biblical Tales for Fathers and Sons*. New York: UAHC Press, 1997.

Wolfson, Paula Ethel. *Jewish Fathers: A Legacy of Love*. Woodstock, Vt.: Jewish Lights, 2004

Bar/Bat Mitzvah

The JGirl's Guide: The Young Jewish Woman's Handbook for Coming of Age
By Penina Adelman, Ali Feldman, and Shulamit Reinharz
This inspirational, interactive guidebook helps pre-teen Jewish girls address the many issues surrounding coming of age. 6 x 9, 240 pp, Quality PB, 978-1-58023-215-9 **$14.99**
 Also Available: **The JGirl's Teacher's and Parent's Guide**
 8½ x 11, 56 pp, PB, 978-1-58023-225-8 **$8.99**
Bar/Bat Mitzvah Basics: A Practical Family Guide to Coming of Age Together
Edited by Cantor Helen Leneman 6 x 9, 240 pp, Quality PB, 978-1-58023-151-0 **$18.95**
The Bar/Bat Mitzvah Memory Book, 2nd Edition: An Album for Treasuring the Spiritual Celebration *By Rabbi Jeffrey K. Salkin and Nina Salkin*
8 x 10, 48 pp, Deluxe HC, 2-color text, ribbon marker, 978-1-58023-263-0 **$19.99**

For Kids—Putting God on Your Guest List, 2nd Edition: How to Claim the Spiritual Meaning of Your Bar or Bat Mitzvah *By Rabbi Jeffrey K. Salkin*
6 x 9, 144 pp, Quality PB, 978-1-58023-308-8 **$15.99** *For ages 11–13*
Putting God on the Guest List, 3rd Edition: How to Reclaim the Spiritual Meaning of Your Child's Bar or Bat Mitzvah *By Rabbi Jeffrey K. Salkin*
6 x 9, 224 pp, Quality PB, 978-1-58023-222-7 **$16.99**; HC, 978-1-58023-260-9 **$24.99**
Also Available: **Putting God on the Guest List Teacher's Guide**
8½ x 11, 48 pp, PB, 978-1-58023-226-5 **$8.99**
Tough Questions Jews Ask: A Young Adult's Guide to Building a Jewish Life
By Rabbi Edward Feinstein 6 x 9, 160 pp, Quality PB, 978-1-58023-139-8 **$14.99** *For ages 12 & up*
Also Available: **Tough Questions Jews Ask Teacher's Guide**
8½ x 11, 72 pp, PB, 978-1-58023-187-9 **$8.95**

Bible Study/Midrash

Abraham's Bind & Other Bible Tales of Trickery, Folly, Mercy and Love *By Michael J. Caduto*
Re-imagines many biblical characters, retelling their stories.
6 x 9, 224 pp, HC, 978-1-59473-186-0 **$19.99** *(A book from SkyLight Paths, Jewish Lights' sister imprint)*
Ancient Secrets: Using the Stories of the Bible to Improve Our Everyday Lives
By Rabbi Levi Meier, PhD 5½ x 8½, 288 pp, Quality PB, 978-1-58023-064-3 **$16.95**
The Genesis of Leadership: What the Bible Teaches Us about Vision, Values and Leading Change *By Rabbi Nathan Laufer; Foreword by Senator Joseph I. Lieberman*
Unlike other books on leadership, this one is rooted in the stories of the Bible.
6 x 9, 288 pp, Quality PB, 978-1-58023-352-1 **$18.99**; HC, 978-1-58023-241-8 **$24.99**
Hineini in Our Lives: Learning How to Respond to Others through 14 Biblical Texts and Personal Stories *By Norman J. Cohen* 6 x 9, 240 pp, Quality PB, 978-1-58023-274-6 **$16.99**
Moses and the Journey to Leadership: Timeless Lessons of Effective Management from the Bible and Today's Leaders *By Dr. Norman J. Cohen*
6 x 9, 240 pp, Quality PB, 978-1-58023-351-4 **$18.99**; HC, 978-1-58023-227-2 **$21.99**
Self, Struggle & Change: Family Conflict Stories in Genesis and Their Healing Insights for Our Lives *By Norman J. Cohen* 6 x 9, 224 pp, Quality PB, 978-1-879045-66-8 **$18.99**
The Triumph of Eve & Other Subversive Bible Tales *By Matt Biers-Ariel*
5½ x 8½, 192 pp, Quality PB, 978-1-59473-176-1 **$14.99**; HC, 978-1-59473-040-5 **$19.99**
(A book from SkyLight Paths, Jewish Lights' sister imprint)

The Wisdom of Judaism: An Introduction to the Values of the Talmud
By Rabbi Dov Peretz Elkins
Explores the essence of Judaism. 6 x 9, 192 pp, Quality PB, 978-1-58023-327-9 **$16.99**
Also Available: **The Wisdom of Judaism Teacher's Guide**
8½ x 11, 18 pp, PB, 978-1-58023-350-7 **$8.99**

Or phone, fax, mail or e-mail to: **JEWISH LIGHTS** Publishing
Sunset Farm Offices, Route 4 • P.O. Box 237 • Woodstock, Vermont 05091
Tel: (802) 457-4000 • Fax: (802) 457-4004 • www.jewishlights.com
Credit card orders: (800) 962-4544 (8:30AM–5:30PM ET Monday–Friday)
Generous discounts on quantity orders. SATISFACTION GUARANTEED. Prices subject to change.

Meditation

Jewish Meditation Practices for Everyday Life
Awakening Your Heart, Connecting with God
By Rabbi Jeff Roth Offers a fresh take on meditation that draws on life experience and living life with greater clarity as opposed to the traditional method of rigorous study. 6 x 9, 224 pp, Quality PB Original, 978-1-58023-397-2 **$18.99**

The Handbook of Jewish Meditation Practices
A Guide for Enriching the Sabbath and Other Days of Your Life
By Rabbi David A. Cooper Easy-to-learn meditation techniques.
6 x 9, 208 pp, Quality PB, 978-1-58023-102-2 **$16.95**

Discovering Jewish Meditation: Instruction & Guidance for Learning an Ancient
Spiritual Practice *By Nan Fink Gefen* 6 x 9, 208 pp, Quality PB, 978-1-58023-067-4 **$16.95**

Meditation from the Heart of Judaism: Today's Teachers Share Their Practices,
Techniques, and Faith *Edited by Avram Davis*
6 x 9, 256 pp, Quality PB, 978-1-58023-049-0 **$16.95**

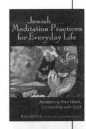

Ritual/Sacred Practice

The Jewish Dream Book: The Key to Opening the Inner Meaning of
Your Dreams *By Vanessa L. Ochs with Elizabeth Ochs; Full-color illus. by Kristina Swarner*
Instructions for how modern people can perform ancient Jewish dream practices
and dream interpretations drawn from the Jewish wisdom tradition.
8 x 8, 128 pp, Full-color illus., Deluxe PB w/flaps, 978-1-58023-132-9 **$16.95**

God in Your Body: Kabbalah, Mindfulness and Embodied Spiritual Practice
By Jay Michaelson
The first comprehensive treatment of the body in Jewish spiritual practice and an
essential guide to the sacred.
6 x 9, 288 pp, Quality PB, 978-1-58023-304-0 **$18.99**

The Book of Jewish Sacred Practices: CLAL's Guide to Everyday & Holiday
Rituals & Blessings *Edited by Rabbi Irwin Kula and Vanessa L. Ochs, PhD*
6 x 9, 368 pp, Quality PB, 978-1-58023-152-7 **$18.95**

Jewish Ritual: A Brief Introduction for Christians
By Rabbi Kerry M. Olitzky and Rabbi Daniel Judson
5½ x 8½, 144 pp, Quality PB, 978-1-58023-210-4 **$14.99**

The Rituals & Practices of a Jewish Life: A Handbook for Personal Spiritual
Renewal *Edited by Rabbi Kerry M. Olitzky and Rabbi Daniel Judson*
6 x 9, 272 pp, illus., Quality PB, 978-1-58023-169-5 **$18.95**

The Sacred Art of Lovingkindness: Preparing to Practice
By Rabbi Rami Shapiro 5½ x 8½, 176 pp, Quality PB, 978-1-59473-151-8 **$16.99**
(A book from SkyLight Paths, Jewish Lights' sister imprint)

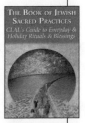

Science Fiction/Mystery & Detective Fiction

Mystery Midrash: An Anthology of Jewish Mystery & Detective Fiction
Edited by Lawrence W. Raphael; Preface by Joel Siegel
6 x 9, 304 pp, Quality PB, 978-1-58023-055-1 **$16.95**

Criminal Kabbalah: An Intriguing Anthology of Jewish Mystery &
Detective Fiction *Edited by Lawrence W. Raphael; Foreword by Laurie R. King*
All-new stories from twelve of today's masters of mystery and detective fiction—
sure to delight mystery buffs of all faith traditions.
6 x 9, 256 pp, Quality PB, 978-1-58023-109-1 **$16.95**

Wandering Stars: An Anthology of Jewish Fantasy & Science Fiction
Edited by Jack Dann; Introduction by Isaac Asimov
6 x 9, 272 pp, Quality PB, 978-1-58023-005-6 **$18.99**

More Wandering Stars: An Anthology of Outstanding Stories of Jewish Fantasy and
Science Fiction *Edited by Jack Dann; Introduction by Isaac Asimov*
6 x 9, 192 pp, Quality PB, 978-1-58023-063-6 **$16.95**

Spirituality

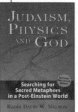

Journeys to a Jewish Life: Inspiring Stories from the Spiritual Journeys of American Jews *By Paula Amann*
Examines the soul treks of Jews lost and found. 6 x 9, 208 pp, HC, 978-1-58023-317-0 **$19.99**

The Adventures of Rabbi Harvey: A Graphic Novel of Jewish Wisdom and Wit in the Wild West *By Steve Sheinkin*
Jewish and American folktales combine in this witty and original graphic novel collection. Creatively retold and set on the western frontier of the 1870s.
6 x 9, 144 pp, Full-color illus., Quality PB, 978-1-58023-310-1 **$16.99**

Rabbi Harvey Rides Again
A Graphic Novel of Jewish Folktales Let Loose in the Wild West *By Steve Sheinkin*
6 x 9, 144 pp, Quality PB Original, Full-color illus., 978-1-58023-347-7 **$16.99**

Ethics of the Sages: *Pirke Avot*—Annotated & Explained
Translation and Annotation by Rabbi Rami Shapiro 5½ x 8½, 192 pp, Quality PB, 978-1-59473-207-2
$16.99 *(A book from SkyLight Paths, Jewish Lights' sister imprint)*

A Book of Life: Embracing Judaism as a Spiritual Practice
By Michael Strassfeld 6 x 9, 528 pp, Quality PB, 978-1-58023-247-0 **$19.99**

Meaning and Mitzvah: Daily Practices for Reclaiming Judaism through Prayer, God, Torah, Hebrew, Mitzvot and Peoplehood *By Rabbi Goldie Milgram*
7 x 9, 336 pp, Quality PB, 978-1-58023-256-2 **$19.99**

The Soul of the Story: Meetings with Remarkable People
By Rabbi David Zeller 6 x 9, 288 pp, HC, 978-1-58023-272-2 **$21.99**

Aleph-Bet Yoga: Embodying the Hebrew Letters for Physical and Spiritual Well-Being
By Steven A. Rapp. Foreword by Tamar Frankiel, PhD and Judy Greenfeld. Preface by Hart Lazer.
7 x 10, 128 pp, b/w photos, Quality PB, Layflat binding, 978-1-58023-162-6 **$16.95**

Does the Soul Survive? A Jewish Journey to Belief in Afterlife, Past Lives & Living with Purpose *By Rabbi Elie Kaplan Spitz; Foreword by Brian L. Weiss, MD*
6 x 9, 288 pp, Quality PB, 978-1-58023-165-7 **$16.99**

First Steps to a New Jewish Spirit: Reb Zalman's Guide to Recapturing the Intimacy & Ecstasy in Your Relationship with God *By Rabbi Zalman M. Schachter-Shalomi with Donald Gropman* 6 x 9, 144 pp, Quality PB, 978-1-58023-182-4 **$16.95**

God in Our Relationships: Spirituality between People from the Teachings of Martin Buber *By Rabbi Dennis S. Ross* 5½ x 8½, 160 pp, Quality PB, 978-1-58023-147-3 **$16.95**

Judaism, Physics and God: Searching for Sacred Metaphors in a Post-Einstein World
By Rabbi David W. Nelson 6 x 9, 368 pp, Quality PB, inc. reader's discussion guide, 978-1-58023-306-4 **$18.99**;
HC, 352 pp, 978-1-58023-252-4 **$24.99**

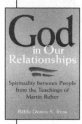

The Jewish Lights Spirituality Handbook: A Guide to Understanding, Exploring & Living a Spiritual Life *Edited by Stuart M. Matlins*
What exactly is "Jewish" about spirituality? How do I make it a part of my life? Fifty of today's foremost spiritual leaders share their ideas and experience with us.
6 x 9, 456 pp, Quality PB, 978-1-58023-093-3 **$19.99**

Bringing the Psalms to Life: How to Understand and Use the Book of Psalms
By Daniel F. Polish 6 x 9, 208 pp, Quality PB, 978-1-58023-157-2 **$16.95**;
HC, 978-1-58023-077-3 **$21.95**

God & the Big Bang: Discovering Harmony between Science & Spirituality
By Daniel C. Matt 6 x 9, 216 pp, Quality PB, 978-1-879045-89-7 **$16.99**

Minding the Temple of the Soul: Balancing Body, Mind, and Spirit through Traditional Jewish Prayer, Movement, and Meditation *By Tamar Frankiel, PhD, and Judy Greenfeld*
7 x 10, 184 pp, illus., Quality PB, 978-1-879045-64-4 **$16.95**

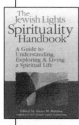

One God Clapping: The Spiritual Path of a Zen Rabbi *By Alan Lew with Sherril Jaffe*
5½ x 8½, 336 pp, Quality PB, 978-1-58023-115-2 **$16.95**

There Is No Messiah ... and You're It: The Stunning Transformation of Judaism's Most Provocative Idea *By Rabbi Robert N. Levine, DD*
6 x 9, 192 pp, Quality PB, 978-1-58023-255-5 **$16.99**

These Are the Words: A Vocabulary of Jewish Spiritual Life
By Arthur Green 6 x 9, 304 pp, Quality PB, 978-1-58023-107-7 **$18.95**

Current Events/History

A Dream of Zion: American Jews Reflect on Why Israel Matters to Them
Edited by Rabbi Jeffrey K. Salkin Explores what Jewish people in America have to say about Israel. 6 x 9, 304 pp, HC, 978-1-58023-340-8 **$24.99**
Also Available: **A Dream of Zion Teacher's Guide** 8½ x 11, 32 pp, PB, 978-1-58023-356-9 **$8.99**

The Jewish Connection to Israel, the Promised Land: A Brief Introduction for Christians *By Rabbi Eugene Korn, PhD* 5½ x 8½, 192 pp, Quality PB, 978-1-58023-318-7 **$14.99**

The Story of the Jews: A 4,000-Year Adventure—A Graphic History Book
Written & illustrated by Stan Mack 6 x 9, 288 pp, illus., Quality PB, 978-1-58023-155-8 **$16.99**

Hannah Senesh: Her Life and Diary, the First Complete Edition
By Hannah Senesh; Foreword by Marge Piercy; Preface by Eitan Senesh; Afterword by Roberta Grossman
6 x 9, 368 pp, b/w photos, Quality PB, 978-1-58023-342-2 **$19.99**

The Ethiopian Jews of Israel: Personal Stories of Life in the Promised Land *By Len Lyons, PhD; Foreword by Alan Dershowitz; Photographs by Ilan Ossendryver* Recounts, through photographs and words, stories of Ethiopian Jews.
10½ x 10, 240 pp, 100 full-color photos, HC, 978-1-58023-323-1 **$34.99**

Foundations of Sephardic Spirituality: The Inner Life of Jews of the Ottoman Empire
By Rabbi Marc D. Angel, PhD 6 x 9, 224 pp, Quality PB, 978-1-58023-341-5 **$18.99**

Judaism and Justice: The Jewish Passion to Repair the World
By Rabbi Sidney Schwarz 6 x 9, 352 pp, Quality PB, 978-1-58023-353-8 **$19.99**

Ecology/Environment

A Wild Faith: Jewish Ways into Wilderness, Wilderness Ways into Judaism
By Rabbi Mike Comins; Foreword by Nigel Savage
Offers ways to enliven and deepen your spiritual life through wilderness experience.
6 x 9, 240 pp, Quality PB, 978-1-58023-316-3 **$16.99**

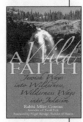

Ecology & the Jewish Spirit: Where Nature & the Sacred Meet
Edited by Ellen Bernstein 6 x 9, 288 pp, Quality PB, 978-1-58023-082-7 **$18.99**

Torah of the Earth: Exploring 4,000 Years of Ecology in Jewish Thought
Vol. 1: Biblical Israel: One Land, One People; Rabbinic Judaism: One People, Many Lands
Vol. 2: Zionism: One Land, Two Peoples; Eco-Judaism: One Earth, Many Peoples
Edited by Arthur Waskow Vol. 1: 6 x 9, 272 pp, Quality PB, 978-1-58023-086-5 **$19.95**
Vol. 2: 6 x 9, 336 pp, Quality PB, 978-1-58023-087-2 **$19.95**

The Way Into Judaism and the Environment *By Jeremy Benstein, PhD*
6 x 9, 288 pp, Quality PB, 978-1-58023-368-2 **$18.99**; HC, 978-1-58023-268-5 **$24.99**

Grief/Healing

Healing and the Jewish Imagination: Spiritual and Practical Perspectives on Judaism and Health *Edited by Rabbi William Cutter, PhD*
Explores Judaism for comfort in times of illness and perspectives on suffering.
6 x 9, 240 pp, Quality PB, 978-1-58023-373-6 **$19.99**; HC, 978-1-58023-314-9 **$24.99**

Grief in Our Seasons: A Mourner's Kaddish Companion *By Rabbi Kerry M. Olitzky*
4½ x 6½, 448 pp, Quality PB, 978-1-879045-55-2 **$15.95**

Healing of Soul, Healing of Body: Spiritual Leaders Unfold the Strength & Solace in Psalms *Edited by Rabbi Simkha Y. Weintraub, CSW*
6 x 9, 128 pp, 2-color illus. text, Quality PB, 978-1-879045-31-6 **$14.99**

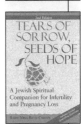

Mourning & Mitzvah, 2nd Edition: A Guided Journal for Walking the Mourner's Path through Grief to Healing *By Anne Brener, LCSW*
7½ x 9, 304 pp, Quality PB, 978-1-58023-113-8 **$19.99**

Tears of Sorrow, Seeds of Hope, 2nd Edition: A Jewish Spiritual Companion for Infertility and Pregnancy Loss *By Rabbi Nina Beth Cardin*
6 x 9, 208 pp, Quality PB, 978-1-58023-233-3 **$18.99**

A Time to Mourn, a Time to Comfort, 2nd Edition: A Guide to Jewish Bereavement *By Dr. Ron Wolfson*
7 x 9, 384 pp, Quality PB, 978-1-58023-253-1 **$19.99**

When a Grandparent Dies: A Kid's Own Remembering Workbook for Dealing with Shiva and the Year Beyond *By Nechama Liss-Levinson, PhD*
8 x 10, 48 pp, 2-color text, HC, 978-1-879045-44-6 **$15.95** *For ages 7–13*

Holidays/Holy Days

Rosh Hashanah Readings: Inspiration, Information and Contemplation
Yom Kippur Readings: Inspiration, Information and Contemplation
Edited by Rabbi Dov Peretz Elkins with Section Introductions from Arthur Green's These Are the Words
An extraordinary collection of readings, prayers and insights that enable the modern worshiper to enter into the spirit of the High Holy Days in a personal and powerful way, permitting the meaning of the Jewish New Year to enter the heart.
RHR: 6 x 9, 400 pp, HC, 978-1-58023-239-5 **$24.99**
YKR: 6 x 9, 368 pp, HC, 978-1-58023-271-5 **$24.99**

Jewish Holidays: A Brief Introduction for Christians
By Rabbi Kerry M. Olitzky and Rabbi Daniel Judson
5½ x 8½, 144 pp, Quality PB, 978-1-58023-302-6 **$16.99**

Reclaiming Judaism as a Spiritual Practice: Holy Days and Shabbat
By Rabbi Goldie Milgram
7 x 9, 272 pp, Quality PB, 978-1-58023-205-0 **$19.99**

7th Heaven: Celebrating Shabbat with Rebbe Nachman of Breslov
By Moshe Mykoff with the Breslov Research Institute
5⅛ x 8¼, 224 pp, Deluxe PB w/flaps, 978-1-58023-175-6 **$18.95**

Shabbat, 2nd Edition: The Family Guide to Preparing for and Celebrating the Sabbath
By Dr. Ron Wolfson 7 x 9, 320 pp, illus., Quality PB, 978-1-58023-164-0 **$19.99**

Hanukkah, 2nd Edition: The Family Guide to Spiritual Celebration
By Dr. Ron Wolfson. Edited by Joel Lurie Grishaver.
7 x 9, 240 pp, illus., Quality PB, 978-1-58023-122-0 **$18.95**

The Jewish Family Fun Book, 2nd Edition: Holiday Projects, Everyday Activities, and Travel Ideas with Jewish Themes *By Danielle Dardashti and Roni Sarig. Illus. by Avi Katz.*
6 x 9, 304 pp, 70+ b/w illus. & diagrams, Quality PB, 978-1-58023-333-0 **$18.99**

The Jewish Lights Book of Fun Classroom Activities: Simple and Seasonal Projects for Teachers and Students *By Danielle Dardashti and Roni Sarig*
6 x 9, 240 pp, Quality PB, 978-1-58023-206-7 **$19.99**

Social Justice

Conscience: The Duty to Obey and the Duty to Disobey
By Rabbi Harold M. Schulweis
This clarion call to rethink our moral and political behavior examines the idea of conscience and the role conscience plays in our relationships to governments, law, ethics, religion, human nature, God—and to each other.
6 x 9, 160 pp, HC, 978-1-58023-375-0 **$19.99**

Judaism and Justice: The Jewish Passion to Repair the World
By Rabbi Sidney Schwarz; Foreword by Ruth Messinger
Explores the relationship between Judaism, social justice and the Jewish identity of American Jews, offering new ways to understand these important aspects of Jewish life.
6 x 9, 352 pp, Quality PB, 978-1-58023-353-8 **$19.99**; HC, 978-1-58023-312-5 **$24.99**

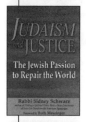

Shared Dreams: Martin Luther King, Jr. & the Jewish Community
By Rabbi Marc Schneier; Preface by Martin Luther King III
6 x 9, 240 pp, Quality PB, 978-1-58023-273-9 **$18.99**

Spiritual Activism: A Jewish Guide to Leadership and Repairing the World
By Rabbi Avraham Weiss; Foreword by Alan M. Dershowitz
6 x 9, 224 pp, HC, 978-1-58023-355-2 **$24.99**

Righteous Indignation: A Jewish Call for Justice
Edited by Rabbi Or N. Rose, Jo Ellen Green Kaiser and Margie Klein; Foreword by Rabbi David Ellenson
Leading progressive Jewish activists are gathered together in one groundbreaking volume as they explore meaningful intellectual and spiritual foundations for their social justice work.
6 x 9, 384 pp, HC, 978-1-58023-336-1 **$24.99**

Inspiration

Happiness and the Human Spirit: The Spirituality of Becoming the
Best You Can Be *By Abraham J. Twerski, MD*
Shows you that true happiness is attainable once you stop looking outside yourself for the source.
6 x 9, 176 pp, Quality PB, 978-1-58023-404-7 **$16.99**; HC, 978-1-58023-343-9 **$19.99**

Life's Daily Blessings: Inspiring Reflections on Gratitude and Joy for Every Day, Based on
Jewish Wisdom *By Rabbi Kerry M. Olitzky* 4½ x 6½, 368 pp, Quality PB, 978-1-58023-396-5 **$16.99**

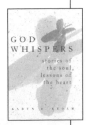

The Bridge to Forgiveness: Stories and Prayers for Finding God and
Restoring Wholeness *By Rabbi Karyn D. Kedar*
Examines how forgiveness can be the bridge that connects us to wholeness and peace.
6 x 9, 176 pp, HC, 978-1-58023-324-8 **$19.99**

God's To-Do List: 103 Ways to Be an Angel and Do God's Work on Earth
By Dr. Ron Wolfson 6 x 9, 150 pp, Quality PB, 978-1-58023-301-9 **$16.99**

God in All Moments: Mystical & Practical Spiritual Wisdom from Hasidic Masters
Edited and translated by Or N. Rose with Ebn D. Leader
5½ x 8½, 192 pp, Quality PB, 978-1-58023-186-2 **$16.95**

Our Dance with God: Finding Prayer, Perspective and Meaning in the Stories of Our
Lives *By Karyn D. Kedar* 6 x 9, 176 pp, Quality PB, 978-1-58023-202-9 **$16.99**

Also Available: **The Dance of the Dolphin** (HC edition of Our Dance with God)
6 x 9, 176 pp, HC, 978-1-58023-202-9 **$19.95**

The Empty Chair: Finding Hope and Joy—Timeless Wisdom from a Hasidic Master,
Rebbe Nachman of Breslov *Adapted by Moshe Mykoff and the Breslov Research Institute*
4 x 6, 128 pp, 2-color text, Deluxe PB w/flaps, 978-1-879045-67-5 **$9.99**

The Gentle Weapon: Prayers for Everyday and Not-So-Everyday Moments—
Timeless Wisdom from the Teachings of the Hasidic Master, Rebbe Nachman of Breslov
Adapted by Moshe Mykoff and S. C. Mizrahi, together with the Breslov Research Institute
4 x 6, 144 pp, 2-color text, Deluxe PB w/flaps, 978-1-58023-022-3 **$9.99**

God Whispers: Stories of the Soul, Lessons of the Heart *By Karyn D. Kedar*
6 x 9, 176 pp, Quality PB, 978-1-58023-088-9 **$15.95**

Restful Reflections: Nighttime Inspiration to Calm the Soul, Based on Jewish Wisdom
By Rabbi Kerry M. Olitzky & Rabbi Lori Forman 4½ x 6½, 448 pp, Quality PB, 978-1-58023-091-9 **$15.95**

Sacred Intentions: Daily Inspiration to Strengthen the Spirit, Based on Jewish Wisdom
By Rabbi Kerry M. Olitzky and Rabbi Lori Forman 4½ x 6½, 448 pp, Quality PB, 978-1-58023-061-2 **$15.95**

Kabbalah/Mysticism

Seek My Face: A Jewish Mystical Theology *By Arthur Green*
6 x 9, 304 pp, Quality PB, 978-1-58023-130-5 **$19.95**

Zohar: Annotated & Explained *Translation and annotation by Daniel C. Matt; Foreword by
Andrew Harvey* 5½ x 8½, 176 pp, Quality PB, 978-1-893361-51-5 **$15.99**
(A book from SkyLight Paths, Jewish Lights' sister imprint)

Ehyeh: A Kabbalah for Tomorrow
By Arthur Green 6 x 9, 224 pp, Quality PB, 978-1-58023-213-5 **$16.99**

The Flame of the Heart: Prayers of a Chasidic Mystic *By Reb Noson of Breslov. Translated by
David Sears with the Breslov Research Institute* 5 x 7¼, 160 pp, Quality PB, 978-1-58023-246-3 **$15.99**

The Gift of Kabbalah: Discovering the Secrets of Heaven, Renewing Your Life on Earth
By Tamar Frankiel, PhD 6 x 9, 256 pp, Quality PB, 978-1-58023-141-1 **$16.95**
HC, 978-1-58023-108-4 **$21.95**

Kabbalah: A Brief Introduction for Christians
By Tamar Frankiel, PhD 5½ x 8½, 208 pp, Quality PB, 978-1-58023-303-3 **$16.99**

The Lost Princess and Other Kabbalistic Tales of Rebbe Nachman of Breslov
The Seven Beggars and Other Kabbalistic Tales of Rebbe Nachman of Breslov
Translated by Rabbi Aryeh Kaplan; Preface by Rabbi Chaim Kramer
Lost Princess: 6 x 9, 400 pp, Quality PB, 978-1-58023-217-3 **$18.99**
Seven Beggars: 6 x 9, 192 pp, Quality PB, 978-1-58023-250-0 **$16.99**

See also *The Way Into Jewish Mystical Tradition* in Spirituality / The Way Into... Series

Men's Interest

A Man's Responsibility
A Jewish Guide to Being a Son, a Partner in Marriage, a Father and a Community Leader
By Rabbi Joseph B. Meszler
A provocative look at how a new generation of Jewish men can grow spiritually, and in doing so, strengthen the intangible bonds of family, love, duty, and truth which ultimately lead to God.
6 x 9, 192 pp, HC, 978-1-58023-362-0 **$21.99**

Congregation Resources

Inspired Jewish Leadership: Practical Approaches to Building Strong Communities
By Dr. Erica Brown
6 x 9, 256 pp, HC, 978-1-58023-361-3 **$24.99**

Becoming a Congregation of Learners: Learning as a Key to Revitalizing Congregational Life *By Isa Aron, PhD; Foreword by Rabbi Lawrence A. Hoffman*
6 x 9, 304 pp, Quality PB, 978-1-58023-089-6 **$19.95**

Finding a Spiritual Home: How a New Generation of Jews Can Transform the American Synagogue *By Rabbi Sidney Schwarz*
6 x 9, 352 pp, Quality PB, 978-1-58023-185-5 **$19.95**

Jewish Pastoral Care, 2nd Edition: A Practical Handbook from Traditional & Contemporary Sources *Edited by Rabbi Dayle A. Friedman, MSW, MAJCS, BCC*
6 x 9, 528 pp, HC, 978-1-58023-221-0 **$40.00**

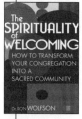

Jewish Spiritual Direction: An Innovative Guide from Traditional and Contemporary Sources *Edited by Rabbi Howard A. Addison and Barbara Eve Breitman*
6 x 9, 368 pp, HC, 978-1-58023-230-2 **$30.00**

The Self-Renewing Congregation: Organizational Strategies for Revitalizing Congregational Life *By Isa Aron, PhD; Foreword by Dr. Ron Wolfson*
6 x 9, 304 pp, Quality PB, 978-1-58023-166-4 **$19.95**

Spiritual Community: The Power to Restore Hope, Commitment and Joy
By Rabbi David A. Teutsch, PhD 5½ x 8½, 144 pp, HC, 978-1-58023-270-8 **$19.99**

The Spirituality of Welcoming: How to Transform Your Congregation into a Sacred Community *By Dr. Ron Wolfson* 6 x 9, 224 pp, Quality PB, 978-1-58023-244-9 **$19.99**

Rethinking Synagogues: A New Vocabulary for Congregational Life
By Rabbi Lawrence A. Hoffman 6 x 9, 240 pp, Quality PB, 978-1-58023-248-7 **$19.99**

Children's Books

What You Will See Inside a Synagogue
By Rabbi Lawrence A. Hoffman and Dr. Ron Wolfson; Full-color photos by Bill Aron
A colorful, fun-to-read introduction that explains the ways and whys of Jewish worship and religious life. 8½ x 10¼, 32 pp, Full-color photos, Quality PB, 978-1-59473-256-0 **$8.99**
For ages 6 & up (A book from SkyLight Paths, Jewish Lights' sister imprint)

The Kids' Fun Book of Jewish Time
By Emily Sper 9 x 7½, 24 pp, Full-color illus., HC, 978-1-58023-311-8 **$16.99**

In God's Hands
By Lawrence Kushner and Gary Schmidt 9 x 12, 32 pp, HC, 978-1-58023-224-1 **$16.99**

Because Nothing Looks Like God
By Lawrence and Karen Kushner
Introduces children to the possibilities of spiritual life.
11 x 8½, 32 pp, Full-color illus., HC, 978-1-58023-092-6 **$17.99** *For ages 4 & up*
Board Book Companions to *Because Nothing Looks Like God*
5 x 5, 24 pp, Full-color illus., SkyLight Paths Board Books *For ages 0–4*

The Book of Miracles: A Young Person's Guide to Jewish Spiritual Awareness
By Lawrence Kushner. All-new illustrations by the author
6 x 9, 96 pp, 2-color illus., HC, 978-1-879045-78-1 **$16.95** *For ages 9 and up*

What Makes Someone a Jew? *By Lauren Seidman*
Reflects the changing face of American Judaism.
10 x 8½, 32 pp, Full-color photos, Quality PB Original, 978-1-58023-321-7 **$8.99** *For ages 3–6*

Spirituality/Lawrence Kushner

Filling Words with Light: Hasidic and Mystical Reflections on Jewish Prayer
By Lawrence Kushner and Nehemia Polen
5½ x 8½, 176 pp, Quality PB, 978-1-58023-238-8 **$16.99**; HC, 978-1-58023-216-6 **$21.99**

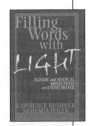

The Book of Letters: A Mystical Hebrew Alphabet
Popular HC Edition, 6 x 9, 80 pp, 2-color text, 978-1-879045-00-2 **$24.95**
Collector's Limited Edition, 9 x 12, 80 pp, gold foil embossed pages, w/limited edition silkscreened print, 978-1-879045-04-0 **$349.00**

The Book of Miracles: A Young Person's Guide to Jewish Spiritual Awareness
6 x 9, 96 pp, 2-color illus., HC, 978-1-879045-78-1 **$16.95** *For ages 9 and up*

The Book of Words: Talking Spiritual Life, Living Spiritual Talk
6 x 9, 160 pp, Quality PB, 978-1-58023-020-9 **$16.95**

Eyes Remade for Wonder: A Lawrence Kushner Reader *Introduction by Thomas Moore*
6 x 9, 240 pp, Quality PB, 978-1-58023-042-1 **$18.95**

God Was in This Place & I, i Did Not Know: Finding Self, Spirituality and Ultimate Meaning   6 x 9, 192 pp, Quality PB, 978-1-879045-33-0 **$16.95**

Honey from the Rock: An Introduction to Jewish Mysticism
6 x 9, 176 pp, Quality PB, 978-1-58023-073-5 **$16.95**

Invisible Lines of Connection: Sacred Stories of the Ordinary
5½ x 8½, 160 pp, Quality PB, 978-1-879045-98-9 **$15.95**

Jewish Spirituality—A Brief Introduction for Christians
5½ x 8½, 112 pp, Quality PB, 978-1-58023-150-3 **$12.95**

The River of Light: Jewish Mystical Awareness
6 x 9, 192 pp, Quality PB, 978-1-58023-096-4 **$16.95**

The Way Into Jewish Mystical Tradition
6 x 9, 224 pp, Quality PB, 978-1-58023-200-5 **$18.99**; HC, 978-1-58023-029-2 **$21.95**

Spirituality/Prayer

My People's Passover Haggadah: Traditional Texts, Modern Commentaries
Edited by Rabbi Lawrence A. Hoffman, PhD, and David Arnow, PhD Diverse commentaries on the traditional Passover Haggadah—in two volumes! Vol. 1: 7 x 10, 304 pp, HC 978-1-58023-354-5 **$24.99** Vol. 2: 7 x 10, 320 pp, HC, 978-1-58023-346-0 **$24.99**

Witnesses to the One: The Spiritual History of the *Sh'ma* By Rabbi Joseph B. Meszler; Foreword by Rabbi Elyse Goldstein 6 x 9, 176 pp, HC, 978-1-58023-309-5 **$19.99**

My People's Prayer Book Series

Traditional Prayers, Modern Commentaries   *Edited by Rabbi Lawrence A. Hoffman*
Provides diverse and exciting commentary to the traditional liturgy, helping modern men and women find new wisdom in Jewish prayer, and bring liturgy into their lives. Each book includes Hebrew text, modern translation, and commentaries from all perspectives of the Jewish world.

Vol. 1—The *Sh'ma* and Its Blessings
7 x 10, 168 pp, HC, 978-1-879045-79-8 **$24.99**

Vol. 2—The *Amidah*
7 x 10, 240 pp, HC, 978-1-879045-80-4 **$24.95**

Vol. 3—*P'sukei D'zimrah* (Morning Psalms)
7 x 10, 240 pp, HC, 978-1-879045-81-1 **$24.95**

Vol. 4—*Seder K'riat Hatorah* (The Torah Service)
7 x 10, 264 pp, HC, 978-1-879045-82-8 **$23.95**

Vol. 5—*Birkhot Hashachar* (Morning Blessings)
7 x 10, 240 pp, HC, 978-1-879045-83-5 **$24.95**

Vol. 6—*Tachanun* and Concluding Prayers
7 x 10, 240 pp, HC, 978-1-879045-84-2 **$24.95**

Vol. 7—Shabbat at Home
7 x 10, 240 pp, HC, 978-1-879045-85-9 **$24.95**

Vol. 8—*Kabbalat Shabbat* (Welcoming Shabbat in the Synagogue)
7 x 10, 240 pp, HC, 978-1-58023-121-3 **$24.99**

Vol. 9—Welcoming the Night: *Minchah* and *Ma'ariv* (Afternoon and Evening Prayer) 7 x 10, 272 pp, HC, 978-1-58023-262-3 **$24.99**

Vol. 10—Shabbat Morning: *Shacharit* and *Musaf* (Morning and Additional Services) 7 x 10, 240 pp, HC, 978-1-58023-240-1 **$24.99**

Theology/Philosophy/The Way Into... Series

The Way Into... series offers an accessible and highly usable "guided tour" of the Jewish faith, people, history and beliefs—in total, an introduction to Judaism that will enable you to understand and interact with the sacred texts of the Jewish tradition. Each volume is written by a leading contemporary scholar and teacher, and explores one key aspect of Judaism. The Way Into... series enables all readers to achieve a real sense of Jewish cultural literacy through guided study.

The Way Into Encountering God in Judaism
By Rabbi Neil Gillman, PhD
For everyone who wants to understand how Jews have encountered God throughout history and today.
6 x 9, 240 pp, Quality PB, 978-1-58023-199-2 **$18.99**; HC, 978-1-58023-025-4 **$21.95**
Also Available: **The Jewish Approach to God:** A Brief Introduction for Christians
By Rabbi Neil Gillman, PhD
5½ x 8½, 192 pp, Quality PB, 978-1-58023-190-9 **$16.95**

The Way Into Jewish Mystical Tradition
By Rabbi Lawrence Kushner
Allows readers to interact directly with the sacred mystical text of the Jewish tradition. An accessible introduction to the concepts of Jewish mysticism, their religious and spiritual significance and how they relate to life today.
6 x 9, 224 pp, Quality PB, 978-1-58023-200-5 **$18.99**; HC, 978-1-58023-029-2 **$21.95**

The Way Into Jewish Prayer
By Rabbi Lawrence A. Hoffman, PhD
Opens the door to 3,000 years of Jewish prayer, making available all anyone needs to feel at home in the Jewish way of communicating with God.
6 x 9, 208 pp, Quality PB, 978-1-58023-201-2 **$18.99**

Also Available: **The Way Into Jewish Prayer Teacher's Guide**
By Rabbi Jennifer Ossakow Goldsmith
8½ x 11, 42 pp, Quality PB, 978-1-58023-345-3 **$8.99**
Visit our website to download a free copy.

The Way Into Judaism and the Environment
By Jeremy Benstein, PhD
Explores the ways in which Judaism contributes to contemporary social-environmental issues, the extent to which Judaism is part of the problem and how it can be part of the solution.
6 x 9, 288 pp, Quality PB, 978-1-58023-368-2 **$18.99**; HC, 978-1-58023-268-5 **$24.99**

The Way Into Tikkun Olam (Repairing the World)
By Rabbi Elliot N. Dorff, PhD
An accessible introduction to the Jewish concept of the individual's responsibility to care for others and repair the world.
6 x 9, 304 pp, Quality PB, 978-1-58023-328-6 **$18.99**; 320 pp, HC, 978-1-58023-269-2 **$24.99**

The Way Into Torah
By Rabbi Norman J. Cohen, PhD
Helps guide in the exploration of the origins and development of Torah, explains why it should be studied and how to do it.
6 x 9, 176 pp, Quality PB, 978-1-58023-198-5 **$16.99**

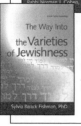

The Way Into the Varieties of Jewishness
By Sylvia Barack Fishman, PhD
Explores the religious and historical understanding of what it has meant to be Jewish from ancient times to the present controversy over "Who is a Jew?"
6 x 9, 288 pp, Quality PB, 978-1-58023-367-5 **$18.99**; HC, 978-1-58023-030-8 **$24.99**

Theology/Philosophy

A Touch of the Sacred: A Theologian's Informal Guide to Jewish Belief
By Dr. Eugene B. Borowitz and Frances W. Schwartz Explores the musings from the
leading theologian of liberal Judaism. 6 x 9, 256 pp, HC, 978-1-58023-337-8 **$21.99**

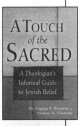

Talking about God: Exploring the Meaning of Religious Life with
Kierkegaard, Buber, Tillich and Heschel *By Daniel F. Polish, PhD*
Examines the meaning of the human religious experience with the greatest theologians of modern times. 6 x 9, 160 pp, HC, 978-1-59473-230-0 **$21.99**
(A book from SkyLight Paths, Jewish Lights' sister imprint)

Jews & Judaism in the 21st Century: Human Responsibility, the
Presence of God, and the Future of the Covenant *Edited by Rabbi Edward Feinstein;*
Foreword by Paula E. Hyman Five celebrated leaders in Judaism examine contemporary
Jewish life. 6 x 9, 192 pp, Quality PB, 978-1-58023-374-3 **$19.99**; HC, 978-1-58023-315-6 **$24.99**

Christians and Jews in Dialogue: Learning in the Presence of the Other
By Mary C. Boys and Sara S. Lee; Foreword by Dr. Dorothy Bass
6 x 9, 240 pp, Quality PB, 978-1-59473-254-6 **$18.99**; HC, 978-1-59473-144-0 **$21.99**
(A book from SkyLight Paths, Jewish Lights' sister imprint)

The Death of Death: Resurrection and Immortality in Jewish Thought
By Neil Gillman 6 x 9, 336 pp, Quality PB, 978-1-58023-081-0 **$18.95**

Ethics of the Sages: Pirke Avot—Annotated & Explained
Translation & Annotation by Rabbi Rami Shapiro
5½ x 8½, 208 pp, Quality PB, 978-1-59473-207-2 **$16.99** *(A book from SkyLight Paths, Jewish Lights' sister imprint)*

Hasidic Tales: Annotated & Explained *By Rabbi Rami Shapiro; Foreword by Andrew Harvey*
5½ x 8½, 240 pp, Quality PB, 978-1-893361-86-7 **$16.95**
(A book from SkyLight Paths, Jewish Lights' sister imprint)

A Heart of Many Rooms: Celebrating the Many Voices within Judaism
By David Hartman 6 x 9, 352 pp, Quality PB, 978-1-58023-156-5 **$19.95**

The Hebrew Prophets: Selections Annotated & Explained
Translation & Annotation by Rabbi Rami Shapiro; Foreword by Zalman M. Schachter-Shalomi
5½ x 8½, 224 pp, Quality PB, 978-1-59473-037-5 **$16.99** *(A book from SkyLight Paths, Jewish Lights' sister imprint)*

A Jewish Understanding of the New Testament
By Rabbi Samuel Sandmel; Preface by Rabbi David Sandmel
5½ x 8½, 368 pp, Quality PB, 978-1-59473-048-1 **$19.99** *(A book from SkyLight Paths, Jewish Lights' sister imprint)*

Keeping Faith with the Psalms: Deepen Your Relationship with God Using the Book
of Psalms *By Daniel F. Polish* 6 x 9, 320 pp, Quality PB, 978-1-58023-300-2 **$18.99**

A Living Covenant: The Innovative Spirit in Traditional Judaism
By David Hartman 6 x 9, 368 pp, Quality PB, 978-1-58023-011-7 **$20.00**

Love and Terror in the God Encounter: The Theological Legacy of Rabbi Joseph
B. Soloveitchik *By David Hartman* 6 x 9, 240 pp, Quality PB, 978-1-58023-176-3 **$19.95**

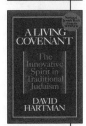

The Personhood of God: Biblical Theology, Human Faith and the Divine Image
By Dr. Yochanan Muffs; Foreword by Dr. David Hartman
6 x 9, 240 pp, Quality PB, 978-1-58023-338-5 **$18.99**; HC, 978-1-58023-265-4 **$24.99**

Traces of God: Seeing God in Torah, History and Everyday Life *By Neil Gillman*
6 x 9, 240 pp, Quality PB, 978-1-58023-369-9 **$16.99**; HC, 978-1-58023-249-4 **$21.99**

We Jews and Jesus: Exploring Theological Differences for Mutual Understanding
By Rabbi Samuel Sandmel; Preface by Rabbi David Sandmel
6 x 9, 176 pp, Quality PB, 978-1-59473-208-9 **$16.99** *(A book from SkyLight Paths, Jewish Lights' sister imprint)*

Your Word Is Fire: The Hasidic Masters on Contemplative Prayer
Edited and translated by Arthur Green and Barry W. Holtz
6 x 9, 160 pp, Quality PB, 978-1-879045-25-5 **$15.95**

I Am Jewish

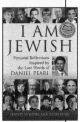

Personal Reflections Inspired by the Last Words of Daniel Pearl
Almost 150 Jews—both famous and not—from all walks of life, from all around
the world, write about many aspects of their Judaism.
Edited by Judea and Ruth Pearl 6 x 9, 304 pp, Deluxe PB w/flaps, 978-1-58023-259-3 **$18.99**
Download a free copy of the *I Am Jewish Teacher's Guide* at our website:
www.jewishlights.com

About Jewish Lights

People of all faiths and backgrounds yearn for books that attract, engage, educate, and spiritually inspire.

Our principal goal is to stimulate thought and help all people learn about who the Jewish People are, where they come from, and what the future can be made to hold. While people of our diverse Jewish heritage are the primary audience, our books speak to people in the Christian world as well and will broaden their understanding of Judaism and the roots of their own faith.

We bring to you authors who are at the forefront of spiritual thought and experience. While each has something different to say, they all say it in a voice that you can hear.

Our books are designed to welcome you and then to engage, stimulate, and inspire. We judge our success not only by whether or not our books are beautiful and commercially successful, but by whether or not they make a difference in your life.

For your information and convenience, at the back of this book we have provided a list of other Jewish Lights books you might find interesting and useful. They cover all the categories of your life:

Bar/Bat Mitzvah	Life Cycle
Bible Study / Midrash	Meditation
Children's Books	Parenting
Congregation Resources	Prayer
Current Events / History	Ritual / Sacred Practice
Ecology / Environment	Spirituality
Fiction: Mystery, Science Fiction	Theology / Philosophy
Grief / Healing	Travel
Holidays / Holy Days	12-Step
Inspiration	Women's Interest
Kabbalah / Mysticism / Enneagram	

Stuart M. Matlins

Stuart M. Matlins, Publisher

Or phone, fax, mail or e-mail to: **JEWISH LIGHTS Publishing**
Sunset Farm Offices, Route 4 • P.O. Box 237 • Woodstock, Vermont 05091
Tel: (802) 457-4000 • Fax: (802) 457-4004 • www.jewishlights.com
Credit card orders: **(800) 962-4544** (8:30AM–5:30PM ET Monday–Friday)
Generous discounts on quantity orders. SATISFACTION GUARANTEED. Prices subject to change.

For more information about each book, visit our website at www.jewishlights.com